THE IMAGE OF AFRICA

VOLUME ONE

THE
IMAGE OF AFRICA

British Ideas and Action, 1780–1850

VOLUME ONE

PHILIP D. CURTIN

The University of Wisconsin Press

To Anne Gilbert Curtin

The University of Wisconsin Press
114 North Murray Street
Madison, Wisconsin 53715

3 Henrietta Street
London WC2E 8LU, England

ISBN 0-299-83025-X (vol. 1); 0-299-83026-8 (vol. 2)
LC 64-10922

CONTENTS · VOLUME 1

CONTENTS · VOLUME 2

FIGURES · VOLUME 1

FIGURES · VOLUME 2

MAPS · VOLUME 1

*Maps by the University of Wisconsin
Cartographic Laboratory*

PREFACE

It was apparent during the 1950's that the West in general, and the colonial powers in particular, were unprepared for the emergence of Africa. The popular mental image of the "dark continent" lived on, in spite of the decades of government over Africans, stretching back to the 1880's and sometimes beyond. This image owed something to the superiority feelings of the conquerors over the conquered, the administrators over those whom they administered. Its roots, however, lie much further back in the history of Western ideas. An image began to emerge out of the haze of the unknown with the first voyages down the West African coast in the fifteenth century. It was strengthened by more frequent contact during the sixteenth century, strengthened still more by intensive commercial contact through the slave trade in the centuries from the seventeenth to the middle of the nineteenth.

The crucial period, however, was the early nineteenth century. Beginning in the 1780's, Europeans began to take a new look at Africa. Now that the slave trade was under sharp attack in England, France, and America alike, a new prospect appeared in Afro-European relations. For the British, this prospect was one of "legitimate" trade, which might soon replace the slave trade, and provide a radically new basis for Anglo-African commerce. From the 1780's, therefore, the British began to see Africa, not merely as it was, but as it might be, and with full consideration for the new Africa in the imperial scheme of things.

Since West Africa was the core-area of the old slave trade, it was the first part of Africa to attract attention; and the British image of "the African," and of African conditions generally, was initially concerned almost entirely with West Africa. South Africa entered the picture only in the 1820's, Central and East Africa only in the 1850's, and the Congo basin only in the 1870's. With each new dimension, the image spread and took on local variations, but for Britain itself the early-nineteenth-century image of Africa was, in fact, the image of West Africa.

The new view of Africa which began to emerge in the 1780's, drew some of its novelty from a new attitude on the part of Europeans, but even more from the flood of new data that began to pour in—first from coastal travellers, then from explorers into the interior (and the early nineteenth century was the great age of African exploration), finally from the refinement and synthesis of these data in the hands of stay-at-home scholars and publicists. As the decades passed, British ideas about Africa became more and more detailed and better publicized. By the 1850's the image had hardened. It was found in children's books, in Sunday school tracts, in the popular press. Its major affirmations were the "common knowledge" of the educated classes. Thereafter, when new generations of explorers or administrators went to Africa, they went with a prior impression of what they would find. Most often, they found it, and their writings in turn confirmed the older image—or at most altered it only slightly.

With the 1850's, British interest in West Africa began to taper off, until it reached a low point about 1865. It then rose gradually as the era of the new imperialism approached, and Britain entered fully into the scramble for Africa of the 1880's and 1890's. For convenience' sake, the period of limited missionary and commercial penetration up to the 1850's can be called the era of humanitarianism. The three decades from about 1850 to about 1880 mark a transition from this to the era of imperialism.

There is no need to enter the period of transition. The hardened image of Africa was complete by the 1850's. It was to change slowly in later years, but the later image of Africa was very largely drawn from Europe's first impressions, taken during the earlier and formative decades. It is not my concern here to trace the later course of these ideas, but it should be apparent that they lived on into the middle of the twentieth century—indeed, that they contributed substantially to the cross-cultural misunderstandings of the recent past.

The aim of the present work is to show how these ideas were formed and integrated with Western thought. The history of political events is therefore carried down to the reaffirmation of the anti-slave-trade blockade in 1850, the capture of Lagos in 1851, and the fall of the Russell Government in 1852. These three events together mark both the last important stand of humanitarian policies, the first step toward more active intervention along the Gulf of Guinea, and the fall of the last British Government that clearly belongs to the era of humanitarianism. The history of British thought about race and its meaning can stop conveniently with the publication of Darwin's *Origin of Species* in 1859. Economic thought and policy took a new direction from the passage of the Sugar Act of 1846 and the end of the Brazilian slave trade in 1850, while European medical technology also reached a new level of achievement at about 1850. Finally, the great age of West African exploration was rounded out by the first really successful steamboat entry into the Niger in 1854 and the emergence of Barth, the greatest explorer of West Africa, in 1855.

It is customary for historians of the British Empire to write about the history of British policy, and British policy can be most conveniently studied with reference to the explicit documentary record of the central administration. It has not usually been thought relevant or useful to consider anything so broad as the national "image" one people may hold of another.

Even from the narrow point of view of policy-formation, however, the broader history of ideas has some importance. Officials in the Colonial Office did not, in fact, write down all that they believed to be true about the world in which they lived or the regions they governed. Beyond the world of despatches, there was also a world of unstated assumptions. The more cohesive the society, the less need to bring these unstated assumptions into the open—and the ruling class of nineteenth century Britain was very cohesive indeed. Officials therefore wrote for other officials, who held very much the same set of beliefs, placed much the same values on their own culture (or on that of foreigners), or shared unstated assumptions about the nature of race and its role in history.

Any attempt to discover the roots of European policy in any part of the world must therefore take account of these unstated assumptions, and a great deal of light can be thrown on them by examining the attitudes, values, and sentiments present in European society at large. The history of European ideas about the African people, the African way of life, or the earlier course of African history, therefore, is something more than the history of African studies—though it is that too. These ideas were formed in a particular historical setting. They, in turn, helped to influence the course of future history.

It can, of course, be argued, that the prominence of an idea in British thought as a whole is no guarantee that any particular body of administrators were moved by it in their decisions. This is quite true: it is no *guarantee*. But it is extremely likely that people who share a common educational background and who are subject to common intellectual influences will share a common denominator of ideas and attitudes. In practice, those who dissented from the common attitudes of the day often said so in their despatches. The best verification, however, comes with the study of the official correspondence against the background of generally held ideas. Once the broader image of Africa is uncovered, it becomes obvious that this image—this combination of attitudes, values, and theory about the world—does in fact provide the set of unstated assumptions that lead rationally to the policies that did emerge.

On another plane, it has been customary for general historians to neglect the technical aspects of European relations with the world overseas. Matters like the history of tropical medicine, however, are more than a sidelight of importance only to historians of medicine. The inability of the Europeans to solve medical problems on the African coast—even to survive in reasonable proportion—was one of the basic determinants of Afro-European relations in any period before the First World War. The state of this problem at any moment in time set limits on the policies that were practicable. This is true not merely of correct knowledge, which led to medical progress: it is equally true of incorrect knowledge. Erroneous medical ideas, the *culs de sac* in the history of medicine, led men to die and policies to be abandoned on the coast of West Africa.

Nor was technical knowledge unrelated to other ideas and attitudes. As it turned out, incorrect information about racial immunities to disease became one of the strongest rational supports for pseudo-scientific racism in the early nineteenth century. Racism, in turn, colored British attitudes toward other peoples across the whole spectrum of thought, from the theory of history at one end to explicit provisions for African education at the other.

In short, the body of knowledge about Africa which influenced African history was much broader than mere "colonial policy." It was also interrelated in curious ways, which carry the investigator across many of the usual divisions of knowledge. By concentrating on the study of what one country thought about one part of Africa, investigation is drawn into many of the nooks and crannies of the history of British ideas themselves. It is hoped that this study, with its first concern for the role of British ideas in African history, will also add something to our knowledge of the way in which ideas originated in Western society, the ways they changed through time, and some of the uses to which they were put by those who tried to carry them into action. Even more, it is hoped that this study of the early origins of the image of Africa will help to illuminate present relations between Africa and the West, and through this example, will say something useful about the role of ideas in the confrontation of differing civilizations.

The trail of debt I have left in the preparation of this book is even more diverse than the material that has found its way into it. The library of the British Museum and the Memorial Library of the University of Wisconsin have been far more than ordinarily helpful. I am especially grateful to Miss Margarite Christensen of the Wisconsin library for searching out and procuring through inter-library loan the books which neither library held. In London, The Institute of Commonwealth Studies of the University of London was extremely generous in making its facilities available, and I am grateful for the intellectual stimulus of its staff and my fellow-visitors during several prolonged visits. In West Africa, I am especially indebted to Mr. Peter Kup, the archivist of Sierra Leone at the time of my visit, to Mr. J. M. Akita of the National Archives of Ghana, and to Dr. K. O. Dike, Mr. L. C. Gwam, and Mr. S. S. Waniko of the National Archives of Nigeria.

Among colleagues and friends, Mr. Christopher Fyfe was generous far beyond the call of duty in supplying citations and guideposts to the literature about Sierra Leone. Drs. David Kimble and J. F. A. Ajayi were kind enough to allow me to read their books on the Gold Coast and Nigeria respectively, prior to publication. Others were generous with their time in reading and commenting on sections of the manuscript. Among those to whom I am especially grateful are Thomas L. Hodgkin, Jeffrey Butler, J. F. C. Harrison, Paul J. Bohannan, Joseph H. Greenberg, Robert Stauffer, Jan Vansina, M. J. Coulbourne, T. H. Silcock, Gerald S. Graham, and Anne G. Curtin, the most exacting critic of all. Needless to say, none of these can be held responsible for those occasions where I may have persisted in error against their good advice, or where I have added error at a later stage of revision.

The Journal of the Historical Society of Nigeria and the *Journal of British Studies* have been kind enough to permit republication of material which first appeared in their pages in a different form.

Still another, and substantial, indebtedness is due to the Research Committee of the University of Wisconsin for generous support during research leaves from my teaching post, and to the Ford Foundation for a year of travel and study in West Africa and Great Britain.

Messrs. Randal Sale, Melvin Albaum, and Rodney Helgeland of the Cartographic Laboratory of the University of Wisconsin have been responsible for the preparation of the maps.

P. D. C.

Madison, Wisconsin
June, 1963

PART I

*The "New World"
of Eighteenth-Century Africa*

KEY TO ABBREVIATIONS

IN THE NOTES

Ad. Mss.	Additional Manuscripts, British Museum
AG	National Archives of Ghana, Accra
ASP	Papers of the Anti-Slavery Society and the Aborigines Protection Society, Rhodes House, Oxford
BT	Board of Trade series, Public Record Office
CMSA	Archives of the Church Missionary Society, Salisbury Square, London. (Microfilm series also available at Memorial Library, University of Wisconsin.)
CO	Colonial Office series, Public Record Office
DNB	Dictionary of National Biography
HO	Home Office series, Public Record Office
H	Hansard
IA	Nigerian National Archives, Western Regional Repository, Ibadan
PP	Parliamentary Papers
PRO	Public Record Office, London
SLA	National Archives of Sierra Leone, Freetown
T	Treasury series, Public Record Office

WEST AFRICA:

THE KNOWN

AND

THE UNKNOWN

The decade between the Peace of Versailles in 1783 and the war with France in 1793 marked a phase of special importance in British relations with the world overseas. The loss of the thirteen American colonies closed an epoch, and seemed to close it decisively. Few in Britain looked back with nostalgia or wanted to found another family of settlement colonies like those in North America. Even fewer were willing to accept the military defeat as final. It was only a temporary decline of British fortunes, and it was met by rapid recovery, reform, and determination to regain some equivalent for the loss.

Britain was then in the middle of the late-eighteenth-century population explosion. The first great burst of industrial growth was just beginning. The way was open to some kind of new overseas activity. But the kind was still undecided, and its geographical focus still undetermined. There were only areas of preference or possibility. The temperate zone as a whole seemed unattractive: its products were competitive with those of Britain. The fur-producing regions on the northern temperate fringes were highly valued, but

Canada and the Hudson's Bay Company territories filled that particular need. The tropical world promised something better—greater material gains, complementary to Britain's own production and without the political inconvenience of managing thousands of importunate settlers.

Several possibilities were open. The trade of China and Southeast Asia was one, calling for the further development of trading-post enclaves in East Asia. (The British had, indeed, begun to show a greater interest in the further East beyond India since the end of the Seven Years' War.) India was a second, and here too British interests had been advancing since the 1750's. Recent decades had seen the transformation of enclaves and informal influence into *de facto* territorial sovereignty in Bengal. The new situation was recognized in North's Regulating Act of 1773 and Pitt's India Act of 1784, but the Indian Empire of the future was still only a very vague promise.

An equal or even greater promise lay in the lands on either side of the tropical Atlantic, where a variety of openings might be exploited. The most valuable form of overseas activity for any of the major European colonial powers was still considered to be the complex of long-distance trade and production centering in the Caribbean. This system as a whole had no contemporaneous name, but in retrospect it may be called the "South Atlantic System."[1] The goal was the production of tropical staples for the European market, and its ramifications stretched out in every direction. The West Indian slave plantations lacked a self-reproducing labor force. Continuous slave trade from Africa was needed to maintain the level of production. Many of the Caribbean islands were so heavily involved in cash-crop production that food supplies, as well as timber and other provisions, had to be imported in a continuous stream from North America or Ireland.

In the European theory of empire, from the later seventeenth century onward, it was thought desirable to have a balanced set of colonies, so that slaves, provisions, and shipping, as well as plantations themselves, could all be monopolized for the benefit of the mother country. Thus, in theory, there was not a single European South Atlantic System, but a series of systems, each completely

1. In naval usage, South Atlantic means the Atlantic south of the equator, but ordinary American usage, which places the South Atlantic more vaguely to the south of the Mason-Dixon line, serves best to describe the extent of the system.

separate from the others. In fact, it never worked out as the theory suggested. By the mid-eighteenth century only France and Britain held the theoretically essential set of colonies in North America and tropical America, plus slave-trade posts on the African coast. Dutch, Danes, Brandenburgers, Spanish, and Portuguese, however, had all participated to some degree or held incomplete sets of colonies. Furthermore, even the French and British sectors were often internally out of balance, having more slaves or more provisions than their own plantations could use, or less tropical production than the home market needed. As a result, the nationals of all countries traded widely, if illegally, between sectors, until the whole system had become most unsystematic. In fact, if not in law, it was a great international network of trade and production.

The South Atlantic System, though principally concerned with tropical agricultural production, had also come to be closely and illegally interlocked with the trade of Spanish America. The gold and silver of Mexico and Peru, mainly acquired by illegal trading on the part of north European nationals, had long since become essential to the monetary operation of the South Atlantic economy. For the British in particular, it was an ancient ambition of colonial policy to pry open a larger access to the trade of Spanish America—either by encouraging smuggling, by direct diplomatic pressure on Spain, or possibly by seizing all or part of the Spanish Empire, if the opportunity presented itself.

At the end of the American War, the British sector of the South Atlantic System was seriously damaged by the loss of the thirteen mainland colonies, and the French sector began to compete more efficiently than ever. The British saw it as a threat that might drive their sugar out of the Continental markets. If Britain were to recover its old position, two alternate possibilities were open. One was to push harder for entry into Latin America. The other was to concentrate on revitalizing the British sector itself. Each course had its advocates, but each had its dangers. Illicit trade with Spanish America was valuable, but to extend it might mean a clash with Spain. The West India interest in Britain preferred government support for their own plantations in the British Caribbean. But the West India interest was narrow and particular, and it was beginning to meet opposition from the anti-slave-trade movement. Humanitarian publicity both underlined moral defects of the South Atlantic System, and pointed out a third possibility. Tropical development might also be encouraged on the eastern shore of the South Atlantic. No other power was so well supplied with African trading posts, and no potential European ally would be alienated by the spread of tropical agriculture in the hinterland of these posts. In the decade after 1783, therefore, the alternative of developing tropical Africa began to have a following.

When Britain or any other European power turned to Africa in the eighteenth century, it was West Africa that counted. Without the Suez Canal, the east coast was far away in the sphere of the Indian "country trade." The Cape was Dutch, and little more than a way station on the route to India. The region of commercial promise was that of the existing slave trade—"the Coast," extending from Benguela in Angola to St. Louis at the mouth of the Senegal. In the later 1780's, all European nations together exported about 75,000 slaves a year from this part of Africa, about half of them carried by British merchants. The annual average "official" value of British exports to Africa in 1783–87 was £691,000, representing 4.4 per cent of the total value of British exports.[2] Export values, however, are misleading by themselves. The importance of the African trade was not merely in the value of goods sold in Africa. The gross income from the sale of slaves in America was nearly twice the value of exports to the Coast, being in the neighborhood of £1,000,000 a year.[3] More important still, West Indian planters depended for their own prosperity on a steady supply of slaves.

But those who favored African development were not concerned with its role in the South Atlantic System. They looked ahead to projected economic growth of astronomical proportions within a few years or decades. As it turned out, they were wrong. West Africa was never again so important to the British sector of the

2. Great Britain. Privy Council. *Report of the Lords of the Committee of Council for . . . Trade and Foreign Plantations . . . Concerning the Present State of Trade to Africa, and Particularly the Trade in Slaves . . .* (London, 1789), Part IV. These figures give a rough indication, but in the 1780's they no longer corresponded to the actual market values of the goods exported. (See Albert Imlah, *Economic Elements in the Pax Britannica* [Cambridge, Mass., 1958], pp. 20–41.)

3. Assuming that British merchants landed about 30,000 slaves annually in the Americas and sold them for the average West Indian price for the period, or about £35 each.

Map 1. West Africa and the Slave Trade

world economy as it was in those last few decades before 1807, but
no one could know this at the time.

Britain had no more than a shadow of sovereignty over any part
of the Coast, though the Portuguese at Luanda and the French at
St. Louis had tiny enclaves. Elsewhere, the relations between
African political authorities and Europeans trading on the Coast were
generally those of equal partners in a commercial transaction. The
question of political sovereignty was seldom raised in the technical
sense of European usage. There were some trading forts on shore,
but the relative power of the European traders and the African states
was roughly in balance. A trading fort did not necessarily imply a

sphere of European influence over its hinterland. In most places, the forts were allowed by the Africans as a mutual convenience for African and European merchants alike; and the Europeans paid for the privilege of trade, either in the form of ground rent for the land occupied by the fort or as a gift in return for good will.

For that matter, British trade was not necessarily centered around the forts, and it was distributed unevenly along the length of the Coast. The region north of the Gambia had been abandoned to France at the end of the American war. Lower Guinea, south of the equator, had traditionally been the special sphere of the Portuguese in their slave trade to Brazil; but the British merchants were active even there, whenever the supply of slaves was plentiful. All along the Coast, indeed, the supply of slaves shifted from time to time with the changing patterns of war or peace in the interior of the continent. Forts and factories, on the other hand, were relatively immobile.

Some British forts were considered to be national property and maintained by grants from the royal government. These were narrowly concentrated along 200 miles on the Gold Coast. The only exceptions were a fort at James Island in the Gambia and a factory at Ouidah (then called Whydah) in Dahomey. All of these were administered by the Company of Merchants Trading to Africa and managed by its elected committee of merchants, informally called the African Committee. A firm trading to Africa was obliged to join the Company, but the membership fee was low and the Company did not engage in trade on its own account.

There was, however, no obligation to trade through the Company's forts, and most trade went elsewhere. Any firm that chose to do so could maintain its own factory wherever it could make suitable arrangements with an African ruler. The circumstances of these private factories varied enormously. In some places a factor was simply left on shore in African territory to purchase slaves between calls from ships. In other places, and especially where African political authority was highly fragmented, a European slave trader with a few hundred armed African followers could set himself up as an authority with power equal to that of the surrounding rulers. In these cases he became a petty king by *de facto* African recognition but not in European international law. Small posts of this kind were most numerous on the "Windward Coast" which is now Portuguese Guinea, the Republic of Guinea, Sierra Leone, and parts of Liberia.[4] To the east of the Gold Coast, however, in the Bights of Benin and Biafra, ships called at established African trading towns and dealt directly with the African merchants, without the permanent European posts, either official or unofficial.

Other European holdings fell into much the same pattern as the British. Along the Gold Coast, where the British forts were most numerous, Dutch and Danish forts were also plentiful; and they were interspersed without regard for nationality. In Accra, Dutch, English, and Danish forts were all within sight of one another and the principal Dutch fort at Elmina was only eight miles from the British administrative center at Cape Coast.

This form of European contact, strictly limited to the coast and a few navigable rivers, was admirably suited to the conditions of the slave trade. European merchants were in no position to go inland to buy or capture slaves, and they were content to let the African middle-men handle that part of the trade. By the later eighteenth century, each of the major partners understood his own function and was supported in it by a body of custom now become traditional. The pattern of commerce, therefore, was not one that could respond rapidly to a flow of new products from Europe or a new economic demand for African products at the coastal ports. If the British in the 1780's hoped to do more in Africa than simply extend the slave trade, some new relationship would have to be worked out between Britons and Africans on the coast; but any assessment of possibilities depended on the existing information about Africa, and theoretical propositions derived from it.

The pattern of empirical information about Africa was itself a product of the peculiar relations built up during the centuries of the slave trade. A great deal was known about the coast in ways that were intimate, detailed, and highly specialized. Almost nothing was known through direct contact with the far interior, but then very little was known about the interior of North or South America or about Central Asia. The image of "darkest Africa," either as an expression of geographical ignorance, or as one of cultural arrogance, was a nineteenth-century invention. Relative to their knowledge of

4. For the variety of slave-trading posts on the Windward Coast, see C. Fyfe, *A History of Sierra Leone* (London, 1962), pp. 1-10.

the world in general, eighteen-century Europeans knew more and cared more about Africa than they did at any later period up to the 1950's.

This knowledge was available in England from a number of sources, often derived from different periods of time, and coming into British consciousness by a variety of routes. Virtually all knowledge about the Western Sudan, the savanna country lying between the forest and the Sahara, came by way of North Africa. This was only to be expected. The centuries-old caravan trade across the desert linked the Maghrib with Sudanese cities like Jenne, Timbuctu, and Gao. The more surprising fact about this source of knowledge is its narrow range of origin in time. The trans-Sahara trade had begun in the very distant past and continued through the nineteenth century; yet the reports of the Western Sudan, transmitted by the Arabs and available in Western Europe at the end of the eighteenth century, dated almost entirely from the period between the tenth century and the early sixteenth.

It was during this period that the great tradition of Arabic geographical studies flourished in the Maghrib, Egypt, and Southwest Asia. Ibn-Hawqal brought back the first surviving Arabic account of the Western Sudan in the tenth century.[5] From that time onward, Arabs crossed and recrossed the desert over a variety of routes, and scholars built up a body of systematic knowledge. Some of the important Arabic manuscripts were available in Western libraries, but the scarcity of Western scholars of Arabic kept them below the intellectual horizon. Neither al-Bakri's geography, ibn-Battūta's travels, nor ibn-Khaldūn's history was available in translation, though much of the substance of Arabic geography and history of the Western Sudan was known through other sources.

Only a few of the major works were known. One of the most important was the *Kitab Rudjar* of al-Idrīsi (c. 1100–1166), completed in 1154 at the court of Roger of Sicily. The sections dealing with Africa were published in Paris in 1619 in both Arabic and Latin, and a further abridged and annotated Latin version appeared in Göttingen in 1796.[6]

5. See E. W. Bovill, *The Golden Trade of the Moors* (London, 1958), pp. 60–65; G. H. T. Kimble, *Geography in the Middle Ages* (London, 1938), pp. 44–68.
6. *Geographia Nubiensis* (Paris, 1619), translated and edited by Gabriel Sionita and Joannes Hesronita; *Africa* (Göttingen, 1796), translated and edited by Joannes Melchior Hartman.

Al-Idrīsi was not a traveller, but a geographical scholar, working with original travel accounts that have since been lost. Only one good travel account of this kind was available. This was the *Description of Africa* of Leo Africanus, which became the most popular of all the Arab works known to Western Europe. Leo Africanus was a Maghribi who had travelled widely in the Western Sudan before his capture by Christian ships in the Mediterranean. He wrote his original narrative in 1526, in defective Italian using Arabic notes. It then appeared in a more literary Italian version in 1550 and was translated into English in 1600. Its eighteenth-century vogue in England came from the fact that Samuel Purchas published certain portions in his enormous seventeenth-century collection of travels.[7]

A third source of Arabic knowledge was Luis del Marmol Carvajal, who wrote a history of North Africa in Spanish toward the end of the sixteenth century, taking a great deal of his material from the work of Ibn Khaldun.[8] Thus something of the Arabic historical tradition joined the geographical.

After Marmol and Leo Africanus, there were only rumors and occasional reports picked up in the North African ports. This piecemeal information might have been systematically collected and used, but it was not. Thus, the interior of western Africa was known at second hand, and the latest solid and systematic information available in the 1780's was already almost three hundred years old.

The sixteenth century, which brought the last of the detailed Arabic accounts of West Africa, also brought the first direct European reports. The Portuguese began sailing down the African coast in the fifteenth century, and they were followed shortly by other Europeans. From the mid-fifteenth to the mid-eighteenth century, several hundred different travellers left some account of their voyage to Guinea. Many of these journals and reports had dropped from sight by the 1780's, but about twenty different works had come to be accepted as a canon of West African knowledge.

These works were easily accessible to the educated English public, in spite of the fact that they had been written in a variety of European languages and sometimes dated from the distant past. Pub-

7. See introduction to recent critical edition: A. Epaulard (Translator and editor), *Description de l'Afrique, par Jean Léon l'Africain*, 2 vols. (Paris, 1957).
8. Luis del Marmol Carvajal, *La descripción general de Affrica, con todos los successos de guerras que a avido . . . hasta el año del Señor 1571*, 3 vols. (Granada and Malaga, 1573–1599).

lished collections of travel accounts had appeared regularly ever since Hakluyt's *Principal Voyages Traffiques & Discoveries of the English Nation* in 1599. The later multi-volume collections of Purchas and Churchill kept the older travellers in print and added the more recent ones. Major publications of world-wide scope were supplemented by local or regional collections, some of which were designed to serve as a systematic source book for an individual part of the world. Father J. B. Labat covered the African coast in this way by gathering both published and unpublished accounts and stringing them together in a scissors-and-paste compilation. One set of five volumes, based mainly on the notes of La Brue, dealt with the Senegambia and the coastal region from Cape Blanc in Mauritania to Sierra Leone. A second set of four volumes, derived more narrowly from the voyages of Des Marchais, carried on from Sierra Leone to Dahomey and across the ocean to French Guiana.[9]

This form of presentation was taken up in England by the publisher, Thomas Astley, whose editors produced the *New General Collection of Voyages and Travels* between 1745 and 1747. Its scope was world-wide, but a quarto volume of some six hundred pages in double columns was devoted to Africa alone. Astley's *Voyages* absorbed both English works and French accounts, arranging the excerpts so as to omit the tales of adventure and emphasize geographic and ethnographic information. All the authorities on any section of the coast were brought together, reprinted in their own words where possible, but otherwise rewritten as necessary and supplied with connecting passages to present a comprehensive account. Here, in short, was the whole canon of travel literature, presented in one place. It became the inevitable mine of information for anyone concerned with African affairs during the second half of the century, serving that generation as Lord Hailey's *African Survey* was to serve another generation some two centuries later.[10]

Alongside the collected travel reports, competent works of synthesis were also available. The most ambitious of these was the great *Universal History* published between 1736 and 1765 in sixty-five octavo volumes, or in a special luxury edition of twenty-three folio

9. J. B. Labat, *Nouvelle relation de l'Afrique occidentale*, 5 vols. (Paris, 1728), and *Voyage du Chevalier des Marchais en Guinée, Isles voisines, et à Cayenne, fait en 1725, 1726, et 1727* . . . , 4 vols. (Paris, 1730).

10. Thomas Astley (Publisher), *A New General Collection of Voyages and Travels*, 4 vols. (London, 1745–1747).

volumes.[11] It was designed to be an epitome of world history and geography, and its balance of emphasis is some indication of the range of British interest. Nearly half the total was allotted to the history of the non-Western world—a generosity toward other peoples' history that would be hard to find in similar publications of the twentieth century. Africa also figured much more heavily than it was to do in future works. Two of the sixteen folio volumes of the Modern History section were devoted to Africa—one-eighth of the total, or the same space given to East, Southeast, and South Asia together. The treatment of individual African countries included a short sketch of European activities; but the body of the work was concerned with the history, manners, and customs of the Africans themselves, and a quarter of the Africa section was given over to West Africa.[12] Measured against modern knowledge, the presentation was not always accurate, nor was it free of ethnocentric prejudice. It was, however, a serious and ambitious effort to understand the African world with a tolerance and interest that was to be slowly eroded away during the course of the nineteenth century.

The established body of knowledge constantly absorbed new information. One source was the movement of individuals back and forth between Africa and Europe. The African posts were highly manned, but there were always a few ex-officials, merchants, or military officers in England who could claim personal knowledge of the Coast, and some of these were eager to make their knowledge available.[13] The age of the "expert" witness had already come, and committees of Parliament or the Privy Council could always round up a dozen or so, who willingly gave their various and contradictory opinions about the present situation and future possibilities. Many of these specialists were, in fact, professional or interested publicists ad-

---

11. Authors attributed by the Library of Congress catalogue are George Sale, George Psalmanzar, Archibald Bower, George Shelvocke, John Campbell, and John Swinton.

12. This relatively heavy concentration on Africa was typical of other works of the period as well. C. T. Middleton's *New and Complete System of Geography*, 2 vols. (London, 1779), for example, gave Africa more space than it gave to all of Asia, and three times as much space as the Americas. West Africa alone received more detailed treatment than India.

13. F. L. Bartels, "Philip Quaque, 1741–1816," *Transactions of the Gold Coast and Togoland Historical Society*, I, 153–77 (Achimota, 1955); John Adams, *Remarks on the Country Extending from Cape Palmas to the River Congo* (London, 1823), p. 144; Matthews, Penny, and Norris to John Tarleton, 16 April 1788, in Privy Council, *Report on the Trade in Slaves*, Part I, Detached pieces, no. 4. See also Kenneth Little, *Negroes in Britain* (London, 1947), pp. 165–94.

vocating particular forms of action or inaction in West Africa. They
were joined by the ever-present group of absentee West Indian proprietors, whose source of labor was in Africa, and who believed they
knew a good deal about the Africans, if not about Africa.

There were also several hundred Africans resident in England.
They rarely supplied information on their own initiative, but they
would often do so if asked; and their information was more or less
reliable according to the length of time they had been away from
home and their level of acculturation. Some of these were the "black
poor," African servants who came to England by way of West Indian
slavery, discharged sailors and soldiers from the American war, and
other Negroes who had become permanent residents in Britain.

As informants, they were not nearly so trustworthy as a second
group of transients direct from Africa. The long contact with the
Europeans had already produced in Africa a need for literacy in
English and for other Western skills. A small group of educated
Africans was to be found at many points along the Coast. There were
a few schools, such as one in Bonny conducted by English-educated
schoolmasters, but most well-to-do Africans who wanted an education for their children had to send them to Europe. At least one of
these, Philip Quaque of Cape Coast, had completed a formal education in Britain and returned to the Coast in 1765 as an ordained
minister and chaplain at Cape Coast Castle. Most had the more mod-
est aim of learning to read and write and do a little commercial arith-
metic. They were usually sent in the charge of English traders who
assured them of some care and supervision. In the later 1780's, about
fifty of these trainees were to be found in and around Liverpool.

In addition to those who travelled in line of business, a new kind
of reporter appeared in West Africa during the latter part of the
eighteenth century. Some Europeans began to travel for the sake
of gathering information. People had, of course, travelled out of
curiosity before this time, but now they were after specific bodies of
knowledge—something to fill in a corner of an intellectual puzzle,
part of which was already known. It was not yet "scientific" investigation but it was heavily influenced by the rationalism of the Enlightenment. At the very least it was scholarly field work, and the
scholarship was up to the best intellectual standards of the time.

Two general ways existed for organizing the flow of data from
overseas for scholarly ends. One method, in occasional use for cen-

turies, was to send a questionnaire to people who were already there. The Spanish Council of the Indies had done this as early as 1517, hoping to base their "native policy" in Hispaniola on systematic ethnographic knowledge. An eighteenth-century variant on a more ambitious scale was organized by Professor Johan Michaelis of Göttingen, a Biblical scholar and linguist. He proposed an expedition of five scholars to the Red Sea to act as emissaries from the "Republic of Letters" in Europe. Through correspondence, Michaelis prepared a questionnaire based on the desiderata of scholars in many fields and from many countries. Fauna, flora, ethnography, medicine, linguistics, economic and commercial matters were all included. The questionnaire itself was published as a book of nearly five hundred pages, and the project received the patronage of the Danish court. There were obvious flaws in this kind of project as a technique of scholarship, but it marked a transitional stage between dependence solely on whatever travellers might choose to report, and scholarly investigation on the spot.[14]

The second alternative was to send junior researchers with specific objects in mind. The naturalists were the first to experiment on a considerable scale with this technique. Karl Linnaeus began sending botanical expeditions from Uppsala in the 1740's. His emissaries went first to the coast of China, later to America, Java, and Egypt. In 1771, Andreas Berlin was sent to West Africa to make a botanical collection, though he died of disease shortly after his arrival.[15] Meanwhile, Sir Joseph Banks followed the same method from his base at Kew Gardens. He had worked overseas himself on Captain Cook's voyage round the world in 1768–71, and later in North America and Iceland. To fill in the botanical picture of Africa, he sent Francis Masson to the Cape of Good Hope and Henry Smeathman to West Africa.

Whether on specific missions from Linnaeus and Banks, or as independent travellers, the naturalists were also the first of the enlightened travellers to visit West Africa, and they came with a curiosity that extended broadly beyond their immediate botanical or zoological objectives. Michel Adanson, who spent the years 1749 to

14. J. D. Michaelis, *Receuil de questions proposées à une Société des savans* . . . (Frankfurt-a.-M., 1763); *Colleción de documentos inéditos relativos al descubrimiento, conquista y organización de las antiguas possessiones españolas,* 42 vols. (Madrid, 1864–1889), XXXIV, 201–29.

15. A. A. Boahen, "British Penetration of North-West Africa and the Western Sudan, 1788–1861 " (Unpublished Ph.D. thesis, London, 1959), p. 17.

1754 in Senegal, was mainly a naturalist, but he also made the first consciously "scientific" effort to carry out ethnographic field work in West Africa. He stayed within the region already known through the slave trade, but he learned Wolof and he made a systematic study of the manners and customs of the people.[16] His successors were mainly Scandinavians, who drew on the combination of Linnaean interest and Danish commercial establishments on the Gold Coast. Ludevig Ferdinand Römer published in 1760 a highly ethnographic account of the region around the Danish forts.[17] Between 1783 and 1787, Paul Erdman Isert, another Danish naturalist, tried consciously to broaden his subject to include the "natural history of man," being especially anxious to record the "manners and customs of savage peoples" before they should be lost or submerged in the advance of civilization.[18]

Still other expeditions bridged the gaps between natural history, ethnography, and a more active interest in African affairs. Banks' emissary, Henry Smeathman, went to the Banana Islands off Sierra Leone in 1771. He settled down for several years and made the first substantial collection of West African plants and insects. In addition to his work for Kew Gardens, Smeathman conducted his own research on termites and followed an interest in ethnography, though he never published in that field. Instead, his experience in Africa led him ultimately to become the first promoter of the English settlement at Sierra Leone.[19]

A Swedish expedition of Arrhenius, Sparrman, and Wadström set out in 1787 with mixed objectives. Sparrman and Arrhenius were naturalists, and Sparrman was a veteran enlightened traveller with ex-

16. M. Adanson, *Histoire naturelle du Sénégal* (Paris, 1757); English translation, *Voyage to Sénégal* (London, 1759). See also A. Chevalier, *Michel Adanson, naturaliste et philosophe* (Paris, 1934). Although Adanson was long an obscure figure in the history of biology, his botanical work in Senegal has recently been recognized as having a place of the first importance in the history of that science. For this rehabilitation, see Bentley Glass, "Heredity and Variation in the Eighteenth Century Concept of the Species," in B. Glass and others, *Forerunners of Darwin, 1745–1859* (Baltimore, 1959), pp. 151–57.

17. L. F. Römer, *Nachrichten von der Kuste Guinea* (Copenhagen and Leipzig, 1769). First published in Danish, Copenhagen, 1760.

18. P. E. Isert, *Reise nach Guinea und den Caräibischen Inseln* (Copenhagen, 1788). See also C. D. Adams, "Activities of Danish Botanists in Guinea, 1783–1850," *Transactions of the Historical Society of Ghana*, III, 30–46 (1957).

19. Henry Smeathman to J. C. Lettsom, 19 October 1782, in J. Fothergill, *The Works of John Fothergill, M.D. . . . .*, 3rd ed. (London, 1784), pp. 575–82.

perience in Cook's second voyage and in South Africa. Karl Bernhard Wadström, the third member, was a Swedenborgian, an enthusiast for colonization, and something of a *philosophe* with an interest in "contemplating human nature in simpler states." All three hoped to penetrate into the Western Sudan by way of the Senegal, but they were held up at Gorée by warfare on the mainland and returned to Europe the next year. Arrhenius died, Sparrman went off alone on a new expedition to South Africa, and Wadström followed Smeathman into a quixotic career as a colonial projector in both England and France.[20]

Sir Joseph Banks was meanwhile working toward an even more systematic organization of enlightened travel in Africa. In 1788 he founded the Association for Promoting the Discovery of the Interior Parts of Africa, and he dominated its operations until 1805 from the post of Treasurer. The organization was commonly called simply the African Association, causing a certain amount of confusion both then and later. There was already an African Committee, which administered the Gold Coast forts, and an African Institution was founded in 1807 to promote humanitarian policies. These three bodies were respectively scientific, mercantile, and Evangelical-humanitarian. Each worked within its own circle of interest, though individuals could and did belong to two or more of them. They continued into the 1820's as important but distinct pressure groups acting in Africa, as well as influencing British policy.

The object of the African Association was exactly what its full name suggests, to send enlightened travellers into the interior of Africa to report on geography, ethnography, and natural history. Three explorers, Ledyard, Lucas, and Houghton, were sent to try an entry of the Western Sudan from three different directions. Ledyard went to Cairo to attempt a westward crossing from the upper Nile. He died there in 1788 before he had moved inland. Lucas went to Tripoli, hoping to move south into Fezzan, then across the desert and west to the Gambia. He reached Murzuk in Fezzan, but then he re-

20. C. B. Wadström, *Observations on the Slave Trade* . . . (London, 1789); *An Essay on Colonization* . . . 2 vols. (London, 1794–1795), I, i; [J. Leyden], *A Historical and Philosophical Sketch of the Discoveries and Settlements of Europeans in Northern and Western Africa at the close of the Eighteenth Century* (Edinburgh, 1799), pp. 107–11.

treated to the coast. Houghton was to move east from the Gambia, but he died somewhere beyond Bambuk in 1791.[21] Thus the triple effort of the first years became a triple failure, though Houghton and Lucas produced some new evidence; but the general effort was only delayed, not abandoned.

In all, British scholars of the later eighteenth century were reasonably well supplied with data, even though the data varied greatly in relative reliability. Geographers found themselves dealing with three different zones of evidence. The first was the coastal zone of constant contact, plus the navigable Senegal and Gambia Rivers. European ships could go as far as the falls of Baracunda on the Gambia, about 200 air miles toward the heart òf the Western Sudan. The Senegal was more difficult for ocean shipping, but here the head of navigation was nearly 350 miles inland. The coastal waters had been described since 1701 by the appropriate volume of the *English Pilot,* predecessor of successive pilot guides published by the Hydrographic Office. Its sectional charts showed each stretch of the coast, with soundings, advice on trade and navigation, and sketches of the seaward appearance of prominent headlands.[22] This zone of coastal knowledge, however, was extremely narrow. Detailed data rarely existed for regions more than twenty miles or so inland.

Beyond, there was a second zone of occasional and unsystematic hearsay evidence. African merchants went inland for slaves. Arab travellers from the Maghrib occasionally came south across West Africa to the Guinea coast. Muslim Africans from as far west as the Gambia travelled eastward to Mecca. Any of these African travellers could have filled in pieces of information, and these pieces could have been fitted into a whole—but the Africans were often unwilling to tell what they knew, and the coastal Europeans were unwilling to spend time collecting and collating such evidence. Commercial routes into the interior were a form of trade secret. Most Europeans on the coast were not sufficiently interested in knowledge for its own sake to report all they picked up by hearsay. Even those European travel-

21. Boahen, "British Penetration of North-West Africa," pp. 3–14, 32, 41–43; A. A. Boahen, "The African Association, 1788–1805," *Transactions of the Historical Society of Ghana,* V, 43–64 (1961); Association for Promoting the Discovery of the Interior Parts of Africa, *Proceedings* (London, 1792).

22. J. Seller and C. Price, *The Fifth Part of the General English Pilot . . . Describing the West-Coast of Africa: From the Straits of Gibraltar to the Cape of Good Hope* (London, 1701).

Map 2. Explorations planned by the African Association, 1788–1791

19

lers who went a few hundred miles inland rarely published what they
had seen. Many such trips are undoubtedly unrecorded; others are
simply known to have taken place. An officer from a French slaver
visited Old Oyo (or Katunga), 180 miles inland from the Bight of
Benin, a full quarter century before Clapperton's publicized visit in
the 1820's.[23] Another traveller went about 120 miles inland from
the Gold Coast and reported, "that the Country, was entirely cleared,
and so immensely Populous that as far as the Eye could carry him
wherever he went, it was covered with Towns, and Villages. Furthermore India goods are in great demand there, so that the African merchants buy a slave for 22 s. worth of India goods and sell him on
the Coast for a profit of 400 per cent."[24]

If the account is accurately reported, the traveller must have been
on the northern fringes of Ashanti, further inland than any publicized penetration of this part of Africa for a century to come, though
not so far as the Portuguese embassy to Mali, which seems to have
used this route in the sixteenth century.

Europeans on the coast were nevertheless able to keep track of
major political changes in the larger African states—in Ashanti, Dahomey, Oyo, or Futa Jallon. North of these states or east of the upper
Senegal, the evidence was very scanty indeed, and in the latitude of
the present-day Nigerian "middle belt" it was almost nil. But even
near the coasts it could be very slight, especially in the hinterland of
modern Liberia and Ivory Coast, and again in the delta of the Niger,
where after centuries of trade the Europeans were still ignorant of
the fact that their ships anchored in the mouths of one of the world's
great river systems.

Beyond the middle belt was a third zone, where information came
in part through North African hearsay evidence, but where it could
be supplemented by the older published information of the Arab
geographers and travellers. Like the coastal sources, this evidence was
spatially limited. It was most complete for the Niger bend, Hausa,
and Bornu—in a sense the other shore of the Sahara, as seen from
the Maghrib. It told little about the powerful but non-Muslim kingdoms like Jukun or the Mossi states. Thus the course of the upper
and middle Niger was known from Arab evidence, but it disappeared

23. J. Adams, *Remarks*, pp. 93–94.
24. Lt. Clarke to William Pitt, 17 March 1785, PRO 30/8/363.

Map 3. European Knowledge of Africa, c. 1780

- - - Approximate Limit of Occasional European Visits And Hearsay Reports on the Coast

///// Approximate Southern Limit of the Sahara Desert

Area of Detailed Knowledge

••••• Approximate Southern Limit of Detailed Reports From the Maghrib

21

over the horizon of systematic Maghribi knowledge when it flowed south into the "middle belt" beyond Nupe.

In spite of the fact that neither the Europeans on the Guinea coast, nor those in the Maghrib, collected the full information that was surely available to them, the geographers in Europe were already at work collating whatever reports they could gather from overseas. The rational and critical spirit of the Enlightenment appeared successively in the geographical work of Guillaume Delisle (1675–1726) and J. B. Bourguignon d'Anville (1697–1782) in France. Both attempted a scholarly reconstruction of the map of Africa, and the final version by d'Anville became the basis on which English geographers were to work. It was remarkably accurate, given his sources. Desert cities such as Agadès were located. The Niger was shown flowing from west to east (correctly enough), but flowing into Lake Chad instead of the Gulf of Guinea. Some of the cities of the Western Sudan appeared, though Kano was confused with the ancient kingdom of Ghana.[25]

D'Anville's British successor was James Rennell, who had been Surveyor-General of Bengal. After his return to England, he began work on a historical reconstruction of the geography of Herodotus, which carried his interest into Africa. In collaboration with the African Association, he became the principal analyst of new reports from Africa, taking account of Houghton's information from the Gambia and Lucas' reports from Fezzan. Rennell incorporated these data and other new information from North Africa into a series of maps and commentaries, the first of which was published by the Association in 1790.[26]

Ethnographic reporting and synthesis necessarily followed the pattern of geographical evidence, but the contrast was much sharper between the relatively well-known coastal area and the virtually unknown interior. Mountains, rivers, and even the vague outlines of political geography could be picked up by hearsay. More complex information about culture was harder to come by, and harder to transmit without the written word. The quality of cultural reporting varied

25. J. B. Bourguignon d'Anville, "Mémoire concernant les Rivières de l'interieur de l'Afrique," *Recueil des Mémoires de l'Académie des Inscriptions et Belles-Lettres*, XXVI, 64–81 (1759). See also J. D. Barbie de Bocage, *Notice sur les ouvrages de M. d'Anville* (Paris, 1802).

26. African Association, *Proceedings* (1792); James Rennell, *Elucidations of the African Geography* (London, 1793); C. R. Markham, *Major James Rennell and the Rise of Modern English Geography* (London, 1895), pp. 122–45.

enormously, even in the coastal regions. Adanson, Römer, and Isert made an effort to understand Akan, Ga, and Wolof culture and to see African society as a functioning whole, but of these authors only Adanson was translated into English. Even the more serious enlightened travellers tended to see Africa through a cultural filter, and the filtering process was even more selective with the non-scholarly travellers whose works made up the bulk of the canon.

Since Europeans mainly came to the Coast for trade, they reported with an eye to matters of commercial importance. An elementary knowledge of political structure was essential for traders, who had to deal with the African authorities. Certain aspects of material culture and the African economic systems were equally crucial, especially when they concerned the slave trade into the interior or the market demand for European goods. With the growth of the anti-slavery movement in Britain, more attention was paid to the place of slaves in African society, and especially to the question of how an individual might be made a slave in the first instance. Social structure as a whole, however, was ignored, and there was little notice that the institution of slavery was part of a wider net of family and group relations. The European concept of slavery, derived ultimately from Roman law, stood in the way of understanding what slavery meant in Africa. Most of the more subtle differences between distinct African cultures were also lost. The fact that all were strikingly different from that of Europe made them seem much the same. But some "tribal" distinctions had to be recognized as a matter of practical necessity—not only on the Coast but in the West Indies, where the planters believed that the African-born slaves had various "national characteristics," and that their market value varied accordingly.[27]

The European travellers wrote to please their audience as well as to inform. Religious beliefs were of no interest: they were mere "pagan error." But spectacular festivals, human sacrifice, judicial ordeals, and polygyny were "curiosities," and were therefore recounted at length. Thus the reporting often stressed precisely those aspects of African life that were most repellent to the West and tended to submerge the indications of a common humanity. This love of the extraordinary was partly the reflection of a much older European interest

27. Bryan Edwards, *The History, Civil and Commercial, of the British Colonies in the West Indies,* 2nd ed., 2 vols. (London, 1794), II, 60–79.

in the exotic—an interest blending genuine intellectual curiosity with
a libidinous fascination for descriptions of other people who break
with impunity the taboos of one's own society. Part of this interest
came with the romantic movement. In the later eighteenth century,
there was an increasing tendency to look whenever possible for diversity in experience as in literary expression. Lovejoy has called this
tendency "diversificationism," replacing the "uniformism" which
dominated the earlier, or Newtonian, phase of the Enlightenment.[28]

This tendency influenced both the first-hand reports and the work
that might be called ethnographic scholarship. Astley's *Voyages* and
the *Universal History* both abstracted or condensed descriptive passages with an eye to the exotic. Other choice bits were gathered together in popular manuals, like the Reverend John Adams' *Curious
Thoughts on the History of Man.*[29] Historical works showed a similar
emphasis. Robert Norris' *Memoirs of the Reign of Bossa Ahadee* was
a vitriolically anti-African history of Dahomey during the middle
decades of the eighteenth century, and it was largely incorporated in
the more inclusive *History of Dahomey* compiled by Archibald Dalzel, the Governor of Cape Coast Castle, to show the savagery of the
Dahomeans as a justification of the slave trade.[30] In spite of their bias,
these two works were the first English attempt to write the history
of any African state south of the forest. At the very least, they represented an admission that African states had a history, a generous attitude compared with the prevailing view a century later.

The scholarly study of West African languages was also in its
infancy in the later eighteenth century. (Perhaps because the *linguae
francae* on the Coast were English and Portuguese, African languages
were not essential as a tool of the trade.) Travellers occasionally
gave a word list in some language they encountered. A vocabulary of
Fetu, one of the Akan languages of the Gold Coast, had been published in Nuremberg as early as 1675, but the only recent result of
linguistic research was a brief study of Fante and Ga grammar by
Christian Protten, a mulatto born on the Gold Coast.[31] The most ex-

28. A. O. Lovejoy, *The Great Chain of Being: A Study of the History of an Idea*
(Cambridge, Mass., 1936). See pp. 233–311 for a detailed discussion of this tendency.
29. J. Adams, *Curious Thoughts on the History of Man* . . . (London, 1789).
30. R. Norris, *Memoirs of the Reign of Bossa Ahadee, King of Dahomey* (London,
1789); A. Dalzel, *The History of Dahomey* (London, 1793).
31. C. Protten, *En nyttig grammaticalsk indledese til tvende hindindtil gadanske
ubekiendte sprog, Fantiesk og Acraisk* (København, 1764). For a brief history of
African linguistic studies, see: R. N. Cust, *A Sketch of the Modern Languages of Africa*,
2 vols. (London, 1883), pp. 24–38.

tensive collection of comparative African vocabularies was also the
work of a German, Christian Oldendorp, a missionary in the Danish
West Indies who compiled a list of numbers from one to ten, plus
thirteen common words, in twenty-six different African languages.
This work was carried out in the spirit of enlightened travel, and
Oldendorp went further still and pieced together a picture of African
religion and customs from his slave informants.[32] Even though Oldendorp's investigation was conducted in the New World rather than
the Old, it was the only recent source of published information about
the peoples of the interior.

Otherwise, information about the Western Sudan was so vague,
ancient, or unsupported that it was possible to believe almost anything. Fact–even the often-erroneous "facts" reported about the
coast–gave way to myth and legend. Some supporters of the slave
trade claimed the people of the interior were even more "degraded"
than those of the coast.[33] (Since slaves for export were largely from
the interior, the more "barbarous" they were, the more they would
gain by transportation to the West Indies.) But this view of a savage
interior was relatively rare.

The main line of speculation dwelt on the great unknown cities
and civilizations, the known fact that gold flowed across the Sahara
to North Africa in the caravan trade, and the reports of the Arab
travellers, in particular Leo Africanus. Even further back in the European past there had been the shadowy figure of Prester John, the
supposedly powerful Christian Prince in the heart of Africa. By the
eighteenth century, Prester John was identified with Christian Ethiopia, but James Bruce's account published in 1790 was the first really
detailed report from that part of the world since the early seventeenth
century. Even before its actual publication, knowledge of his travels
and discoveries lent color to the possibility of an equivalent civilization further west.[34]

The possibility was further supported by a variety of reports from
the fringes of European activity in West Africa. La Brue wrote a
glowing description of the country beyond the upper Senegal, which

32. C. Oldendorp, *Geschichte der Mission der Evangelischen Brüder auf den
Caraibischen Inseln S. Thomas, S. Croix, und S. Jan* (Barby, 1777), pp. 270–347.

33. John Matthews, *A Voyage to the River Sierra-Leone . . .* (London, 1788),
pp. 93–94.

34. Bruce returned to Europe in 1773, and the general findings of his journey were
immediately publicized. The full account first appeared as *Travels to Discover the
Source of the Nile,* 5 vols. (Edinburgh, 1790).

was printed by Labat in 1728 and reprinted by Astley. The promise
of the interior could be taken upon several sides—by merchants who
had come to suspect the rate of profit made by African middle-men
in the slave trade, or by humanitarians who wished, at least in some
moods, to show that Africa was capable of civilization. Among these,
John Wesley himself painted a very favorable picture of the West
African interior, and Wesley was widely read by the faithful.[35]

The strongest religious interest in the Western Sudan, however,
was shown by Emanuel Swedenborg. His information ostensibly came
by direct divine revelation, rather than human agency, but it was
important in directing European efforts to West Africa in the 1780's
and 1790's. According to Swedenborgian doctrine, God had created
not one church but a series of "true churches," each of them founded
in whatever part of the world men have the most perfect knowledge
of God. Each church in turn declined from its original purity. As
this happened, each in turn was "consummated" and underwent its
"last judgement." A new "true church" was then founded among another, previously heathen, nation. Swedenborg held that, up to the
eighteenth century, there had been four churches, the "Adamical
Church," the "Noahtical Church," the "Israelite Church," and the
Christian Church as it was known in Europe. Having fallen into decay, the European Christian Church had undergone its "last judgement" in 1757, and God was even then in the process of founding a
new church.[36]

There was a strong presumption in Swedenborg's writings that this
church would be in Africa. He praised the Africans of the interior regions for thinking "more internally" than other people and living a
more spiritual life. He even reproduced a map of Africa showing the
"celestial" region at the center and the corrupted nations surrounding
it. The worst of these corrupt people were shown in Egypt, those at
the Cape were a little less corrupt, and those who lived in the east
toward Asia still less so. There was no specific mention of the West
coast, but it was a possible inference from corruption elsewhere that
the best approach to the interior would be from that side.[37] Many

35. John Wesley, "Thoughts upon Slavery," in *Works* (London, 1872), XI, 59–79.
First published 1774.

36. "That the Lord now establishes a Church in Africa," *The New Jerusalem Magazine* (London, 1890), pp. 181–82. For a guide to Swedenborg's references to Africa
see J. F. Potts, *The Swedenborg Concordance*. 4 vols. (London, 1888), I, 99–100.

37. E. Swedenborg, "Continuation of the Last Judgement," in *The Last Judgement*
(London, 1951), pp. 103–5. First published 1763.

Swedenborgians both then and now reject the view that the new church was being raised in Africa and only in Africa, but some did not. Spelled out, their view came to this:

According to Swedenborg, all the nations who live in the earth may be reduced to two general species, the white and the black, the habitation of the former is chiefly in Europe and corresponds with the spiritual kingdom of the Lord. The latter dwell in Africa and correspond to the celestial kingdom of the Lord. The whites have cultivated only their understanding, but the blacks have cultivated their will and affections; the ancient Christian Church being a spiritual church, was instituted among the European nations; but this New Church being celestial cannot easily be established in Europe, by reason that the nations of which Christendom is now composed, are in a very great degree worse than the nations which do not belong to the Christian world, and whom we call Heathens; of which the Africans are the best of all; therefore the Church of the New Jerusalem becomes established among those who are situated in the interior parts of Africa.[38]

This view went beyond the present condition and possibilities of Africa. By introducing the concept of two separate species of man it went beyond the conclusions possible from current observation, and on to those that might be derived from a consideration of assumed and innate racial qualities. The Swedenborgian speculations about the interior of Africa thus merged with another and intricate body of European thought about the Africans' place in nature.

38. *New Jerusalem Magazine*, p. 183. See also Henry Serventé to James Glen, 12 August 1805, printed in *Monthly Observer, and New Church Record*, I, 313 (London, 1857); Sten Lindroth, "Adam Afzelius: A Swedish Botanist in Sierra Leone, 1792–1796," *Sierra Leone Studies*, I (n.s.), 196 (June 1955).

2

THE AFRICANS'
"PLACE IN NATURE"

The terms "racism" and "racist" have become highly emotive since the 1930's, when a special variety of racism was taken up and carried to power in Germany by the National Socialist Party. The atrocities committed during the 1940's in the name of pseudo-scientific racism give special overtones to any discussion of the history of Western thought about race differences. Race prejudice, racial consciousness, and racism can mean many things. At one level, there is the simple and unavoidable fact that major racial differences are recognizable. In every racially mixed society, in every contact between people who differ in physical appearance, there has always been instant recognition of race: it was the first determinant of inter-group social relations.

Beyond this point of recognition, the further interpretations have varied enormously. These variants have all felt the weight of a second factor—that of plain xenophobia. People tend to fear and dislike the strange and the unknown, and racial difference immediately brands the individual of another race as a stranger, and as a member of an alien group. When this happens, racial recognition may lead naturally to the assumption that such a person will have all the characteristics imputed to his group. To this extent, race difference has always played a role in history and surely will continue to play a role.

But beyond these underlying constants of race relations, more elaborate sets of ideas about race have also played an important part in history. Some people, perhaps most people, have been conscious of their own racial type. Some have assummed that they were a "chosen people," especially favored by God. Some have assumed that they, and they alone, were human. Most have preferred their own type as the esthetic standard of human beauty. Most have assumed that people of their own type were physically or mentally or culturally superior to other races.

Any of these views may be labelled "racism" of some variety, but they need to be kept separate from the full-blown pseudo-scientific racism which dominated so much of European thought between the 1840's and the 1940's. The difference lay in the fact that "science," the body of knowledge rationally derived from empirical observation, then supported the proposition that race was one of the principal determinants of attitudes, endowments, capabilities, and inherent tendencies among human beings. Race thus seemed to determine the course of human history.

These rationalized and elaborate theories about race difference were not "pseudo" in their beginnings. They were the teachings of science at its best for its own time. In the twentieth century, when earlier science is recognized to have been mistaken, they have continued as truly pseudo-scientific. That is, they claim the backing of science for propositions which the consensus of authoritative science denies, and in the face of overwhelming evidence to the contrary. It is more difficult to assess the degree of pseudo-science in the racial doctrines of the eighteenth and nineteenth centuries. Many were stated by men who pursued truth for its own sake. Others were stated by men who pursued political ends, wished to find support for their prejudice, or were merely misled by a little learning into wild speculations which the best science, even of their time, would not sustain on the basis of reason and evidence. For us, it makes little difference whether error followed the pursuit of truth or the pursuit of other ends. It received, in time, the backing of Western science, and it was, perhaps, the most disastrous error scientists have ever made.

Even today, when rationalized, "scientific" racism is no longer tenable, many people of middle age half remember the teachings of their early training and half believe, if only at an emotional level, that physical race is an outward sign of other inborn characteristics. In addition, today as in the eighteenth century, many people are subject to a variety of xenophobic feelings about people who are racially different from themselves. In this same emotional sense, the recognition of racial difference dominated European thought about Africans even before the rise of scientific and pseudo-scientific racism. If "racism" can be defined as any of the various doctrines holding that human culture and behavior are strongly influenced by physical race, then even this vague xenophobic sentiment is a form of racism. It should, however, be distinguished from the rationalized racial theories attempting to explain the nature of society in racial terms, and even more sharply distinguished from the extreme political creeds which hold that "racial inferiority" justifies inequality of treatment, enslavement, or genocide for the "inferior races." These things may follow from racism, but they are not a necessary part of racist beliefs as such.

Europeans in the later eighteenth century had already had several centuries of contact with Africans, both with the sellers of slaves on the African coasts and with the slaves in the New World. Whatever their views in detail, one assumption was almost universal. They believed that African skin color, hair texture, and facial features were associated in some way with the African way of life (in Africa) and the status of slavery (in the Americas). Once this association was made, racial views became unconsciously linked with social views, and with the common assessment of African culture. Culture prejudice thus slid off easily toward color prejudice, and the two were frequently blended in ways that were imprecise at the time—and even harder to separate after the passage of almost two centuries.

There is a further problem here. Even today, when pride of race has weakened in the West, pride of culture has continued. Many otherwise well informed people continue to think of pre-colonial Africa as a series of "primitive" societies, still in the stone age or only just emerging from it under the impact of Europe. They tend to accept an older historical tradition, which held that Africa was static, while Europe and, to a lesser extent, Asian and American civilizations advanced during the past few millennia. This view derives some of its continuing force from the general Western ignorance of the African past. It draws as well from our tendency to emphasize technology as the principal measure for the "advancement" of any society. Technology is, indeed, the one field of human culture where it is legitimate to make value judgments of general validity. (A repeating rifle is clearly superior to a bow and arrow for its purpose in hunting and warfare, but no such certainty is possible in comparing artistic culture—the bronze heads of Ife with Greek sculpture, for example.)

In technology, then, it was obvious that nineteenth-century Europe was far ahead of nineteenth-century Africa, but to see this fact alone gives too much emphasis to the short run of history. Pre-colonial Africa had long been within the iron age. Perhaps as many as a third of the people south of the Sahara lived in societies that were literate in the sense that Europe was literate during the middle ages—that is, at least a class of scribes could read and write. While there was certainly a technological lag between Africa and the West, it has to be seen against the perspective of human history. If Africa was behind, it was hardly more than a thousand years behind. The technology of most African societies of about 1750 A.D. had reached and in some respects passed the level of technology prevalent in northwest Europe in 750 A.D. If the line of comparison is pushed back further still, and centered specifically on Britain and the Western Sudan in 750 B.C., the two societies were very much on a par.

A similar comparison can be set in broader, and somewhat different, terms. Robert Redfield has made a distinction between the "little community" and the larger society of which it may form a part. This distinction can be made in Africa, separating the peasant village of the forest or savanna from the centers of learning and commerce in the towns or the courts of rulers in Abomey, Jenne, Kumasi, or Kuka. It can also be made in Europe, where peasant culture, peasant values, and quality of peasant life were historically sharply different from those of the upper classes. Taking one European century with another, from the middle ages through the seventeenth century, European peasant life did not change very radically. Neither did African peasant life change very radically from the middle ages to the end of the nineteenth century. Nor were the conditions of peasant life in Africa very markedly different from the conditions of peasant life in Europe. Both were subordinate communities, suffering from peace and war, famine and plague, and other external factors that were the normal lot of mankind. There were, of course, differences within

Africa and differences between Africa and Europe; but both shared, at the level of the "little community," the conditions common to all little communities between the invention of settled agriculture and the coming of the industrial revolution.[1]

The cultural difference between the great communities is another matter. For Europe, much is known about the life of the great communities at many periods in the past: they have too often been the sole object of historical investigation. For Africa, almost nothing is known about the distant past—about the life and thought of Ife, for example, at the period when the bronzes were cast. Comparisons are therefore difficult, but it is clear that the European great community entered a period of unusual creativity about one millennium ago. This in turn was based on a period of similar creativity in the Mediterranean basin stretching back about two millennia further. Even if we assume no such creativity in African great communities during these three millennia, three millennia are a relatively short period in the whole of man's history, and African society was far from static.

Eighteenth-century Europeans, however, were not able to look at the world with this perspective. Their ignorance of Africa was enormous, and they were only beginning the serious study of early human history. Most of their thought on the matter was still set in a Biblical frame of reference, carrying back about six thousand years. European contacts with non-Western societies outside of the Mediterranean basin were not yet really extensive. They had been increasing for the past three hundred years, but they were still contacts on the periphery. The only Europeans who had yet tried the experiment of ruling over a non-Western society were the two Hispanic powers.

The Spanish theorists and administrators had faced in the sixteenth century a whole series of questions about their proper relations with the Middle American and Andean Indians. Among these were problems of the right of Christian conquest, the nature of the Indians in law and religion, and the practical means Christians should use in dealing with them. During that century the Spanish had gathered information, quarrelled over its meaning, and beat out a "native policy" in both theory and practice. Their conclusions were further supported by the authority of the papacy. Paul III in the bull *Sublimis Deus* of

1. R. Redfield, *The Little Community and Peasant Society and Culture* (Chicago, 1960).

1537 condemned as heretical the opinion that American Indians were not rational or were incapable of receiving the True Faith, and this position was confirmed and repeated in various forms in later centuries. By extension, whatever else might be said of non-Westerners, they were officially human beings and potentially Christians with full spiritual equality.[2]

Because of the religious difference, this position did not necessarily extend to Protestant Europe. Nor did English overseas activity from the sixteenth century to the mid-eighteenth involve them in practical situations where these questions had to be met as they were by sixteenth-century Spain. The English trading posts in the East had an indigenous population, but the principal purpose was commercial, and there was no serious concern with the way men of a different culture should be ruled. In the West Indies the dominant social form by the middle of the seventeenth century was the slave plantation. Uprooted individuals from Africa were forced into a social mold that was not distinctly English—and certainly not African. In this case, the English simply took over the social forms created in the Mediterranean, and developed further in Brazil and the Hispanic West Indies. There was no need to innovate, and hence no need to consider seriously what policy to follow. Even in North America, the confrontation of the English and the Indians was not so much a "native problem" as a "frontier problem." The relatively sparse Indian population was pushed westward, rather than being absorbed into the settlers' society. Before the 1780's, it was only in Ireland that a persistent and troublesome "native problem" had developed, and here the racial and cultural difference between the metropolis and the empire was much less than that between the overseas world and the West.

In any case, the British Empire before 1783 was loosely organized. The North American settlers on one hand and the West Indian planters on the other were allowed to make their own internal policy without metropolitan interference. It was only when imperial control began to tighten in the reign of George III that British imperial theory had to take account of the questions discussed in Spain some two cen-

2. See J. H. Parry, *The Spanish Theory of Empire in the Sixteenth Century* (Cambridge, 1940); S. A. Zavala, *New Viewpoints on the Spanish Colonization of America* (Philadelphia, 1943); L. U. Hanke, *The Spanish Struggle for Justice in the Conquest of America* (Washington, 1949).

turies earlier. Especially after 1783, in the shadow of the lost war and
in a spirit of general reform, British publicists began to consider the
Africans' "place in nature" and its bearing on imperial policy.

In its early stages, with little background in conscious or rationalized theory, British consideration of African race and African culture
was highly dispersed. It was not a central problem discussed as such,
but a peripheral question that had to be taken into account by several
groups of writers. "The Negro's place in nature" naturally had a role
in whatever reporting came from Africa or the West Indies. It was
discussed from another point of view by biologists, who were just then
concerned with the problem of explaining human varieties. In quite
another context, men of letters used the convention of the "noble savage" for their own purposes. Finally, the anti-slavery writers of a
dominantly Christian and humanitarian turn of mind were forced into a discussion of race by their efforts to reform imperial policy.

Of these four groups, only the travel writers had adequate access
to empirical data. Their information, therefore, had to serve the
others as a store from which they could draw as it suited their needs
and interests. Travel reports contained something for everyone, with
accounts varying from the most bitter condemnation of Africans and
their way of life to an equally broad-minded tolerance. If there was
a principal thread running through the whole body of information,
it was one of moderate xenophobia. Slave traders, officials, and planters were all men sent out to live in dangerous tropical conditions.
They were there to do a job, and one that necessarily brought them
into contact with alien peoples whose culture they did not understand. Their resentments were those of foreign visitors in any country. In Africa they often thought they were cheated, and they disliked the strangeness of African customs. In America they took the
slaves to be obstinate, rebellious, thievish, and lazy—which they
probably were: these are the expected attributes of slaves in any society.

But for all their xenophobia, the travellers were unusually free of
racial antagonism. Most men connected with the slave trade, and
even the West Indian planters (to say nothing of the enlightened
travellers with their ethnographic and humane interests), were less
inclined to emphasize racial factors than those who stayed in England. This was especially true of their accounts of day-to-day dealings
with the Africans. In 1789, for example, sixteen recent visitors to

West Africa reported to a Privy Council Committee on the African trade. While most of them had been concerned in one way or another with the slave trade, none mentioned an assumed African racial inferiority as a bar to future development.[3] They had little respect for the African way of life, but those who belonged to the Company of Merchants Trading to Africa had in Philip Quaque, their official Chaplain at Cape Coast, an African who was later the most highly paid man on their staff, except the Governor himself.

The travellers often condemned individual Africans as bad men— or all Africans as savage men—but they left the clear impression that Africans *were* men. The African way of doing things might be curious or unpleasant, but individual Africans were shown with abilities, faults, and virtues in much the same proportion as Europeans. Merchants on the African coast (in contrast to planters in the West Indies) dealt with Africans as partners in trade—not, perhaps, equal partners, or the partners an Englishman might choose, but nevertheless men of substance whose views could not safely be ignored.[4] Thus the image of Africans in Africa was radically different from the stereotype of the servile Africans of the Americas.

Moderate xenophobia, with emphasis on the fact of moderation, was reproduced in the popular attitude toward Africans in England, especially among those in day-to-day contact. Negro servants who came to England from the colonies were popular with their masters and were often valued by the aristocracy in preference to white servants. They were also popular with their European fellow-servants, and with members of the English working class who came to know them. Some racial tension was present, but it came from the normal distrust of strangers, from sexual competition or the belief that Negroes took away employment from Englishmen.[5] However wrongheaded these attitudes might be, either on the Coast or in England,

3. Great Britain. Privy Council. *Report of the Lords of the Committee of Council for . . . Trade and Foreign Plantations . . . Concerning the Present State of Trade to Africa, and Particularly the Trade in Slaves . . .* (London, 1789), Part I.

4. The most accessible sample of mid-eighteenth century attitudes is T. Astley (Publisher), *A New General Collection of Voyages and Travels,* 4 vols. (London, 1745–1747). For representative later works see: William Snelgrave, *A New Account of Guinea and the Slave Trade* (London, 1754); Bryan Edwards, *The History, Civil and Commercial, of the British Colonies in the West Indies,* 2nd ed., 2 vols. (London, 1794); John Matthews, *Voyage to the River Sierra-Leone . . .* (London, 1788), esp. pp. 91–94. See also B. Davidson, *Black Mother* (London, 1961), pp. 101–2.

5. J. J. Hecht, *Continental and Colonial Servants in Eighteenth Century England* (Northampton, Mass., 1954), pp. 33–36, 45–47.

they arose from the practical concerns of one people dealing with another. As such, they were in touch with social reality. Race as such was a *mark* identifying the group—not a *cause* of the group's other characteristics.

A different kind of attitude emerged when the travellers abstracted from qualities of individuals and began to talk about the group—not individual men but the collective "Negro." Reporting of this kind became increasingly common in the 1780's, as the Africa interest felt itself threatened by the rise of the anti-slave-trade movement. Several writers began to project a double image, relatively friendly to individual Africans but unfriendly to the collective African. Individuals in Norris' *Memoirs of the Reign of Bossa Ahadee,* for example, are clearly living portraits of men not especially different from men elsewhere, while "the African" in his collective image is an inhuman savage.[6]

As the element of political purpose made its appearance, so did a certain degree of circularity between the works of travellers to Africa and those of theorists in Britain. Lt. John Matthews, the pro-slavery author of an account of the Coast in 1785–1787, wrote from what were ostensibly his own observations. Some parts of his works were in the matter-of-fact tradition of earlier reports, but some were clearly derived from Edward Long, an early "scientific" racist resident in Jamaica, who had never visited Africa. Long's low assessment of "the Negro's place in nature" thus found its way into Matthew's book, where it could later be picked up as a piece of first-hand evidence from Africa.[7]

The tendency to write about the abstract and collective "Negro" was strongest among biological writers, whose business it was to deal with abstractions of this kind. Where the travellers set out to report what they saw, without the necessity of building their evidence into a system, the eighteenth-century biologists began with a system and used empiricism to make it as accurate as they could. Their principal aim was to examine, classify, and arrange the whole order of nature in a rational pattern.

6. R. Norris, *Memoirs of the Reign of Bossa Ahadee, King of Dahomey* (London, 1789).

7. Matthews, *Voyage to Sierra-Leone,* pp. 158–59; Edward Long, *History of Jamaica,* 3 vols. (London, 1774), II, 373–74.

This emphasis on the creation of a large-scale system tended to distract attention from the systematic study of man. The first concern of naturalists like Linnaeus and Banks was the world-wide collection of specimens to build up a picture of botany and the zoology of the "lower animals," which made up the largest part of the whole order of nature. No individual or group of scholars was concerned with anthropology, defined a century later as "that science which deals with all phenomena exhibited by collective man, and by him alone, which is capable of being reduced to law."[8] The physical structure of man belonged institutionally to anatomical studies, as a branch of medicine. Data about human culture and society outside of Europe was collected by whatever travellers happened to have the interest to write down what they saw. Analysis of these data was mainly left to a rather vague and still-undifferentiated social science, most often under the rubric of "moral philosophy." The scientific study of human varieties therefore fell by default to the biologists, as a kind of appendix to their general systems of nature.

The major eighteenth-century classifications of nature began with Linnaeus' *Systema Naturae,* first published in 1735, and later revised with additions. This work and its successors formed the basic framework of modern biological classification, and they were decidedly set in the eighteenth-century modes of thought. One of the important items of intellectual lumber common to educated men was the ancient belief that God (or Nature, according to taste) had so organized the world that all creation was arranged in a "Great Chain of Being"— that all living things could be classified and fitted into a hierarchy extending "from man down to the smallest reptile, whose existence can be discovered only by the microscope."[9]

Since man had a place as the highest term on the scale, the varieties of mankind had also to be taken into account, and the biologists assumed from the beginning that they too could be arranged in hierarchic order. Linnaeus himself included a racial classification, which changed slightly in different editions of his work. Initially it was a simple system based on skin color, with a white, red, yellow, and black race, each of them placed on one of the four major continents.

8. T. Bendyshe, "The History of Anthropology," *Memoirs Read Before the Anthropological Society of London,* I, 335 (1863–1864).

9. Charles White, *An Account of the Regular Graduations in Man* . . . (London, 1799), p. 1. See also A. O. Lovejoy, *The Great Chain of Being* (Cambridge, Mass., 1936).

In 1758 he divided *genus homo* into two species to make room for
orang-outangs and certain rumored wild men without speech.[10] This
later division seemed to be called for by another assumption implicit
in the Great Chain of Being: since God in His perfection must have
created a perfect hierarchy of living things, the gap between any
two creatures was not expected to be very great—not, certainly, so
great as that between man and the higher apes.

Other authorities used a four-fold classification like that of Linnaeus, or else dropped back to the ancient and familiar Biblical distinction between the descendents of Ham, Shem, and Japhet, and thus
to a three-fold division. Or, the three-fold division could be extended
to five by introducing mixed races. J. F. Blumenbach of Göttingen
worked with three primary races, the Caucasian, Ethiopian, and Mongolian. American Indians were taken to be a mixture of Caucasian
and Mongolian, and a Malay race was supposedly a mixture of Mongolian and Ethiopian. Blumenbach's term "Caucasian" for the European variety lasted into the twentieth century, but later authorities
using the five-fold system adopted their own variants. Thus, John
Hunter in England took the European, American, and African to be
three primary varieties, with two other mixed races to fill out the
scheme.[11] By any of these systems of classification, the African variety
was always considered a primary stock, if only because of its skin
color, so strikingly different from that of Europeans.

Whatever the number of races, the second problem was to arrange
them in order of quality. Since there is no strictly scientific or biological justification for stating that one race is "higher" than another,
the criteria of ranking had to come from non-scientific assumptions.
All of the biologists gave some order of classification, but few of
them stated their basis for doing so. Their unstated assumptions,
however, were clear enough, even when they were not explicit. All of
them began by putting the European variety at the top of the scale.
This was natural enough, if only as an unthinking reflection of cul-

10. A. C. Haddon, *History of Anthropology*, 2nd ed. (London, 1934), p. 71.
11. J. F. Blumenbach, "On the Natural Variety of Mankind" (1775 and 1795),
p. 264; John Hunter, "An Inaugural Disputation on the Varieties of Man" (1775),
pp. 366–67. Both translated in T. Bendyshe (Ed.), *The Anthropological Treatises of
Johann Friedrich Blumenbach* (London, 1865). This John Hunter, a physician (d.
1809) should not be confused with his more famous namesake, the anatomist (1723–
1793). See DNB biographies. It is an interesting commentary on the staying power of
these first formulations that Blumenbach's terminology and the substance of his classification was still in use by the United States Immigration Service in 1961.

tural chauvinism. It could be held to follow from their assessment of European achievements in art and science, or even from the "fact" that God had given the One True Religion to the whites. It was taken for granted that historical achievement was intimately connected with physical form—in short, that race and culture were closely related.

The first term of the series was thus accepted by common agreement. Disagreement came only with the ranking of the others. One solution was to concentrate on skin color. If whiteness of skin was the mark of the highest race, then darker races would be inferior in the increasing order of their darkness. On this basis, and with no further evidence, Africans could be put at the bottom. Esthetic judgements could also be introduced. Blumenbach, who became in his later years a champion of the Negro, fell into this form of racio-esthetic pride. He described Caucasians as having, "in general the kind of appearance which, according to our opinion of symmetry, we consider most handsome and becoming." His description of Africans was less flattering:

Ethiopian variety. Colour black; hair black and curly, head narrow, compressed at the sides; forehead knotty, uneven, malar bones protruding outwards; eyes very prominent; nose thick, mixed up as it were with the wide jaws; alveolur edge narrow, elongated in front; upper primaries obliquely prominent; lips very puffy; chin retreating. Many are bandy-legged. To this variety belong all the Africans, except those of the North.[12]

This description was hardly accurate, and even where it was accurate it took the European type as a standard of comparison. Blumenbach, however, was more kind to the Africans than his colleagues. He gave primacy to the "Caucasian" variety, but he placed the others below it on the same level. Here at least, Negroes were not automatically put at the bottom of the human family. Blumenbach was also conscious that qualitative descriptions of this kind were not sufficiently precise, and he experimented with head shape as a possible basis for a more accurate system of classification.

The most important of the eighteenth century attempts to quantify racial distinctions, however, was the work of Pieter Camper (1722–1789) in Holland. "Camper's facial Angle," as it was later called, was essentially a measurement of prognathism, derived by looking at a human head in profile. One line was drawn from the meeting of the lips to the most prominent part of the forehead, and another

12. Blumenbach, "Varieties of Mankind," pp. 265–66.

from the opening of the ear to the base of the nose. The crucial angle was formed where these two lines met. Presumably, the wider the angle, the smaller the degree of prognathism, and prognathism was suggestive of the headshape of animals. A wide angle was also supposed to indicate a higher forehead, a greater skull capacity, a better esthetic appearance, and greater intelligence. Camper claimed that, if this angle were measured for men of various races (or even for animals), the measurements would fall into an ordered series, from Greek statuary as the ideal form, through the European races, to Negroes as the lowest human variety, and finally to the "lower animals."[13] After a vogue of popularity in the later eighteenth century, Camper's angle died out of respectable usage, principally because it was extremely difficult to measure accurately. But the suggestion that skull shape had something to do with ability was to have a long future.

The attempts to classify and grade human races were damaging enough to the reputation of Africans, but the efforts to explain the origin of race were more serious still. The traditional and orthodox view was that of Christian revelation: God created man, a single pair, at a finite time in the not-very-distant past. Scientific versions of this belief in a single creation came to be known as "monogenesis." If the basic tenets of monogenesis were accepted, all the biologist had to do was explain the origin of later variations among Adam's descendants.

There were many suggestions. Moreau de Maupertuis believed the original creation included the creation of all the racial varieties to emerge later in time. They were latent in the original female egg and the original male sperm given to Adam and Eve, though Adam and Eve were themselves of the white race. When Negro variants appeared, the "normal" part of mankind drove them off into Africa, a less desirable part of the world. Once there, they continued to breed true to their Negro form and color, though it was still possible that they might one day change back into their original European race.[14]

A more common view held that African form and color were acquired traits, strengthened through generations of life in the tropics,

13. Haddon, *History of Anthropology,* p. 16: W. E. Mühlmann, *Geschichte der Anthropologie* (Bonn, 1948), p. 60.

14. P. L. Moreau de Maupertuis, "Venus Physique" (1745), II, pp. 106–10, 129–30, in *Oeuvres de Maupertuis,* 4 vols. (Lyon, 1756).

not unlike a heritable and constantly deepening suntan. This was authoritatively restated in Buffon's *Histoire naturelle,* which began to appear in 1749, and it was repeated by later monogenists like Blumenbach and John Hunter.[15] Kant's position was midway between this and the opinion of Moreau de Maupertuis. He thought that Negro features and skin color were not simply acquired characteristics. They were latent in the original stock and appeared when it was subject to heat and humidity.[16]

The unconscious assumption in all these ideas was that God had created man "in His image," which was necessarily the image of the biologist. Other varieties must therefore be worse varieties, and thus "degenerations" from the original stock. Even at its worst, however, the usual monogenetic view allowed all races a place in humanity, and peoples who had "degenerated" in a few thousand years might well "improve" again in a relatively short time.

The opposing theory of polygenesis was less favorable. It held that each race was a separate creation, distinct from the children of Adam and permanently so. Although polygenesis was a minority position in eighteenth-century Europe, it has probably been the most common explanation of race throughout human history. Several European suggestions to this effect had appeared from time to time, in spite of the open contradiction of the Bible. One of the most widely read was Isaac LaPeyrere's *Prae-Adamitae,* published in 1655, which held that Adam and Eve had been the last of a series of special creations, and some of the living non-Europeans were descended from the earlier pre-Adamites. Another possibility was that of the anonymous *Co-Adamitae* of 1732, which held that all races were created simultaneously but not endowed with equal ability. The idea was specifically applied to Africans in 1734 by John Atkins, a naval surgeon who had visited the Coast.[17]

Polygenesis was especially attractive to the eighteenth century *phi-*

15. Blumenbach, "Varieties of Mankind," pp. 209–13; Hunter. "Inaugural Disputation." See also J. C. Greene, "Some Early Speculations on the Origin of Human Races," *American Anthropologist,* LVI, 33 (February 1954).

16. E. W. Count, "The Evolution of the Race Idea in Modern Western Culture during the Period of the Pre-Darwinian Nineteenth Century," *Transactions of the New York Academy of Sciences,* VIII (2nd series), 143–45 (February, 1946); A. O. Lovejoy, "Kant and Evolution," in B. Glass and others, *Forerunners of Darwin, 1745–1859* (Baltimore, 1959), pp. 186–87.

17. Bendyshe, "History of Anthropology," pp. 345–49; Count, "The Race Idea," p. 158; John Atkins. *Navy Surgeon* . . . (London, 1734), pp. 23–24.

losophes who were concerned to find a plausible and systematic explanation of the world, and not especially concerned either with religious orthodoxy or with the kind of evidence they used. Both Voltaire and Rousseau suggested that Negroes were naturally inferior to Europeans in their mental ability. David Hume argued that, "There never was a civilized nation of any other complexion than white, nor even any individual eminent either in action or speculation. No ingenious manufactures amongst them, no arts, no sciences. . . . Such a uniform and constant difference could not happen, in so many countries and ages, if nature had not made an original distinction betwixt these breeds of men."[18] He thus incorporated the two key assumptions—that white Europeans had a superior culture, and that race and culture were causally connected.

New evidence for polygenesis was brought to light by the publication of Buffon's *Histoire naturelle,* even though Buffon himself was a monogenist. His comparative anatomy showed that there were amazing similarities in physical structure between all animals, and especially between men and certain apes. This information fitted in with the Great Chain of Being and the expected close gradation between species. As early as 1713 naturalists began looking for a "missing link" between men and apes and speculated on the possibility that Hottentots and orang-outangs might be side by side in the "scale of life," separated only by the fact that orang-outangs could not speak.[19]

By the mid-century anatomical knowledge was improving and the structural similarities seemed even clearer. Linnaeus changed his classification in 1758 to allow for lower species of *genus homo.* In 1773 James Burnet, Lord Monboddo, stretched the classification still further and included men and orang-outangs in the same species. The following year, his friend, Lord Kames, published *Sketches of the History of Man,* where he developed a fully fledged polygenist theory. Kames held that God had created the varieties of men in order to adapt each to a particular climate. But neither Monboddo

18. David Hume, "Of National Character," *The Philosophical Works of David Hume,* 4 vols. (London, 1898), III, 252. The essay was first published in 1742, but the passage quoted was added as a footnote in the edition of 1753–54. See also M. Cook, "Jean Jacques Rousseau and the Negro," *Journal of Negro History,* XXI, 294–303 (July, 1936).

19. Lovejoy, *Great Chain of Being,* pp. 233 ff.; A. O. Lovejoy, "Some Eighteenth Century Evolutionists," *Popular Science Monthly,* LXV, 327 (1904).

nor Kames were biologists. Monboddo merely wanted to cite an example of a human society without language, and Kames was struck by the distinct physical appearance of Europeans and Africans. Neither statement was well supplied with evidence that could pass for "scientific," and both were shocking to orthodox Christians.[20]

Another work of 1774 was to be immensely more important in giving a pseudo-scientific base to polygenist theories already in the air. This was the *History of Jamaica* by Edward Long, who, as a resident of the island, was in a position to bring forward "evidence" about the African slaves. In spite of the title, the book was a multivolume compendium of history and description, and a guide to future British policy in Jamaica. In a key section, Long tried to assess the place of the Negro in nature, drawing partly on Buffon and partly on the xenophobia natural to his home, where lines of caste and race ran parallel. Africans, in his opinion were "brutish, ignorant, idle, crafty, treacherous, bloody, thievish, mistrustful, and superstitious people." Their skins were dark, their features different, and they had "a covering of wool, like the bestial fleece, instead of hair." They were inferior in "faculties of mind," had a "bestial and fetid smell," and were even parasitized by black lice instead of the lighter-colored lice of the Europeans.[21] All of this was the common prejudice of the West Indies.

Long's importance in biological thought was not simply his restatement of old prejudice, but the fact that he gave his prejudice the backing of technical biological arguments. He claimed that Europeans and Negroes did not belong to the same species. Since species were generally held to have been created in the beginning by God, while varieties were produced after the creation, it was a distinction of some importance. Species also had a technical meaning that still persists: individuals that can breed together and produce fertile offspring are considered to be of the same species.

Long tried, among other things, to associate Negroes with animals by claiming that Negro children, like animals, mature more rapidly than whites. According to him, Negro women bear children after

20. A. O. Lovejoy, "Monboddo and Rousseau," *Modern Philology*, XXX, 275–96 (February, 1933); James Burnet, Lord Monboddo, *The Origin and Progress of Language*, 8 vols. (Edinburgh, 1773–1792), I, 279–90; Henry Home, Lord Kames, *Sketches of the History of Man*, 2nd ed., 4 vols. (Edinburgh, 1788), I, 11–13, 36–40.

21. Long, *Jamaica*, II, 353–56.

only brief labor and practically without pain. This point could be taken to "prove" that Negro women escaped the Divinity's curse on Eve's female descendants. (It might equally well have "proved" that Negroes were without original sin, but Long went no further in his theological speculations.) Finally, as the key argument, Long claimed that mulattoes were unfertile hybrids. This particular point was a little difficult to sustain in the face of evident race mixture in the West Indies, but most of his readers had no access to the evidence, and his specific argument was subtle enough to pass with people who might otherwise know better. He admitted that Europeans and Africans could breed together in the first generation and produce fertile children, but the mulatto children would only be fertile when breeding with one or the other of the "pure" races. Mulattoes breeding with other mulattoes could not in his opinion, produce a permanent mixed race.[22]

On this basis, Long divided *genus homo* into three species: Europeans and similar people, Negroes, and "orang-outangs." This last group included not only the real orang-outangs of Southeast Asia, but also the larger African tailless apes, such as chimpanzees. Using the evidence from Buffon that so impressed Lord Monboddo, he argued that these "orang-outangs" differed from other men only in the formation of the feet and the *os ilium,* and in their inability to speak or reason. But this failing was only a matter of education. The apes would be able to talk and think well enough, if only they were properly trained.[23]

Long's system also met the demands of the Great Chain of Being. There were three species of man, with many gradations within the species. He arranged Africans on an ascending scale from the half-legendary Jagas of Angola upwards through Hottentots, Fulbe and Mandinka peoples of West Africa, to the Wolof and Ethiopians, the highest type of African man.[24] He could thus claim a certain credibility on grounds of symmetry alone: "The system of man will seem more consistent, and the measure of it more complete, and analogous to the harmony and order that are visible in every other line of the world's stupendous fabric. Nor is this conclusion degrading to human nature, while it tends to exalt our idea of the infinite perfections

22. Long, *Jamaica,* II, 336–37, 380.
23. Long, *Jamaica,* II, 358–71.
24. Long, *Jamaica,* II, 373–74.

of the Deity; for how vast is the difference between inert matter, and matter embued with thought and reason."[25]

Long's ideas on race are so obviously nonsense by any modern standard, their importance has sometimes been neglected. He was widely read by the naturalists of his time, and his thought had a place in the background of the theory of biological evolution. Even though he published later than Monboddo and knew about Monboddo's theory, he seems to have "discovered" the human qualities of the orang-outang independently, and he stated his case with more "scientific" care than Monboddo had done. Long's West Indian background also gave a note of authority, even though the "facts" he claimed to have observed himself were often false. Where Monboddo was laughed at for thinking that apes were men, Long was not laughed at for saying that Negroes were less than men. The idea fitted all too well into the pattern of racial and cultural pride already prevalent in English thought.

Long's greatest importance was in giving an "empirical" and "scientific" base that would lead on to pseudo-scientific racism. The part of the *History of Jamaica* dealing with race was reprinted in America in the *Columbia Magazine* of 1788, where it became a support for later American racism.[26] It was used again and again for three-quarters of a century by British and Continental polygenists of scientific repute, and it provided a set of ready made arguments for any publicist who wanted to prove the "fact" of African inferiority.

Long was more of a pro-slavery publicist than a scientist, but his views influenced even those scientists who believed in a more liberal social policy. One of the more important restatements of the polygenist case toward the end of the eighteenth century was that of Charles White, a Manchester physician. White favored the abolition of slavery throughout the world—an advanced position for his day, when only the slave trade was under direct attack in Parliament—but his attention was drawn to the similarities between human and animal skulls by the lectures of John Hunter on comparative anatomy. Hunter himself was a monogenist, but White discarded that position largely on the strength of Long's evidence. Like many of his contemporaries, he was also impressed by an inordinate admiration for European physical beauty and the expectation of a symmetrical and graded order of nature.[27]

White's thesis was first presented in 1795, and new biological work over the two decades since Long had published made it possible for him to clear up some of Long's patent inaccuracies. He straightened out the difference between chimpanzees and orang-outangs. By reference to Camper's dissection of apes, he showed that they could never be taught to speak. Thus the "orang-outangs" were down-graded and sent back to become two different species of *simiae*. But the greater care and precision merely made polygenesis scientifically respectable, without saving the reputation of the Africans. Indeed, new "evidence" had been produced by S. T. von Soemmering in Germany, whose comparative anatomy of Negroes and Europeans showed striking physical differences between the two races.[28] Soemmering's work had been badly done, but it was enough to satisfy White, who checked it by measuring a single Negro skeleton. He was even more impressed by the alleged mental inferiority of the Africans—a "fact" which he accepted on the authority of Thomas Jefferson, Edward Long, and a single visitor to the East Indies. His conclusion was to produce a new division of mankind into four separately created species. In descending order, these were the European, Asian, American, and African. The one saving grace was that all four species had souls.[29]

It is clear that the biologists, as well as the travellers, were influenced by the tendencies of "diversificationism." They were actively looking for differences between human races. On one hand, this tended to blind them to similarities. On the other, it made them more willing to accept popular myths. There was, for example, a belief going back to antiquity, that southern people are more lascivious than northerners. It was sometimes re-expressed in racial terms, and Negroes were given credit for extraordinary sexual prowess. In the guarded language of a popular pamphlet of 1772: "The lower class of women in *England,* are remarkably fond of the blacks, for reasons too brutal to mention. . . ."[30] The biologists were less timid.

27. White, *Regular Gradations in Man,* pp. iii, 1, 125–29, 134–35.
28. S. T. von Soemmering, *Über die Köperlich Verschiedenbeit des Negers vom Europäer* (Frankfurt am Main, 1785).
29. White, *Regular Gradations in Man,* pp. 26–29, 41–44, 63–66, 83–85, 125–33.
30. *Candid Reflections Upon the Judgement Lately Awarded by the Court of King's Bench in Westminster-Hall, on What is Commonly Called the Negro-Cause, by a Planter* (London, T. Lownes, 1772), p. 49.

Both monogenists and polygenists thought the penis of Negro men was larger than that of Europeans, and that Negro women were sexually more desirable for physiological reasons left unexplained.[31] Thus a great deal of the popular xenophobia already prevalent on the fringes of Empire came to be expressed in terms of race difference and endowed with "scientific" authority.

There were only occasional efforts to redress the balance and recall the unity of mankind. Adam Smith pointed out the relativity of physical beauty: "What different ideas are formed in different nations concerning the beauty of the human shape and countenance? A fair complexion is a shocking deformity on the coast of Guinea. Thick lips and a flat nose are a beauty."[32]

John Hunter held that, "Travellers have exaggerated the mental varieties far beyond the truth, who have denied good qualities to the inhabitants of other countries, because their mode of life, manners and customs have been excessively different from their own."[33]

But only Blumenbach among the biological writers made a serious effort to correct the dominant tendencies of the science as a whole. In some of his later writings he not only moderated his own earlier racial chauvinism but tried to make a reasoned case for Negro equality. His defense significantly stressed the non-biological factors which had contributed so heavily to the ranking of human races. Since the Negro race was so often condemned by reference to African culture, Blumenbach compiled brief biographies of Africans who had made a name for themselves in European society. His list of notable Negroes included an author of Latin poetry, a Prussian counsellor of state, a meteorologist, and a variety of literary figures.[34]

Blumenbach's authority was undoubted, and his work was enormously influential far into the nineteenth century, especially with English anthropologists like Prichard and Lawrence. His positive and scientific anti-racism was therefore of the greatest importance in stemming the eighteenth-century tendencies toward pseudo-scientific racism, even though his was a minority voice in his own time—in much the same way that full-scale polygenesis was a minority position on

31. Long, *Jamaica,* II, 383–84; Blumenbach, "Varieties of Mankind," p. 249; White, *Regular Gradations in Man,* p. 61.

32. A Smith, "The Theory of Moral Sentiments," *Essays* (London, 1869), p. 175. First published 1757.

33. Hunter, "Inaugural Disputation," p. 392.

34. J. F. Blumenbach, "Observations on the Bodily Conformation and Mental Capacity of the Negroes," *Philosophical Magazine,* III, 141–47 (1799).

the anti-Negro side. The majority view of the biological writers was still monogenesis, but monogenesis with strong overtones of racial pride.

While the reputation of the Africans lost something in the chance tendencies of eighteenth-century biological thought, it gained from the literary convention of the "noble savage." The alien or savage literary hero began to appear as a stock figure of English *belles lettres* toward the end of the seventeenth century and reached a kind of peak of popularity toward the end of the eighteenth.

This literary African had some characteristics of the biological African of the same period. He was just as much an abstraction, and drawn just as much from the needs of European thought without concern for the empirical evidence. The noble savage as a literary hero was not only removed from reality, he was necessarily so. Any literary hero of this period was something of an abstraction, designed to point moral lessons. His exceptional qualities of strength, intellect, or virtue reflected, while at the same time they reinforced, the ethical standards of the age. From the later seventeenth century onward, some heroes were drawn for the purpose of criticizing the artificialities of European civilization. It was the fashion to show virtue or nobility springing from nature itself, rather than from training or birth. The hero's origin was of little consequence, as long as he was alien to the social class of the reading public. He could be from the lower orders, by preference from the peasantry and thus close to the soil. He could be from an exotic overseas society, in which case the author could indulge the romantic taste of the public in still another way.

The exotic hero drew on several aspects of European thought. It was an ancient device of social criticism to describe a golden age—a time and place infinitely better than the real world, necessarily beyond the view of the audience, either in the past, the future, or a far country. European explorations in the sixteenth century had opened the possibility of setting all manner of utopias in the half-known lands of the non-Western world. Even before the discoveries, some European traditions had associated simplicity and moral excellence. The medieval Franciscans laid great stress on the value of unadorned nature, apostolic poverty, and a simplicity that was thought of as "primitive."[35] Perhaps because they expected to find a golden age of

35. J. L. Phelan, *The Millennial Kingdom of the Franciscans in the New World* (Berkeley, 1956), pp. 64–65.

primitive simplicity overseas, the travellers' reports often described
the moral superiority of savage life. Not all, of course, were en-
chanted by the world beyond Europe, but the belief in actual "good
savages" was strong enough in the eighteenth century to support such
visions as Swedenborg's dream of a new Church to be founded in the
heart of Africa. All the more reason to draw the literary hero from
a "savage" society.[36]

The first popular African hero appeared in English literature with
Aphra Behn's *Oroonoko*, before the end of the seventeenth century,
but he was merely the standard hero in fancy dress. The fully con-
ventionalized "noble savage" made his entrance only in the second
half of the eighteenth century along with the cult of nature. Rousseau's glorified "state of nature" was widely misunderstood, but it
gave color to the alleged virtues of savage society.[37] The savage himself became more and more like Pope's poor Indian,

> . . . whose untutor'd mind
> Sees God in clouds, or hears him in the wind;
> His soul proud Science never taught to stray
> Far as the solar walk, or milky-way;
> Yet simple Nature to his hope has giv'n
> Behind the cloud-topt hill an humbler heav'n; . . . .[38]

By the 1760's the literary fad was fully developed in England, with
pride of place going to the American Indian, the noble savage *par
excellence*. The publicity attending Cook's voyages added the Poly-
nesians, and Africans came in especially with the 1770's, as the anti-
slavery movement enlisted the sympathy and talents of literary men.[39]

Beyond any doubt, the use of the savage hero as a literary device
helped to create a much more favorable emotional climate for
Africans than they would otherwise have enjoyed, but it was not so
wholly favorable as might appear. The writers in this vein had no
intention of suggesting that Africans were better than Europeans, or
that their culture, on balance, measured up to the achievements of

36. For the theme of the noble savage, the best general treatment is H. N. Fairchild,
The Noble Savage (New York, 1928), on which much of the following account is
based.

37. A. O. Lovejoy, "The Supposed Primitivism of Rousseau's Discourse on Inequality," *Modern Philology*, XXI, 165–86 (November, 1923); Cook, "Rousseau and
the Negro."

38. Alexander Pope, *Essay on Man* (1732), Epistle I, lines 95–104.

39. For a discussion of this literature see Wylie Sypher, *Guinea's Captive Kings*
(Chapel Hill, 1942) and E. B. Dykes, *The Negro in English Romantic Thought* (Washington, 1942).

Europe. A poet, such as William Roscoe, might lavish praise on
African art:

> The sable artist; to the jav'lin's shaft,
> The ebon staff; or maple goblet, gave
> Fantastic decorations; simply carv'd
> Yet not inelegant: beneath his hand,
> Oft too a cloth of firmer texture grew,
> That steep'd in azure, mocks the brittle threads,
> And fleeting tincture, of our boasted arts.[40]

But Roscoe's sentiments should not be mistaken. He was not suggesting that Europeans should import African textiles or buy African
carvings. Neither he nor his audience believed for a moment that
Africans had a superior art. He merely points with slight wonder to
the fact they had any art at all. In the same way, the nobility of the
savage hero was not a greater nobility than might well be achieved
by a European. The lesson to be drawn was that *even* a savage could
rise to nobility of action because he was close to nature. The attitude
was mildly patronizing, and the impact of the literature depended in
part on the superiority feelings of the audience. It did not even imply
liberal views about race or social policy on the part of the author.
Racists and defenders of West Indian slavery could and did use the
device of the noble Negro in their literary work.[41]

When the theme of the noble savage merged with Christian humanitarianism of the anti-slavery movement, the patronizing attitude
persisted. Christians could not very well depict people without knowledge of God's word as equal in all respects to themselves. Spiritual
equality, they certainly had, but even so Christian and humanitarian
a poet as William Blake could couple a belief in spiritual equality
with pejorative references to the dark skin of the Africans.

> My mother bore me in the southern wild,
> And I am black, but O! my soul is white;
> White as an angel is the English child,
> But I am black, as if bereav'd of light.[42]

The mixture of attitudes in the anti-slavery poets varied widely.
In Day and Bicknell's *Dying Negro,* one of the earliest and most
popular of the longer poems, the theme is that of superiority to

40. *The Wrongs of Africa, a Poem* (London, 1787), p. 10.
41. Sypher, *Guinea's Captive Kings,* pp. 6–7.
42. From "Songs of Innocence and of Experience," in *Poetical Works of William Blake* (London, 1914), p. 68. First published 1789.

circumstances drawn from nature, but equality drawn from God. The combination is summed up in the authors' picture of Africa:

> There too Heav'n planted man's majestic race;
> Bade reason's sons with nobler title rise,
> Lift high their brow sublime, and scan the skies,
> What tho' no rosy tints adorn their face,
> No silken ringlets shine with flowing grace?
> Yet of etherial temper are their souls,
> And in their veins the tide of honour rolls;
> And valorous kindles there the hero's flame,
> Contempt of death, and thirst for martial fame.[43]

Here the portrait of the noble African was at its most favorable, as might be expected from an author trying to make a political argument as well as a work of literature. But even here he took for granted an esthetic prejudice in favor of "silken ringlets" and "rosy tints." The contrast on which this literary effect depends is still (though less skillfully used) the same as Blake's.

After its phase of greatest popularity in the last three decades of the eighteenth century, the theme of the noble Negro died out slowly, with an occasional re-appearance throughout the first half of the nineteenth. Its importance for English thought about Africa is very difficult to assess. It certainly helped to form a vague and positive image of the "good African," and it was widely used by the anti-slave-trade publicists for exactly this purpose. On the other hand it was very much a literary convention, not a rationally supported affirmation about savage life. Aside from those who used it for polemic anti-slavery ends, literary men had no intention of speaking as ethnographic popularizers. They were principally social critics of their own world. As Fairchild put it, "The true Noble Savage arises from a combination of disillusion about the here and now and illusion about the there and then."[44] In some instances, at least, the illusion was consciously an illusion, which the author himself considered a form of poetic license, though many readers probably mistook poetry for reality. Curious assumptions about the nobility of savages recur during the next half century in unexpected quarters outside the field of *belles lettres,* as though the writers were still echoing a belief picked up in casual reading when young.

---

43. Thomas Day and John Bicknell, *The Dying Negro* (London, 1775), pp. 7–8. First published 1773.

44. *The Noble Savage,* p. 127.

Just as literary men who used the convention of the noble savage
were not principally concerned to describe Africa or Africans, humanitarians of the anti-slavery movement were not principally interested in "the Negro." Their own aim was to eradicate evil as they
saw it from the world. The more emotional Christianity of the later
eighteenth century, especially the Wesleyan movement and its coun-
terpart, the Evangelical wing of the Church of England, made new
moral demands on Christians. It was not enough for them, to live
by a negative code—to abide by the "Thou shalt not's" and be present
once a week at Church services. The Christian life included positive
responsibilities. Whatever talent, wealth, or training a Christian
might have was not his alone. He was obliged to dispense some part
of it for the relief of his fellow creatures, and he was accountable to
God for the use he made of it.[45]

The African slave trade was one of the first evils to catch the
attention of the humanitarians. It was perfectly evident that the trade
produced suffering in Africa, more loss of life in transit to the Coast
and to America, and still further cruelty on the American plantations.
The Religious Society of Friends had opposed both slavery and the
trade on moral grounds since the seventeenth century. The secular
rights-of-man philosophy of the eighteenth century added another
thread of opposition. The continuing body of travel literature from
West Africa and the West Indies called attention, often unconsciously, to the amount of human suffering necessarily involved in the
customary form of labor supply to the South Atlantic System.[46]

Whatever the source of opposition, there was no need in the beginning to enquire what *kind* of men the Africans were. For secular
reformers, they were simply men, entitled as such to their natural
rights. For Christians they were "fellow creatures." (Even the most
anti-Negro racist could hardly deny this minimum claim and still
remain a Christian.) In either case, it could be argued that Africans
were entitled to the benevolence and protection of the "civilized

45. Thomas Clarkson, *History of the Rise, Progress, and Accomplishment of the
Abolition of the African Slave Trade by the British Parliament*, 2 vols. (London, 1808).
I, 7.
46. For the varying points of view on the anti-slave-trade movement, see, in addi-
tion to Clarkson: R. Coupland, *The British Anti-Slavery Movement* (London, 1933);
R. Coupland, *Wilberforce: A Narrative* (Oxford, 1923); F. J. Klingberg, *The Anti
Slavery Movement in England* (New Haven, 1926); G. R. Mellor, *British Imperia
Trusteeship 1783–1850* (London, 1951); Eric Williams, *Capitalism and Slavery* (Chape
Hill, 1944).

world"—at the very least, against the evils caused by Christian and civilized men. The initial issue was thus that of slavery as such, without concern for racial status, the supposed barbarism of African culture, or the place of Africans on the Great Chain of Being.

Individual reformers came into the movement with a variety of opinions about the Africans, or with no opinion at all. Granville Sharp, the principal leader of the fight against slavery in England itself, rested his initial case on purely legal arguments. The laws of England took no account of slavery, therefore any slave brought to England should automatically become a free man.[47] This view already had some support in judicial decisions, and it was sustained in 1772 by Lord Mansfield.[48] Even as late as this first victory, Sharp himself was uncertain about the nature of the Africans. He wrote to Jacob Bryant, the antiquarian, asking for information and saying: "I am far from having any particular esteem for the Negroes; but as I think myself obliged to consider them as *men,* I am certainly obliged also to use my best endeavours to prevent their being treated as *beasts* by our unchristian countrymen; . . ."[49]

Bryant answered that Negroes were human, descended from Adam through the line of Ham, like all dark-skinned peoples. This was clear enough to satisfy the needs of the moment, but it was not the only image of "the African" reflected in Evangelical thought. John Wesley himself was, at best, ambivalent in his attitude toward Africans and their culture. Through the bulk of his printed work, he treated "savages" in general as a moral lesson—an example of the influence of untrammeled original sin on corrupt mankind. African culture was thus degenerate, showing the common lot of man without Christianity.

On the specific issue of the slave trade, however, Wesley joined the general humanitarian hue and cry. He borrowed freely from the common stock of abolitionist arguments. Since the slave traders claimed African life was so "degraded" that even slavery in the West Indies was preferable, the humanitarians had to provide an answer. In Wesley's case, the answer was taken from the works of the enlightened travellers, from which the favorable passages could be

47. Granville Sharp, *A Representation of the Injustice and Dangerous Tendency of Tolerating Slavery in England* (London, 1769).
48. Hecht, *Continental and Colonial Servants,* pp. 37–39.
49. G. Sharp to J. Bryant, 19 October 1772, quoted in Sharp, *The Just Limitation of Slavery in the Laws of God* . . . (London, 1776), pp. 44–46.

abstracted. Wesley claimed, for example, that Africans were "far more mild, friendly, and kind to strangers than our forefathers were."[50] Other humanitarians took up the same case in greater detail, especially the Quaker Anthony Benezet in *Some Historical Account of Guinea.*[51] Here the literary figure of the noble savage, so often painted in fiction, reappeared as "fact."

Granville Sharp also began to interest himself in the facts of "savage" culture. He made it a point to meet whatever specimens of noble savagery might turn up in England, such as Omai, a Polynesian visitor in 1776. Through his conversations with Omai, Sharp became convinced that "natural man" could be made to understand civilized morality through reason alone. By the later 1780's he was convinced of the high natural endowment of Africans; but he was never a cultural relativist. He continued to believe, for example, that Hindu religion and Hindu law were quite literally the devil's work.[52]

Many of the prominent anti-slave-trade leaders kept to the adverse opinion of African culture throughout the 1780's. Wilberforce in particular argued that Africans were men, but "fallen men," degraded by their savagery and by the equally savage Christians that carried out the slave trade. He was supported in this line by both Burke and Pitt, though something of Wesley's ambivalence was present too. If only to counter the accusation that "degradation" was the natural state of the Africans, Wilberforce occasionally came to the defense of at least some aspects of African culture, pointing to the relatively benign system of household slavery in Africa—and to the cheerfulness, love of peace, and hospitality to strangers.[53] By the 1790's some such mild defense had become a usual part of the humanitarian case, though not inevitably so.

The humanitarians' treatment of race followed much the same course as their treatment of African culture. They began with little

50. John Wesley, "Thoughts upon Slavery" in *Works* (London, 1872), XI, 65. First published 1774; M. T. Hodgen, "The Negro in the Anthropology of John Wesley," *Journal of Negro History,* XIX, 308-23 (July, 1934).

51. *Some Historical Account of Guinea,* new ed. (London, 1788), esp. pp. 2, 81-87.

52. Prince Hoare, *Memoirs of Granville Sharp,* 2nd ed., 2 vols. (London, 1828), I, 221-22, 224-26; Sharp, *A General Plan for Laying out Towns and Townships, of the New Acquired Lands,* 2nd ed. (London, 1804), pp. 21-23. First published 1794.

53. William Wilberforce, Commons, 12 May 1789, *Parliamentary Register,* XXVI, 147; 18 April 1791, *Parliamentary Register,* XXIX, 184, 196-97; Edmund Burke, Commons, 21 May 1789, *Parliamentary Register,* XXVI, 201; Coupland, *Wilberforce,* pp. 170, 292-93.

more than the vague belief that Africans were men, but the growing
theory of polygenesis was a double threat. It could be used to "prove"
that Africans were separately created by God, specifically to serve the
children of Adam as slaves. More serious still, it seemed to deny the
truth of revelation and thus strike at Christianity itself. In this case,
the first line of defense was the Bible. By his own word, God had
made all men "of one blood" (Acts 7:26). Granville Sharp in particular undertook the detailed examination of the legal and scrip-
tural case against the slave trade and in favor of the equality of
man.[54]

But this appeal to authority would only be valid for those who
accepted the authority itself. By the later 1770's, Sharp was searching
for counter arguments to meet polygenesis on its own ground, looking into such matters as the alleged infertility of one mulatto breeding with another. The most comprehensive humanitarian effort in
this direction, however, came from another source. After nineteen
years on St. Kitts, the Reverend James Ramsay returned to England
with a claim to speak from personal knowledge. His principal work,
*Essays on the Treatment and Conversion of African Slaves in the
British Sugar Colonies,* published in 1784, was the best anti-racist
tract of the eighteenth century.

Ramsay used the arguments from revelation, but he went on to
counter the biologists with biological arguments, and at several points
at once. He attacked the assumption that "the Negro" could be considered a valid abstraction by showing that, even in their physical
features, Africans were a diverse lot. Furthermore, the biologists had
not really established a definite relationship between physical form
and ability, or between ability and climate. Until they did so, their
arguments would have to be set aside. On the more detailed anatomical points, he showed that, even if Negro skulls could be proven to
stand between those of Europeans and those of apes, there was no
evidence that skull shape or size had any relation to intelligence or
any other quality. Even if it could be shown that the cranial capacity
of Negroes was smaller than that of other people, there was still no
proof that this characteristic was permanent and independent of such
factors as mental exercise. He contradicted Long's assertion that

54. G. Sharp, *Just Limitation of Slavery;* Sharp, *The Law of Liberty* . . . (London,
1776); Sharp, *The Law of Passive Obedience* . . . (London, 1776); Hoare, *Granville
Sharp,* II, xiii–xvi.

mulattoes were relatively infertile from his own observations in the West Indies. Finally, even if Negroes could be proved to be a distinct race or even a separate species, there was no proof that they were inferior. If they could be proved to be both distinct and inferior *as a group,* there was no proof that individual Africans were inferior to individual Europeans. Even if *all* were inferior, there was still no moral case for their enslavement.[55] All in all, Ramsay used the critical rationalism associated with science in a way the "scientists" had neglected to do.

Ramsay's essay was especially effective for catching a maximum following for the anti-slavery cause. On questions of race there were many stopping places, and the alignment of anti-slavery and anti-racist opinion was never complete. Humanitarians in general were less overtly arrogant in their writings than the defenders of the slave trade, but the possible variety of opinion was enormous. As a minimum common denominator, all humanitarians believed that Africans should not be carried to the West Indies against their will. Beyond this point, views ranged from Ramsay's own egalitarianism through to Charles White's belief that Negroes were a distinct species and the lowest species of man—and yet ought not to be enslaved. Most humanitarians, however, believed in the spiritual equality of all men before God. Perhaps a majority believed that Africans might achieve equality with the Europeans on this earth as well, but only a very few saw much value in African culture as it was.

Within any one of the four distinct traditions of thought about the Africans there was a similar range of opinion. Most biologists were within the pale of orthodox monogenesis, even though some were laying the foundations of "scientific" racism. Among those who used the theme of the noble savage, some believed "the African" was "natural man," yet others simply wrote within a literary convention. Among those who defended the slave trade, several were relatively free of racial prejudice, yet racists could also be humanitarians. Taken as a group, the travellers to Africa were less prejudiced than those who stayed at home. They were often annoyed in petty ways by contact across cultures in the tropics, but they also came closest to an understanding of Africans as men like themselves with an integral

55. James Ramsay, *Essay on the Treatment and Conversion of African Slaves in the British Sugar Colonies* (London, 1784), pp. 179–263.

culture that was more than mere savagery. As a group they were less anxious to reduce individual Africans to an inhuman and abstracted "African." Many of the travellers, however, were in the slave trade, and they defended it before their countrymen in Britain. But the defense they found most convincing to themselves was not race difference. It was, instead, the intractable and unfamiliar conditions of tropical life.

3

THE PROMISE

AND THE TERROR

OF

A TROPICAL ENVIRONMENT

For eighteenth-century Europe, the world between the tropics was much more a "New World" than North America had ever been. In its newness it held out both promise and terror—the promise of tropical wealth and the terror of the unknown. Even though Englishmen had been sailing southern seas since the reign of Elizabeth I and had settled on Barbados in the reign of Charles I, the tropical environment was still alien and forbidding and barely understood. But the most crucial fact *was* known: Europeans died there with considerably greater frequency than they did in Europe. Whatever else it held out, a visit to the tropics meant running the gauntlet of disease and death.

Add to this the factor of sheer unfamiliarity. North Europeans, then as now, preferred being a little cold all the time to being a little warm all the time, and a temperature of eighty-five degrees Fahrenheit seemed an uncomfortable extreme of summer heat. Plants, animals—even the feel of the wind was different. If the tropical world broke in some respects the expected pattern of natural behavior, who could tell how far and in what ways natural law was set aside? Something of the medieval legends of intolerable heat, monstrous animals and plants, strange diseases, and strange people remained in the popular imagination. Even though some Englishmen had spent most of their lives in the tropics, their specialized knowledge did little to correct the apprehension of those who stayed at home. Travellers, as much as any, helped to preserve the mixture of legend and fact. With no rational limit to the credulity of their listeners, one generation after another of "Old Coasters" told their stories. They could still be heard in the middle of the twentieth century on the verandah of the European club or in the smoking room of a ship outward bound from Liverpool to West African ports.[1]

On the other side, in the popular belief of the eighteenth century, the tropical world was a place of immense wealth, from which the "Nabobs" and the absentee West Indian planters drew the funds to buy their country houses and their seats in Parliament. Popular imagination had also been caught by the discoveries of Captain Cook in the South Seas, just as more learned circles were taken with a new curiosity about natural history beyond Europe. The trend of awakening interest was heightened by the romantic movement. As the exotic in all forms came into vogue in Europe, what part of the world could be more exotic? Untouched and unfamiliar natural beauty met the new esthetic standard. The supposed "primitive simplicity" of "savage" life offered a much advertised contrast of the artificiality of Europe.

Enlightened travellers from Michel Adanson onward felt this lure of the tropics especially keenly. Once arrived in West Africa, they found what they were looking for. Henry Smeathman caught the mood of the times as he looked back on his three years of botanical work on the Banana Islands:

Pleasant scenes of vernal beauty, a tropical luxuriance, where fruits and flowers lavish their fragrance together in the same bough! There nature animates every embryo of life; and reigning in vegetable or animal perfection; perpetually glows in wild splendour and uncultivated maturity!

I contemplate the years I passed in that terrestrial Elysium, as the happiest of my life. The simple food, which my solitude usually afforded, was sweetened with rural labour; and my rest was not broken by those corroding cares and

1. For a recent and effective use of environmental xenophobia to create "atmosphere" see Graham Greene's novel, *The Heart of the Matter,* set in Freetown at the period of the Second World War.

perplexing fears, which pride and folly are ever creating in the ambitious emulations of populous communities.[2]

The dream of tropical wealth was much older, going back to the fabulous profits of the sixteenth-century spice trade, or to the gold and silver of New Spain and Peru. By the eighteenth century it centered on the South Atlantic System and the production of tropical staples. The very success of the West Indian plantations reinforced an early and serious European misconception about the wet tropics. When they first saw the exuberant growth of vegetation in the West Indies and coastal Brazil, European explorers thought they had encountered a new relationship between man and nature. Nature seemed to supply the necessities of life freely, and human labor was not needed. As Sir Walter Raleigh reported of the Orenoqueponi: "They never eat of any thing that is set or sowen; and as at home they use neither planting nor manurance, so when they come abroad, they refuse to eat of aught, but that which nature without labour bringest forth."[3]

Similar quotations about many parts of the tropical world could be strung out from the sixteenth century into the twentieth. By the eighteenth century a full-fledged myth of tropical exuberance had been created. In fact, some tropical soils could support very dense populations, even at existing levels of technology, but all tropical soils were not that good. The exuberance of tropical foliage was no true indication of possible agricultural wealth, and quick growth by no means released man from labor, even in the best of circumstances.[4] But appearance was more striking than reality, and eighteenth-century travellers or publicists described the Guinea Coast in rapturous terms. John Wesley believed it was "one of the most fruitful, as well as the most pleasant countries in the known world," a place where: "the soil is in general fertile, producing abundance of rice and roots. Indigo and cotton thrive without cultivation; fish is in great plenty; the flocks and herds are numerous and the tree loaden with fruit."[5]

Or, as Henry Smeathman reported in his famous description of

2. H. Smeathman to J. C. Lettsom, 19 October 1782, in J. C. Lettsom (Ed.), *The Works of John Fothergill, M.D.*, Rev. ed. (London, 1784), p. 577.

3. Quoted in H. N. Fairchild, *The Noble Savage* (New York, 1928), p. 21.

4. See Pierre Gourou, *The Tropical World* (London, 1953). pp. 13–24.

5. John Wesley, "Thoughts Upon Slavery" in *Works* (London, 1872), XI, 61. First published 1774.

Sierra Leone, "the woods and plains produce spontaneously great quantities of the most pleasant fruits and spices, from which may be made oils, marmalades, wines, perfumes, and other valuable articles, to supply the markets of Great Britain and Ireland."

And he continued: "Such are the mildness and fertility of the climate and country that a man possessed of a change of cloathing, a wood axe, a hoe, and a pocket knife, may soon place himself in an easy and comfortable situation. All the cloathing wanted is what decency requires; and it is not necessary to turn up the earth more than two or three inches, with a light hoe, in order to cultivate any kind of grain."[6]

Similar ecstatic reports figured in the works of almost every traveller to West Africa, and the witnesses before the Committee of Privy Council in 1789 told the same story of agricultural wealth.[7] The most obvious implication was perfectly clear. Britain at the dawn of the Industrial Revolution would need more tropical products, and West Africa could supply them in an endless stream, to the profit of those Englishmen who took part.

This implication was not the only one, nor the first to be drawn by the theorists of Europe. From the earliest times, exuberant vegetation of tropical America had seemed to confirm the medieval legend of an earthly paradise in the Fortunate Islands. Men who lived without labor ("strangers alike to luxury and toil," as William Roscoe called the Africans)[8] could hardly help creating a good society. Thus the legend of tropical exuberance lay behind many early reports of the "good savage" and led on to the "noble savage" of literature.[9]

Most eighteenth-century social theorists continued to believe that some intimate relationship existed between tropical vegetation and tropical society; but the paradisaic view of the earlier period gave way to a new interpretation, which was to dominate European thought about tropical environments for more than a century to come. The new view in typical form was laid down in 1770 by James Steuart as a law of tropical society: "If the soil be vastly rich, situated

6. Henry Smeathman, *Plan of a Settlement to be Made Near Sierra Leone* (London, 1786), pp. 8–9.

7. See especially John Matthews. *A Voyage to the River Sierra-Leone* . . . (London, 1788); Great Britain. Privy Council. *Report of the Lords of the Committee of Council for . . . Trade and Foreign Plantations . . . Concerning the Present State of Trade to Africa. and Particularly the Trade in Slaves* . . . (London, 1789). Part I, Produce.

8. William Roscoe, *The Wrongs of Africa. a Poem* (London, 1787), p. 9.

9. See Fairchild. *Noble Savage*, pp. 1–22.

in a warm climate, and naturally watered, the productions of the earth will be almost spontaneous: this will make the inhabitants lazy. Laziness is the greatest of all obstacles to labour and industry. Manufactures will never flourish here. . . . It is in climates less favoured by nature, and where the soil produces to those only who labour, and in proportion to the industry of every one, where we may expect to find great multitudes."[10]

Thus tropical exuberance was a curse rather than a blessing. Far from causing the nobility of the noble savage, it caused his savagery; and his savagery was far from good.[11] The crucial change was the value set on labor. In the Bible man had been cursed and driven from the Garden of Eden to earn his bread by the sweat of his brow (Genesis 3:19). In this view, as in that of sixteenth-century Europe, work was an unpleasant necessity. Eighteenth-century theorists, however, began to see labor as good in itself, even as the mother of civilization and of all progress.

Max Weber and others have traced a similar attitude to the influence of the Protestant ethic and especially to the Calvinist form of Protestantism. It is therefore of some interest that the proposition was stated with special emphasis, but without theological reference, by the Scottish moral philosophers and the Evangelicals in England. Both these groups had a background of Calvinist influence. Economic thought in the later eighteenth century also stressed the value of labor, and the tendency led in time to the central role of the labor theory of value in classical economics. All of these cross-currents, plus the less explicit sense of a need for disciplined and regular wage labor in the new British industries, played their role in producing, by the 1790's, an attitude that was virtually universal. In its most simple form it could be expressed as an equation: labor equals civilization.

The discussion of tropical exuberance and its consequences was only one among a number of points where European social theorists

10. Sir James Denham Steuart, "An Inquiry into the Principles of Political Economy," (1770) in *The Works, Political, Metaphisical, and Chronological of the late Sir James Steuart* (London, 1804), I, 44.

11. See James Burnet, Lord Monboddo, *The Origin and Progress of Language*, 8 vols. (Edinburgh, 1773–1792), I, 252; *Candid Reflections Upon the Judgement Lately Awarded by the Court of King's Bench in Westminster-Hall, On What is Commonly Called the Negro-Cause, By a Planter* (London, 1772), pp. 64–65; Robert Norris, *Memoirs of the Reign of Bossa Ahadee, King of Dahomey* (London, 1789), pp. 145–47; and works cited in note 7 above.

were beginning to think more broadly about the world beyond Europe. The proper study of mankind, especially in the wide ranging reports of the travellers, could take in all kinds of men, and it could be approached from a variety of different backgrounds. There was still no specialized body of ethnological theory, except within the broad realm of moral philosophy. Before the days of ethnographic field work, armchair speculations were open to any educated man who cared to try his hand at amateur scholarship. Some began, as the enlightened travellers in West Africa had commonly done, searching for diversity in human culture through the study of "primitive peoples." Others, like Sir James Mackintosh at the end of the century, sought the least denominator common to all mankind: "under the most fantastic multitude of usages and rites which have prevailed among men, the same fundamental, comprehensive truths, the sacred master-principles which are the guardians of human society, recognized and revered (with few and slight exceptions) by every nation on earth. . . ."[12]

In either case, whether diversity or uniformity was the goal, important subsidiary questions followed in very short order—questions of environmental influence on human culture, the possibility and mode of cultural diffusion, and the nature of human progress. Before they were finished, the eighteenth-century philosophers had raised and given rudimentary answers to many of the problems that still concern social scientists. Most of these discussions were not directly concerned with African affairs, but they set the patterns of British thought. Hence they gave the starting point for any consideration of tropical life.

One of the most common assumptions even then was to hold that non-Western civilizations represented earlier stages in human progress, frozen, as it were, while the European world advanced. If so, it might be possible to explore the earlier stages of man by taking the overseas world as a kind of living museum of human cultures. Some eighteenth-century writers, like Jean Jacques Rousseau in his *Origins of Inequality,* were willing enough to describe the earliest ages of human history without benefit of empirical data, but the more common course was to begin with deductive reason, then to add examples from a convenient compendium like the *Universal History.*

12. Sir James Mackintosh, *A Discourse on the Study of the Law of Nature and Nations* (London, 1799), p. 27.

The most active British theorists in this line of effort were the Scottish moral philosophers. Like their counterparts in England or on the Continent, they sketched the outlines of human history as a story of progress, passing through a series of stages. The number of stages might vary from one philosopher to another, but the nature of the schema was remarkably consistent. The Scottish school were especially attached to the economic system as the principal touchstone for assessing the stage reached by any society.

Among a welter of variants, the common tendency is well represented by John Millar's influential four-stage pattern. For Millar, the earliest men were hunters and gatherers, who moved on to the second stage of pastoralism. From there, they rose to settled farming, and finally to the fourth level of commerce and manufacture. These four stages were thought to parallel a similar four stages of political organization from (1) the family alone, to (2) the tribe or village of several families, to (3) the federation of smaller units or the imposition of a feudal control from above, and on to (4) the further elaboration of the modern stage. Millar, more than others, laid special stress on the position of women as an additional guide to the level reached by a society. The course of progress in this respect began with women merely as servants, reduced to this status by the greater physical strength of men. It then passed through a series of gradual improvements until, at the fourth stage, women were especially valued for their alleged special ability to acquire the arts and graces.[13]

Others might arrange the stages in slightly different ways, sometimes having only three instead of four. In this case, savagery, barbarism, and civilization could be technical terms for a three-part schema, but the progression of hunting, pastoral, agricultural, and commercial was the normal pattern. African societies did not fare badly by this scheme of things. They were mainly agricultural rather than hunting or pastoral peoples. Thus they were near the top and generally assessed as "barbarous" rather than "savage" in a technical sense.[14]

13. John Millar, *Observations Concerning the Distinction of Ranks in Society* (London, 1771). For the Scottish moral philosophers see Gladys Bryson, *Man and Society: The Scottish Inquiry of the Eighteenth Century* (Princeton, 1945); W. C. Lehman, *John Millar of Glasgow* (Cambridge, 1960).

14. See, for example, Montesquieu, *The Spirit of Laws*, 2 vols. (New York, 1949), Bk. XXI, pt. 2. First published 1748.

But the establishment of a pattern and series of stages for advancement was only a preliminary step. The crucial question was to explain why some societies advanced more rapidly, while others seemed relatively static. One answer was implicit in Steuart's analysis: the lag in tropical social development came from the environment, but indirectly so, out of laziness by way of tropical exuberance. West African "barbarism" was most often explained in this way, but other and more direct environmental explanations were also popular. Among these, Montesquieu's belief that climate acts directly on the human psyche was most influential. Montesquieu said little about West Africa, being specifically concerned with "national character" within Europe; but his theory that northerners were generally more active in mind and body, while southerners were more sensitive in soul and spirit, had broader possibilities and echoed an ancient belief.[15]

It was very widely spread by the 1780's and repeated on every side, even being reported back by visitors to the tropics as a piece of empirical information. Dr. Benjamin Mosely, for example, who practiced medicine for twelve years in the West Indies, claimed that Europeans "degenerated" after a long residence in that part of the world, if not in actual mental powers at least in mental activity. "There is, in the inhabitants of hot climates, unless present sickness has an absolute control over the body, a promptitude and bias to pleasure, and an alienation from serious thought and deep reflection. The brilliancy of the skies, and the levity of the atmosphere, conspire to influence the nerves against philosophy and her frigid tenets, and forbids their practice among the children of the sun."[16]

If this were the result for a people of northern origin, it was natural to use Montesquieu's ideas even more systematically to explain human societies native to the tropics. Adam Ferguson and especially William Falconer brought non-European societies more decidedly into the picture. In Falconer's view, both the far north and far south produce unpleasant extremes. Northerners are insensitive, but southerners are overly passionate. Northerners are too kind, while southerners are vindictive. Northerners are brave to a fault, while southerners are timid. Northerners are active, while southerners are indolent. In each case, the northern quality was described in terms a little less pejorative than the southern equivalent. The conclusion is

15. Montesquieu, *The Spirit of Laws*, Bk. XIV. pts. 1–3.
16. Benjamin Mosely, *A Treatise on Tropical Diseases; and on the Climate of the West Indies* (London, 1787), p. 48.

easy to foresee. In Falconer's opinion, the best possible balance of human qualities is to be found near the northern edge of the temperate zone—in short, in Britain.[17]

Social theories of direct environmentalism, whether in the version of Montesquieu, Falconer, or Ferguson, were not very favorable to the prospects of a rapid African advance toward "civilization." Whatever the Africans' other faults or virtues, they were, for the environmentalists, timid, lazy, oversensitive, and oversexed. But the possibility remained that these faults could be overcome. In their specific discussions of West Africa, Falconer and Ferguson allowed for the possible influence of diet, soil, and location. Montesquieu explained the lag in African development by the lack of easy commercial contact across the Sahara: Africa had been cut off from the main trade routes of the Eurasian land mass, but this failing could presumably be remedied by introducing sea-borne trade.[18]

Opposition to direct environmentalism came principally from the polygenists, and especially from the white West Indians. As a tropical people themselves, they resented the implication that they were cowardly (though Bryan Edwards of Jamaica admitted that his fellow West Indians did tend to be lazy). More important still, they preferred to view the "faults" of African society as the congenital faults of the African race as such. Thus the racial and environmental explanations of African "backwardness" were to some extent rivals, though the two views might be squared in the light of recent scientific knowledge.[19]

The most enterprising effort in this direction was made by Alexander Wilson, who was impressed by Priestley's recent chemical investigations. He took up the discovery that respiration and combustion had much the same chemistry, pointing out that animal respiration produced "phlogiston," the material or principle of fire. Living vegetable matter, in turn, needed "phlogistonated air" in order to survive, while at the same time it purified the air for reuse by ani-

17. W. Falconer, *Remarks on the Influence of Climate* . . . (London, 1781), especially pp. 6–24.

18. Montesquieu, *The Spirit of Laws*, Bk. XXI, pt. 2; Falconer, *Influence of Climate*; Adam Ferguson, *An Essay on the History of Civil Society* (Edinburgh, 1767), pp. 171, 177.

19. Edward Long, *History of Jamaica*, 3 vols. (London, 1774), II, 277; Bryan Edwards, *The History, Civil and Commercial, of the British Colonies in the West Indies*, 2nd ed., 2 vols. (London, 1794), II, 6–15; David Hume, "Of National Character," *The Philosophical Works of David Hume*, 4 vols. (London, 1898), III, 249 and 252 n.

mals. The decomposition of organic bodies was also thought to be a source of phlogiston, while water had the capacity to absorb it.[20]

With these elementary "facts" as a starting point, it seemed obvious that greater heat in the tropics speeded the process of decomposition, thus producing highly phlogistonated air. As the air approached the point of saturation with phlogiston, it was less able to absorb phlogiston produced by human respiration. Europeans and others unaccustomed to the tropics were therefore unable to throw off enough phlogiston, while Negroes and other tropical peoples had acquired the ability to get rid of phlogiston through more profuse perspiration. But they paid a price for their physical adjustment. According to Wilson, this price was a weaker power of the mind plus an extreme tendency to indolence. Therefore, no high civilization had ever occurred, nor was one possible, in any part of the tropical world, though the agricultural riches of the tropics were themselves a result of the same highly phlogistonated air that made tropical civilization impossible.

The more pessimistic views of Africa's future came from "natural philosophy," while "moral philosophy" held out a little hope. The most optimistic of all was the view that African faults were merely institutional failings. Henry Smeathman, for example, admitted that Africans were "indolent," but added:

Whatever may be said of the effects which local situation and extremes of heat and cold have on the human body, it will probably be found hereafter, that all men in regard to their dispositions and conduct in life are formed more on artificial than natural causes, by the laws which impel and the education which trains them, in short by custom and habit. A very singular jurisprudence, and customs, which in some respect are wise, but in this pernicious, operate [at Sierra Leone] like enchantment upon the inhabitants of this part of the globe, and till the charm is broken, must continue to keep them in indigence, indolence, and contempt.[21]

He went on to say that the hold of custom discouraged enterprise,

20. A. Wilson, *Some Observations Relative to the Influence of Climate on Vegetable and Animal Bodies* (London, 1780). Wilson's theory of the origin of the Negro race seems to be derived from the similar theory published by Kant in 1775, and amplified in 1785. Kant, however, did not draw out the implications about racial inferiority which Wilson suggests, and both were decisively contradicted by Lavoisier's discovery of oxygen, announced in 1777, and amplified in 1783. (See A. O. Lovejoy, "Kant and Evolution," in B. Glass and others, *Forerunners of Darwin, 1745–1859* [Baltimore, 1959], pp. 186–87.)

21. Smeathman to Knowles, 21 July 1783, printed in *New Jerusalem Magazine*, I, 286 (1790).

innovation, and reform, but that these weaknesses could be corrected by a new form of government and better education.

Each of the various theories about the cause of African "backwardness" implied its own form of cure. Those who believed African indolence came directly or indirectly from the climate, or from basic racial endowment, already had an answer. Their remedy was the slave trade itself, which transported the "indolent" Africans to the West Indies. They could be put to work there under coercion, which alone makes possible a productive tropical society.[22] The idea occurs again and again in the defense of the slave trade and later of slavery: they were illicit in temperate regions, but necessary in the tropics.

In answer, the humanitarians came increasingly to the defense of African society, showing first that its faults were not insuperable and, second, that the slave trade itself was to blame. Wilberforce argued in Parliament that the Africans could hardly be very lazy, seeing the efforts they made to catch one another for the slave trade. Their activities were merely misdirected.[23] Thomas Clarkson made a large collection of African products. It included some twenty polished specimens of tropical woods, pepper, ivory, musk, gum, spices, tobacco, indigo, food crops, and a further selection of manufactured articles such as cotton cloth, pottery, iron, and leather work. He carried this display around to government committees, "that they might really know what Africa was capable of affording instead of the Slave-trade, and that they might make a proper estimate of the genius and talents of the natives."[24]

The humanitarian panacea for improving Africa grew partly from the attack on the slave trade. If the trade were to blame for African barbarism, its abolition would be the first step in bringing about the cure. The humanitarians' further case rested on existing social theory. If the Africans had reached the "agricultural stage," then commerce was the missing element to raise them another step. If, as Montesquieu had suggested, lack of commerce held Africa back, then the introduction of commerce could push her forward. Admiration of commercial life had grown with the expansion of British trade. Most

22. *Candid Reflections . . . ,* pp. 64–65; Wilson, *Observations on Climate,* pp. 278–80.
23. William Wilberforce, Commons, 12 May 1789, *Parliamentary Register,* XXVI, 148.
24. Thomas Clarkson. *History of the Rise, Progress, and Accomplishment of the Abolition of the African Slave Trade by the British Parliament,* 2 vols. (London, 1808), II, 13–16.

writers took for granted the superiority of a commercial society, and William Falconer explained in detail why they were right in doing so. He held that commerce not only encourages the desirable qualities of frugality, peacefulness, justice, and honesty; it also improves the mind: "A commercial life may, in several respects, be accounted favorable to the intellectual faculties. Thus it tends to exercise, and consequently to improve, the memory; it introduces a methodic arrangement into the business of life, which facilitates it greatly, by instructing us to apply our abilities separately to their proper purposes. Commerce also enlarges the ideas, teaches nations their true interests, and is a cure for the most pernicious prejudices."[25]

Against this background, it was only natural to call for the substitution of "legitimate commerce" in place of the slave trade. Wilberforce in particular publicized legitimate commerce as the hope of Africa. What he had in mind was quite clearly a system of enterprise largely in African hands, at least in its African aspect. The European traders would come to Africa with their manufactures and take off the African raw materials, much as the slave traders in the past had worked with and through the enterprise of African middlemen. Such a system would not only help Africa. As Wilberforce told the House of Commons, "we shall find the rectitude of our conduct rewarded, by the benefits of a regular and growing commerce."[26] Legitimate traders, in short, would reap the reward for their morality in the form of higher profits. This in turn rested on a tacit assumption of many Calvinists and Evangelicals—that virtue would be rewarded, both in this world and the next.

Others saw African economic development in terms of temporal rewards alone. It required no feat of economic reasoning to see that the South Atlantic System was to some extent wasteful. It carried labor to the American tropics, whereas, in the light of tropical exuberance in Africa, it might be employed just as effectively at home. As early as the 1680's, the Royal Africa Company had experimented with indigo plantations on Bance Island in the Sierra Leone River, and corn for the supply of slave ships became a regular export of the Gold Coast at about the same period. From the middle of the eighteenth century, suggestions for still more extensive development of

25. Falconer, *Influence of Climate*, p. 415.
26. William Wilberforce, Commons, 12 May 1789, *Parliamentary Register*, XXVI, 150. K. G. Davies, *The Royal African Company* (London, 1957), pp. 220–21 and 228.

African agriculture began to appear. Malachy Postlethwayt became a kind of apostle for the relocation of British enterprise in the tropics. In Africa, he argued: "the fruitful soil lies waste, a very extended country, pleasant vallies, banks of the fine rivers, spacious plains, capable of cultivation to unspeakable benefit, in all probability remain, fallow and unnoticed: Why do not the *Europeans* enclose such lands for cultivation, as by their nature and situation appear proper for beneficial production?"[27]

Postlethwayt's suggestions were significantly different from those put forward by the advocates of legitimate trade. Where the legitimate traders merely wanted to substitute one kind of commerce for another, keeping the basic forms of African commercial organization, Postelthwayt looked to the more drastic innovation of setting Europeans ashore in West Africa in a managerial capacity. They would then be able to apply the considerable European skill and experience in tropical agriculture.

During their centuries of activity in the West Indies, the English had developed the production of certain tropical crops to a high point of efficiency. Especially in the major staples of sugar and coffee they were technologically well ahead of the West Africans, and they could call on a considerable body of published technical literature, as well as the practical knowledge of the West Indian planters. Among the several manuals on sugar or coffee planting, James Granger produced something of a tour de force in 1764 in the form of a planter's guide entirely in verse, and Labourie's *Coffee Planter of Saint Domingo* outlined a technique so developed that it was still in use into the twentieth century.[28]

But these specialized skills also had their limitations. They had been developed mainly in the West Indies and in the light of West Indian conditions. They were not necessarily transferable to the different soils and different plants of the African tropics. Next to the misjudgment of tropical exuberance, perhaps the most serious and common mistake of eighteenth-century European thought about the

27. M. Postlethwayt, *The Importance of the African Expedition Considered* . . . (London, 1758), p. 93. See also, "Africa" in his *Universal Dictionary of Trade,* 2 vols. (London, 1774) and Postlethwayt, *The National and Private Advantages of the African Trade Considered* (London, 1746).

28. J. Grainger, *The Sugar Cane* (London, 1764); P. J. Labourie, *The Coffee Planter of Saint Domingo* (London, 1798). For further references to this literature see L. J. Ragatz, *A Guide to the Study of British Caribbean History, 1763–1834* (Washington, 1932), pp. 239–338.

possibilities of African agriculture was to see West Africa as poten-tially a second and larger West Indies.

Tropical medicine, however, was far more important than tropical agriculture as an essential technique for the mastery of the African tropics. West African mortality figures were not widely publicized or given statistical precision, but the region's general reputation for having a "deadly climate" rested on a basis in fact. Somewhere between 25 and 75 per cent of any group of Europeans newly arrived on the Coast died within the first year. Thereafter, the death rate was much less, perhaps on the order of 10 per cent per annum, but still substantial. Any European activity demanded a price in European lives that was not only intrinsically high, but considerably higher than the cost of similar activity in the West Indies or South Asia. Slightly later calculations of military mortality over twenty years show a loss of 483 per thousand mean strength among European troops in West Africa, against only 78.5 per thousand in the West Indies. Civilian life insurance premiums charged by British firms for different tropical regions tell a similar story: European mortality was roughly four times as high in West Africa as it was in India or the West Indies.[29] Even though these facts were not emphasized, nor even quantitatively understood at the time, they suggest a perfectly valid reason for main-taining the South Atlantic System and one of the probable reasons for establishing it in the first place.

The facts of tropical mortality were not, however, something the Europeans accepted as beyond their control. Their study of tropical medicine went back to the first expansion into the tropical world. By the middle of the seventeenth century, there were important medi-cal studies by Garcia da Orta based on Goa, Nicholas Monardes on the American tropics, and Bontius on Southeast Asia. Further medical studies followed, especially in Britain where the problem of tropical survival took on military implications during the eighteenth-century wars for empire.

All of these works were solidly set in the theoretical framework of medicine inherited from classical antiquity, re-expressed in the eighteenth-century tendency to build medical systems. The essence of any of these systems was to see all pathological conditions as the result of some single cause. Thus the eighteenth-century re-expression

29. PP, 1837–38, xl (138), p. 5; PP, 1840, xxx [C. 228], p. 7; North British Insurance Office to Macgregor Laird, 27 June 1842, in PP, 1842, xi (551), p. 585.

of the classical humoral pathology considered all disease to be the result of an imbalance or impurity of the bodily fluids. Treatment therefore aimed at readjusting the liquid balance by bleeding, purging, or some other general treatment. A second kind of system concentrated instead on the "tone" of the nervous system. In this case the cure consisted of stimulating or relieving tensions. Thus, if the body were "overstimulated" by heat, diet, or mental exertion, stimulation could be reduced by bleeding, purging, or tonics of various kinds. In either case, the treatment was much the same.[30]

By any modern standard, the whole of medical theory was completely erroneous, but improvements in medical practice were possible none the less. Critical standards of observation were improving gradually throughout the eighteenth century, following the tradition of Thomas Sydenham (1634–1689). The clinical description of tropical disease was increasingly accurate, and any of the systems allowed a good deal of latitude to the skill and knowledge of the individual practitioner. Warfare in the tropics gave many European doctors a field training that would otherwise have been impossible, and this experience was passed on through a growing body of literature.[31] By the 1780's the most authoritative summary of British tropical medicine was the work of James Lind (1716–1794), who had served on the Guinea coast as a naval surgeon. He is better known today for his *Treatise on Scurvy* (1754); but his *Diseases of Hot Climates* was equally important in its own time, passing through five editions between 1768 and 1808.[32]

When it came to the specific problems of West Africa, the medical

30. R. H. Shryock, "Nineteenth Century Medicine: Scientific Aspects," *Journal of World History*, III, 881–82 (1957); T. Trotter, *Medica Nautica*, 3 vols. (London, 1797–1803), I, 334–44.

31. The following may be considered representative of the literature as a whole: John Atkins, *Navy Surgeon . . .* , (London, 1734); J. Huxham, *An Essay on Fevers* (London, 1750); Sir John Pringle, *Observations on the Diseases of the Army in Camp and Garrison* (London, 1752); W. Hillary, *Observations on the Changes of the Air and the Concomitant Epidemical Diseases in the Island of Barbados*, 2nd ed. (London, 1766); C. Bisset, *Medical Essays and Observations* (Newcastle-upon-Tyne, 1766); Philippe Fermin, *Traité des maladies les plus frequent à Surinam . . .* (Masstricht, 1764); James Lind, *Essay on the Diseases Incidental to Europeans in Hot Countries* (London, 1768); L. Rouppe, *Observations on Diseases Incidental to Seamen* (London, 1772); J. P. Schotte, *A Treatise on Synochus Atrabiliosa, A Contagious Fever which Raged in Senegal in the Year 1778* (London, 1782); B. Mosely, *A Treatise on Tropical Diseases; And on the Climate of the West Indies* (London, 1787).

32. For Lind's career and contribution, and for naval medicine in general during this period, see: C. Lloyd and J. L. S. Coulter, *Medicine and the Navy 1200–1900. Volume III, 1714–1815* (Edinburgh and London, 1961).

men of the eighteenth cenutry concentrated their attention on "fevers." Malaria, yellow fever, typhus, typhoid, and minor fevers like dengue were all present, but the undifferentiated "fevers" of the Coast were in fact mostly malaria. Virtually the whole of West Africa was and is still an extremely favorable environment for the mosquitoes, *Anopheles gambiae* and *Anopheles funestus.* Both are among the most effective vectors for carrying plasmodial parasites from one individual to another, and their presence is the most important reason why mortality in West Africa was high compared with other tropical areas. *Plasmodium falciparum,* the prevalent West African parasite, is also especially dangerous, since it often kills in the first attack, while the *P. vivax* of the West Indies is more often enervating than fatal.

Even today West Africa is classified as a hyperendemic area for *P. falciparum.* The chance of an individual living there as long as a year with out receiving an infective mosquito bite is negligible. In some areas the average number of infective bites may range upward to one hundred or more. This fact implies different conditions for different groups of people. For the local population, a child is normally infected shortly after birth. During the first years of life it fights a perilous struggle with the parasites, and the rate of infestation is close to 100 per cent of the population under five years of age. Infant mortality from this cause is extremely high, but those who survive attain an apparent immunity in later life. This immunity, however, is not completely effective, either against other kinds of malaria or even against other strains of *P. falciparum.* It can also decline unless the individual is reinfected at frequent intervals. But, if the rate of reinfection is high, there will be no clinical symptoms of the disease; and even if the rate of reinfection drops, the clinical symptoms will rarely be more serious than chills and a slight fever. An absence of several years spent in a non-malarial area, however, may weaken or even destroy the immunity.[33]

Europeans coming to West Africa for the first time had no such

33. A distinction is sometimes made between holoendemic areas, where the rate of reinfestation is so great that adults rarely show clinical symptoms, and hyperendemic areas, where symptoms are more frequent. For historical discussion, this distinction is too fine to be useful, and the term hyperendemic will be used for all areas of high malarial infestation. For recent studies of malariology in West Africa see M. F. Boyd (Ed.), *Malariology,* 2 vols. (Philadelphia, 1949); F. B. Livingstone, "Anthropological Influences of Sickle Cell Genes in West Africa," *American Anthropologist,* LX, 533–62 (June, 1958); M. J. Colbourne and F. N. Wright, "Malaria in the Gold Coast," *West African Medical Journal,* IV, 3–17, 161–74 (1955), and works there cited.

immunity, even though malaria was endemic in some parts of the Mediterranean basin and in the fen country of England itself. In Europe or the West Indies they were accustomed to other types of *plasmodia,* or to other strains of *P. falciparum* which gave little or no protection in West Africa. Thus they paid the same kind of price in adult mortality that African populations paid in infant mortality. After a few years on the Coast, Europeans too acquired an apparent immunity, perhaps not quite so effective as the childhood immunity of the Africans, but sufficient to establish a pattern for newcomers— either a speedy death, or else a reasonable chance of survival over years or decades.

This pattern of disease can be seen clearly in retrospect from the eighteenth-century reports, but it was not so clearly perceived at the time. Neither was the disease itself well understood, though Europeans had been familiar enough with their own kind of malaria for millennia. It was described by Hippocrates, who distinguished the different types according to periodicity, dividing them into quotidian, tertian, and quatran varieties. The enlarged spleen, typical of chronic malaria, was also known to the ancients, and it was commonly associated with marshes and stagnant water.[34] All of this was substantially correct observation, but the problem came from another direction. European pathology still confused the disease and the symptoms. Thus "fever" was thought of as a generic term for a pathological condition. Lind defined it as "an indisposition of the body, attended commonly with an increase of its heat, a thirst, often a headache, and oftener a remarkable quietness of the pulse; or at least a great change from its natural state; accompanied, for the most part, with other symptoms of distress; and which in a few days, will certainly terminate, either in recovery, in a remission, or the death of the patient."[35]

This description would cover not only malaria, but a fair proportion of the other ailments known to man. Sub-classification was therefore necessary, and it took the direction of describing the symptoms with greater accuracy. The ancient Greek classification was still one of the most common, dividing fevers roughly according to the apparent degree and duration of the patient's increased body temperature. There were *ephemera,* or fevers lasting less than twenty-four

34. P. F. Russell, *Man's Mastery of Malaria* (London, 1955), pp. 7–8.
35. Lind, *Diseases in Hot Countries,* pp. 17–18.

hours; *synochus non putris,* or a mild continual fever; *synochus putris,* or a more critical fever; and *causus,* a very high fever which commonly killed the patient in the third or fourth day. (Serious fevers were called putrid because of the association between heat and decay.)

A second form of classification was more suitable for tropical fevers, since it stressed the periodic peaks of high temperature typical of malaria. Lind used this system, with a three-fold distinction between continual fevers, remitting fevers which were irregular in their periodicity and might leave some clinical symptoms during remissions, and intermitting fevers which returned regularly. The intermitting fevers were further sub-divided into the old classes of quotidian, tertian, and the like. Any of the three major classes could be bilious or non-bilious, mild or malignant.[36]

Variants of this classification were used throughout the nineteenth century, and the confusion they caused was not merely a question of terminology. Malaria could be fitted into the scheme at several points. It was, of course, intermittent, but it was also remittent in the sense that the series of closely spaced peaks of fever would die away, only to return weeks or months later without subsequent reinfection. It might also appear to be bilious, on account of jaundice and vomiting which sometimes accompanies the disease, or non-bilious in its milder forms. Thus even a single type of malaria. like *Plasmodium falciparum* would be identified as two or three different kinds of fever, each of which might well be treated in a different manner. In addition, typhus and even typhoid fever could easily be mistaken for malaria, though in West Africa the most serious confusion occurred between malaria and yellow fever.

Yellow fever was also common on the Coast, but its behavior and social consequences were very different. Its vector is another mosquito, *Aedes aegypti,* which ultimately turned out to be more easily controlled than *Anopheles gambiae.* Instead of giving the victim a long struggle that might result in apparent immunity, the disease either kills within five to seven days or allows the victim a rapid recovery followed by life-long and complete immunity to further attacks. Once immune, the victim cannot even serve as an intermediate host for the parasite. Since the disease is also much less serious for

---

36. Rouppe, *Diseases Incidental to Seamen, passim:* Lind, *Diseases in Hot Countries,* pp. 10–14.

children than for adults, it was possible for an entire tropical population to acquire immunity in childhood. When this happened, the disease might die out for a time, even though the vector was still present. Thus, among a stable population an entire generation of non-
immunes might grow up and be subject to a devastating epidemic if
the parasite was reintroduced from the outside. This had already happened several times in the medical history of the West Indies, but in
West Africa it appears that infection of the African population, and
hence its immunity, was maintained at most times. Non-immune
strangers, however, were extremely susceptible to the parasite normally present among the African children. The disease would appear
periodically as an epidemic passing rapidly among the European population before it died out again to await the arrival of a new group
of non-immunes from Europe. The chance appearance of these epidemics accounts for a great deal of variability in European mortality
rates in West Africa.[37]

Like malaria, yellow fever was classified by medical men along
with the other fevers, but certain occurrences were recognized as a
specific type of fever and the name, yellow fever, was already in use.
Both diagnoses and terminology were nevertheless extremely confused. It was very easy to mistake yellow fever not only for malaria
but also for scurvy, the relatively harmless dengue fever, and a number of other diseases. Very commonly, both yellow fever and some
forms of malaria were called "bilious remittent fever, even though
the epidemic quality of the former was already recognized and a good
clinical description of the disease in West Africa was published by
Schotte in 1778. In this case the terminology was even further confused by Schotte's insistence on calling yellow fever *Synochus atrabiliosa* and reserving the name "yellow fever" for what is now called
malaria.[38] It followed from both the confusions of clinical description and terminology, and from the prevalent systems of one-
cause pathology, that any and all of these various fevers were attributed to the same set of causes.

In seeking the cause of fevers, eighteenth-century medical men had
two salient facts on which all were agreed. First, they "knew" that
men came down with fevers more readily in wet or marshy areas

37. Henry H. Scott, *A History of Tropical Medicine,* 2 vols. (London, 1939), I,
322–23; P. M. Ashburn, *The Ranks of Death* (New York, 1947), pp. 135–36.
38. Schotte, *Synochus Atrabiliosa, passim.*

than in dry areas. This point was reasonably accurate for most malarial areas, since most mosquitos breed in marshes. It was not especially the case for West Africa, however, since *A. gambiae* can breed in any tiny pool or puddle and was thus found virtually everywhere and not simply near swamps.

Second, they knew that men came down with fevers more readily in the tropics than they did in Europe. This point was quite accurate, but it led to a serious and persistent confusion. Since the prevalence of disease altered with the climate, the climate was thought to be in some way the cause of the disease. Thus, the expression, "a bad climate" came to mean a place where the mortality rates were high, and not necessarily a place where it was physically uncomfortable to live. At the same time, talk of a "bad climate" between the tropics conjured up a picture of burning heat and great physical discomfort. Some travellers tried to correct the impression. Long pointed out, quite correctly, that summer in Jamaica is not so hot as summer in New York, and others made the same point in regard to West Africa; but the false impression of West Africa as a kind of humid oven beyond all experience in temperate lands lived on.[39] From the start, then, the visual picture of West Africa in the mind of the British non-traveller was false, but it colored a great deal of British thinking about West Africa.

In the serious medical works, the nature of climatic influence was more precisely considered. Marshes were thought to be the point of origin for some form of poison which found its way into the air. For some authorities the poison came from water vapor itself. For others, it was a product of the soil or of wet vegetation. Thus one emphasized the dangerous dampness of tropical air, or its saturation with phlogiston, while another would stress the stink of the mangrove swamps, and still a third the "thickness" of tropical air compared with the air of England. Atkins had even explained that the "thick" air of the African coast was the very factor that kept Guinea from being unpleasantly hot, in spite of its equatorial location.[40]

Most authorities tried to associate the poison and the climate by considering malarial poison an "exciting cause" of fevers, after the body had already been prepared by "predisposing causes." These

39. Atkins, *Navy Surgeon,* p. 2; Lind, *Diseases in Hot Countries,* p. 46; Long, *Jamaica,* I. 363–75.
40. Atkins, *Navy Surgeon,* p. 2.

were, of course, the heat and humidity of the tropics, acting according to one of the more popular medical systems, or a combination
of several. Ludovicus Rouppe's explanation of heat as a predisposing
cause of disease illustrates the line of argument.

> It is a physical truth that heat rarifies all bodies, excepting some few not
> necessarily to be mentioned here; by getting into their most secret recesses, it
> separates the parts from their mutual contact, and increases their porosity,
> whence we daily observe that bodies increase by heat, and decrease by cold;
> but by this diminishing and cohesion of the parts, it not only relaxes the solid
> parts of our body, and weakens them, but expands the fluids and increases
> their compass; it diminishes the force of cohesion of the globules, by which
> means they become looser and more slippery; but when it proceeds to act upon
> the moist parts of the body, they resolve into vapours, and the intestine motion
> is greater, by which means the thinner parts of the blood are too much thrown
> off, and the glutinous part which nourishes the body is too much divided and
> dissipated.[41]

Others would have agreed with the main points of this analysis,
that heat relaxes the "animal fibres" and thins the blood.[42] The belief led naturally to a vital concern with the liquids entering and
leaving the body—especially with the intake of wine and spirits and
the output of perspiration. This was a crucial point. Even in England
perspiration brought on by hard exercise might well be the cause of
ephemeral fevers. That, at least, was the obvious suggestion of the
humoral pathology. In the tropics, fevers were empirically associated
with heat. Heat was an obvious cause of a changed liquid balance
through perspiration. Thus, if liquid balance was the key, then perspiration was also the key to the understanding of tropical fevers, and
Alexander Wilson merely echoed the common understanding in
stressing perspiration in his phlogiston theory.[43]

From this point, speculation could lead out in several directions.
One possibility was to show the special dangers of quick change in
temperature. Mosely, for example, held that the body could become
accustomed to heat by increasing the quantity of perspiration, but
then it became especially sensitive to "the slightest impression from
cold," and "cold is the cause of almost all diseases of hot climates."[44]

41. Rouppe, *Diseases Incidental to Seamen*, p. 382.
42. See, for example, Hillary, *Changes of the Air*, p. vii.
43. Huxham, *Fevers*, pp. 2–4; Rouppe, *Diseases Incidental to Seamen*, pp. 371–72,
390–91; Hillary, *Changes in the Air*, p. 146.
44. Mosely, *Tropical Diseases*, pp. 38–47. See also Bisset, *Medical Essays*, p. 38.

Another principal concern was physical exercise, since this too increased perspiration. Still another was the question of drink.

All of these could be referred back to the humoral theory, and they led in turn to a somewhat diverse set of rules for a healthy tropical life. The rules agreed in stressing the importance of perspiration, exercise, temperature change, and diet, but the specific recommendations varied greatly. Edward Long of Jamaica described the dangerous habits imported into that Island. "The European keeps late hours at night, lounges abed in the morning; gormandizing at dinner and supper on loads of flesh, fish, and fruit; loves poignant sauces; dilutes with ale, porter, punch, claret, and madeira, frequently jumbling all together; and continues this mode of living till, by constantly manuring his stomach with such a heterogeneous compost, he has laid the foundation for a plentiful crop of ailments."[45]

For Long, the safer course would be to drop these ways and take plenty of light exercise, bathe frequently, stay out of fogs and damp, especially in the evening, and keep a fire going or smoke tobacco in order to purify the air. The European should also keep himself psychologically fit by avoiding "strong passions," a way of preserving the proper tone of the nervous system. He should use spirits only moderately, properly aged rum being especially recommended. His clothes should be light in weight and color and loose fitting, and his diet should contain more vegetable and less animal food than it did at home.[46] Mosely gave another set of West Indian rules, recommending as little exercise as possible, the avoidance of cold baths, of all spirits, and especially of rum. Light wines and water were, however, permitted.[47]

Each authority thus had his own set of taboos—except James Lind, who showed that neither drinking water, nor diet, nor excesses of food and drink correlated very well with the pattern of fever. Fevers came seasonally, and when they came they struck down the most moderate of men along with the gluttons and drunkards.[48] While Lind was certainly correct in thinking that personal excesses could be nothing more than minor contributing causes of disease, he was

45. Long, *Jamaica*, I, 375.
46. Long, *Jamaica*, II, 505–70.
47. Mosely, *Tropical Diseases*, pp. 49–51. See also Schotte, *Synochus Atrabiliosa*, pp. 158–62 for another detailed code of conduct.
48. Lind, *Diseases in Hot Countries*, pp. 6–7.

not followed in this respect by later writers. It seems to have been a psychological necessity to have some set of rules for personal hygiene. Especially in the high-mortality posts like those in West Africa, to think that life and death were pure chance beyond human knowledge would have been intolerable. It was much more satisfying to believe the dead had broken one or another of a numerous and complex system of taboos.

A second set of rules for tropical conduct were topographical rather than personal, and they depended more heavily on actual experience and observation. The Europeans had already gained a certain amount of experience in trying to pick a healthy spot for a trading post or a settlement. By general agreement, high, dry places, exposed to the wind were preferred. Winds blowing off shore were more dangerous than sea breezes, presumably because they picked up moisture and "noxious vapours" from the land over which they passed. Marshes were, of course, dangerous, but if one had to live near them, it was better to live on the windward than the leeward side. Places where insects were common were also considered dangerous, and bush and forest were more dangerous than cleared and planted fields. Barbados' freedom from malaria was sometimes thought to be caused by its much greater degree of cultivation than other West Indian islands or the Guinea coast. Lind placed the greatest emphasis on following these rules and would have preferred never to let Europeans go ashore in West Africa if it could possibly be avoided. At the very least, they should stay away from the shore in the evening and early morning, and avoid the forest country during the rainy season.[49]

Most of these suggestions were based on experience in the Americas, but they could also be justified by reference to Alexander Wilson's phlogiston theory. Phlogiston, as a product of decay, was naturally produced most abundantly in swamps. It was carried by the winds; but, since water could absorb it, passage over water cleared the air. Islands and ships at sea were therefore relatively healthy. Cleared and cultivated lands were also safe, because living vegetation absorbed phlogiston in the presence of sunlight. In wooded country, however, the phlogiston produced by decay in the undergrowth was too great for the absorptive capacity of the sunny treetops. Cutting

49. Fermin, *Traité des maladies*, pp. 4–5; Bisset, *Medical Essays*, p. 11; Lind, *Diseases in Hot Countries*, pp. 51–52, 127–28, 132–42, and 159–63; Long, *Jamaica*, II, 506.

the tall trees would admit the sunlight and purify the air; and experimental proof was available in North America, where clearing and cultivation had been followed by the decline of fever.[50]

Both the rules of medical topography and the suggestion of clearing the brush in order to improve the climate were substantially correct for America, and they undoubtedly did reduce European mortality in North America, where the common vector was *Anopheles quadrimaculatus*. *A. gambiae*, however, would not have been appreciably disturbed by these changes. It breeds in small natural collections of water exposed to sunlight, especially small pits, drains, pools made by hoofprints, receding rivers, or rain water collections in small depressions. Its most important breeding places are those made by men, and it stays close to human habitation and outside of the deep forest.[51] Clearing and cultivation were therefore precisely the measures most likely to increase its numbers, but the ubiquity of infective mosquitos in West Africa made the situation there very different from North America. It is unlikely that any preventive measures, short of staying aboard ship well offshore, could have done more than delay the first attack of malaria by a few months.

The treatment of fevers in the later eighteenth century followed the indications of the medical systems, and it varied greatly with the individual practitioner. It generally consisted of some combination of bleeding, blisters, purges, hot or cold baths, diaphoretics, and chinchona bark, each of them "exhibited" at some particular phase of the disease. Of these treatments, chinchona bark (*Cortex peruvianus*) had real therapeutic value. Quinine and some of the other alkaloids derived from it have been until recently the best of the known antimalarial drugs. Even in its raw form, "the bark" could be effective, both for treatment of the disease and for prophylaxis against an expected attack. Taken regularly and in sufficient quantities it built up a resistance to plasmodial parasites that could greatly reduce both morbidity and mortality.

Thus a genuinely valuable form of treatment was known, and had been known in England since the 1670's. But it was not univer-

50. Wilson, *Observations on Climate*, pp. 21–22. 272–76.

51. E. H. Acherknecht, *Malaria in the Upper Mississippi Valley 1760–1900* (Baltimore, 1945), pp. 75–78; B. Rush, "An Inquiry into the Causes of the Increase of Bilious and Intermitting Fevers in Pennsylvania. Read in the American Philosophical Society, December 16, 1785," *Medical Inquiries and Observations*, II, 265–76 (1797); Boyd, *Malariology*, I, 380 and 458.

sally respected as a proper treatment for fevers, and its use went through phases of popularity followed by neglect. These shifts occurred because chinchona is a specific only for malaria, and malaria was not yet clearly distinguished from other fevers. A few failures would turn an experimenting physician back to the traditional purgatives and bleeding, with the occasional addition of mercury and arsenics. When negative results were widely reported by a prominent doctor, the drug could fall into general disuse for decades.[52]

In the 1780's chinchona bark was passing through a phase of relative popularity. The great Sydenham had disapproved of it in the seventeenth century, but in the middle of the eighteenth it received the backing of Fothergill and especially of Lind. Even then, it was not unanimously favored, and some doctors thought that heavy dosages might lead to madness.[53] Lind himself gave the bark along with emetics and blisters, though he advised against bleeding. In the general practice of tropical medicine, the bark seems to have been used widely by British doctors, but not in the way that would have been most effective. In particular, prophylactic treatment with bark was not common, though it was an occasional preventive measure among others of less value. Lind, for example, advised people in malarial areas to smoke tobacco, wear a bit of garlic or camphor sewed in a piece of linen, to take light laxatives regularly, and, "For further prevention, a wine glass of an infusion of the bark and orange peel in water, or what will prove more effectual, a table spoonful of a strong tincture of the bark, in spirits, diluted occasionally with water, may be taken every morning before breakfast."[54]

If this practice were regularly followed, it would certainly have been helpful, more or less so according to the quality of the bark available. Other variants, however, recommended prophylactic bark to be taken only at each change of the moon and before the full moon, a practice that lacked the special benefits of regular treatment.[55]

Eighteenth-century doctors also recognized that those who had lived for some time in the tropics were more resistant to disease than

52. Russell, Man's Mastery of Malaria, pp. 97–104.
53. J. Fothergill, Works . . . (London, 1781), pp. 268–69; Lind, Diseases in Hot Countries, passim, esp. pp. 38 and 55–67; Hillary, Changes of the Air, pp. 156–64; Mosely, Tropical Diseases, pp. 115–18, 416–56.
54. Lind, Diseases in Hot Countries, p. 286. See also Russell, Man's Mastery of Malaria, pp. 132–33.
55. Wilson, Observations on Climate, pp. 190–91.

newcomers were. They were thought to be "acclimatized" or "seasoned." One school believed that the first sickness, or the "seasoning sickness," was the necessary hurdle. Once the patient had lived through this he was relatively safe. In this belief they were, of course, quite correct, but it was no solution to the problem of avoiding high initial mortality. Various forms of prophylaxis to produce the same effect were therefore suggested. One very old practice was to bleed newcomers periodically. The Portuguese had long before justified this measure by assuming that immunity was connected with diet. Blood manufactured by the body from local food was supposed to be resistant to local diseases. They therefore removed the European blood a little at a time to allow for its replacement by the local product. British doctors often followed the same practice with a different justification drawn from the humoral pathology. If increased heat made the blood expand, the unaccustomed pressure could be relieved with occasional use of the lancet.[56]

The apparent immunity of Africans was even more striking than that of the "acclimatized" Europeans. Africans not only lived in health where the Europeans died of fevers, they also seemed to have diseases of their own which Europeans rarely contracted. Among these, sleeping sickness, yaws, and Guinea worm were all recognized and described by Atkins as early as 1734. They were a common problem both for the surgeons on the slavers and those on West Indian plantations, whose job it was to care for the health of the slaves. Negroes were known to suffer from the "vice," as it was considered at the time, of "dirt-eating," now recognized as a symptom of infestation with hook worm (*Necator Americanus*). They were also mysteriously susceptible to "dry belly-ache," especially on the slave ships and shortly after their arrival in America. In all probability, this complaint was lead poisoning from the white lead used to treat slaves for worms. Elephantiasis and several varieties of leprosy were also considered peculiar to the Negro race.[57]

Medical opinion was divided on the question of race and its relation to disease. Some believed there was an absolute racial immunity, which saved Africans from the European diseases and Europeans from those of the Africans. Others thought the immunity was merely

56. Lind, *Diseases in Hot Countries*, pp. 4–5 and 146; Long, *Jamaica*, II, 517–18.
57. Atkins, *Navy Surgeon*, Appendix, pp. 19–28; Hillary, *Changes of the Air*, pp. 182–85; Ashburn, *The Ranks of Death*, pp. 36, 168–70.

relative. The consensus of West Indian opinion was in this direction: apparent racial tendencies toward certain kinds of illness were recognized, but Africans were held to suffer from all tropical diseases.[58] No authority of importance believed that all races were equally endowed in respect to immunity. The different racial mortality rates on the African coast alone were too striking, and men of the time had no way of knowing the real causes. James Lind gave the idea of racial immunities the prestige of medical opinion. John Wesley added the sanction of humanitarian theology. Anthony Benezet claimed it was part of the divine plan—that God had endowed Africans with immunity to fevers so they could live their lives in their own way without interference. In his view, the slave trade was a special sin against the divinely ordained geography of race.[59] Thus the humanitarians, who generally defended the racial equality of all men, accepted the unanimous evidence that, at least in resistance to disease, racial difference was significant. In the end this "fact" rebounded to the favor of the polygenists, and they used it as the one clear argument on which all had to agree.[60] In this way the misunderstanding of the medical men came ultimately to be enshrined at the core of "scientific" racism.

Meanwhile, medical writers tried to explain the differential immunities, occasionally giving a role to custom as well as race. It could be held that Negroes avoided the Europeans' fevers because they

58. Privy Council, *Report on the Trade in Slaves,* Part III. The possibility of a degree of racial immunity is still held open by some authorities, but recent investigations indicate that it is either unlikely or insignificant. Recent studies in serology, however, show that some hemoglobin characteristics in human blood improve the individual's chance of successfully resisting certain diseases. Some of these traits might be thought of as "racial characteristics," since they are inherited; but they do not parallel the recognizable physical features of the major racial stocks. The most widely investigated so far has been the sickle-cell trait, which seems to improve childhood resistance to *Plasmodium falciparum.* [See A. B. Raper, "Malaria and the Sickling Trait," *British Medical Journal,* II 1955), 1186–89 (24 May 1955).] Some West African peoples have a very high incidence of this trait, while others have a very low one. It also occurs in Greece and some other parts of the Mediterranean basin. [See Livingstone, "Anthropological Influences of Sickle Cell Genes in West Africa."] It is probable that further studies in serology will reveal other blood characteristics which may also have the effect of producing relative immunities. Meanwhile, the answer is sufficiently clear for historical purposes. The really important immunities apparent in eighteenth and nineteenth-century West Africans were acquired in childhood, and not inherited.

59. Lind, *Diseases in Hot Countries,* pp. 224-25; Wesley, "Thoughts upon Slavery," p. 61; A. Benezet, *Some Historical Account of Guinea,* Rev. ed. (London, 1788), pp. 3-4.

60. See, for example, Charles White, *An Account of the Regular Gradations in Man. . . .* (London, 1799), pp. 73-79.

lived in "happy Want and Ignorance of luxurious living." Or it
was possible that Negro slaves in the West Indies were more susceptible to their own ills because they were worse fed, clothed, and
housed than their masters.[61] The more common explanation returned
to the question of bodily fluids and the greater Negro capacity for
perspiration. Schotte in particular seized on the difference between
African and European body odor and suggested that Negroes were
better able to throw off "foul and nasty vapours" which poisoned the
European body.[62] Most authorities, however, simply took it for
granted that in some way or other the Africans were differently
constituted.

These medico-racial considerations were crucial to any planning
for European activity in tropical lands. They had been a matter of
practical experience ever since the early-seventeenth-century attempt
to colonize Barbados with European settlers. The dominant view of
the West India interest in the 1770's and 1780's was the solidified
opinion that whites could not settle in the tropics except as a managerial class. Some believed that whites could not even do hard labor
as far north as South Carolina. In the West Indies, physical work
for Europeans was considered to be certain death.[63]

To an uncertain extent, however, this position was merely a justification for continuing the slave trade. Earlier in the century, when
the facts of mortality were equally well known, most West Indian
colonies had been anxious to have a high proportion of European
overseers and had encouraged immigration from Britain as best they
could. In 1774, Edward Long had put forward a complex scheme for
settling white farmers in Jamaica. He believed the island suffered
from a lack of provisions that might be raised by yeoman farmers,
and the central highlands seemed both healthy and unused. His plan
called for a settlement scheme managed by the island government.
It should acquire tracts of land, divide them into townships, and lay
them out in plots of twenty acres for each farming family, or five
acres for artisans. The size of these plots could be smaller than was
common in North America, since the special exuberance of the tropics
would make the land more productive. Each community was to be a

61. Atkins, *Navy Surgeon*, p. 17; Hillary, *Changes of the Air*, p. 206.
62. Schotte, *Synochus Atrabiliosa*, pp. 104–5.
63. *Candid Reflections*, p. 21; Privy Council, *Report on the Trade in Slaves*,
Part III.

balanced group of twenty-eight farming families and sixteen artisans. The land was to be cleared and prepared in advance, and each settler was to receive one male mulatto slave in return for a fixed annual rent. Once the state had been repaid for its outlay on slaves, they would become free and constitute a class of farm laborers.[64] Nothing came of Long's plan, but it foreshadowed later West African projects in both conception and detail. It shows, moreover, that some informed West Indian opinion still favored European settlement in spite of the known dangers of mental "degeneration" and disease.

There were no equivalent plans for West Africa before 1783, and it was known in any case that West Africa was much more dangerous than the West Indies. The best medical opinion was, indeed, opposed to the kind of establishment that already existed there. Lind argued that European garrisons for the West African posts should be reduced to the smallest possible numbers and moved to hulks anchored off shore. As much work as possible should be entrusted to Africans, trained for commercial positions. These men "should be naturalized; should be entitled to rise to a certain rank in the government or army; and they should be entitled to the other privileges of British subjects."[65] Lind's precedent was the earlier assimilationist policy of the Portuguese along the Guinea coast, and the idea returned again and again in other hands during the century that followed.

No matter how discouraging Lind might be about the dangers of West Africa, he himself suggested the possibility of a contingent and limited safety for Europeans. Just as Long assumed that the Jamaican highlands would be safe enough, Lind pointed out that most parts of the Coast had their healthy seasons. Some places were thought to be healthy all year round. Among these were the Banana Islands and the "high hills of Sierra Leone, upon whose summits the air is clear and even, while thick mists and noisome vapours overspread the lower grounds."[66] Thus some few healthy spots were "known," while others could be guessed at. Even as the African Association reported the mediocre results of its first explorations, it added a sanitary element to the myth of the better interior by supposing that, "the long descent of the rivers is a proof that the elevation of the inland country is raised above the level of the coast, and consequently that the

64. Long, *Jamaica*, II, 404–32.
65. Lind, *Diseases in Hot Countries*, pp. 224–25.
66. Lind, *Diseases in Hot Countries*, pp. 52–53, 151, 225–26.

climate is much more temperate, and probably more salubrious."[67]

While the British thus knew both the promise and the dangers of the West African tropics, neither the one nor the other was well enough known to be a cause for unqualified optimism or complete discouragement. The practical difficulties of exploiting African resources were hardly suspected, while the dangers were recognized in a way that still gave room for hope.

67. Association for Promoting the Discovery of the Interior Parts of Africa, *Proceedings* [1790] (London, 1792), p. 206. In fact, they were quite wrong on this point. Recent studies indicate that the incidence of infective bites by malaria-carrying mosquitos is, if anything, higher in the more open savanna country of the interior than it is on the coast or in the forest belt. [Colbourne and Wright, "Malaria in the Gold Coast." (1955), p. 167.]

4

NEW

JERUSALEMS

It was clear by 1781 that Britain was losing the American war, and, as the old empire crumbled, it was equally clear that some basic adjustments would take place in her relations with the overseas world. Many of those with a special interest in Africa began to turn their attention to specific projects or suggestions for a new African policy. After a period of gestation in the first years of peace, the projects began to appear in quantity. Between 1788 and 1793 (and the new war with France) a few actually materialized in a series of attempts to colonize the West African coast.

The planning and promotion took place against a background of shifting British attitudes. In the first postwar years, the pressing problem seemed to be the rivalry with France, and it led to the hope of redressing the balance of the lost American colonies by creating a new empire in Africa. As time passed, and the lost war slipped further behind, a more optimistic mood set in. Those who believed in empire could then begin thinking not merely of a new empire but of a better empire. Pitt's Government showed a spirit of moderate reform at home, even among the ruling classes. On the fringes of political life, still more radical reformers wanted to move with the spirit of the revolution which had just shaken America and would soon shake France. The eighteenth-century faith in man's potential achievement reached its British peak in this decade. It seemed, in the light of reason, that men could both remove the evils of the world around them and build anew on better foundations.

For Africa, this meant first of all the abolition of the slave trade, and the anti-slave-trade movement very nearly succeeded in the early 1790's. It also meant that new plans for Africa could be drawn on a clean slate, designed from the beginning to produce both wealth and a degree of human happiness which would be harder to achieve in the corrupt "Old World" of Europe. Africa was thus peculiarly open to utopian dreaming of a sort that fastened on America in other decades.

The planning of utopias was not merely an exercise for the radical fringe, though it was most common there. Respectable and practical people accepted some elements of utopianism. In spite of the knowledge in the hands of medical men, the general public had not yet formed an image of West Africa as the "white man's grave." The Africans themselves were thought of as a malleable and oppressed people, who would accept with gratitude whatever might be done for them. (The slave rebellion on Saint Domingue in 1791 had not yet destroyed France's richest plantations and created the first independent ex-colony ruled by non-Europeans.) The reform movement in Europe had a broad momentum, unopposed as yet by the backwash from the French Revolution and the Jacobin scare of the 1790's.

The first new project for West Africa, however, came directly out of the pressing problems created by the wreckage of the old empire. Convicts sentenced to transportation were crowding English jails. The dumping ground in America was closed, and some alternative had to be found. It was accepted on grounds of custom, conviction, and economy that transportation was preferable to building more prisons in Britain. No important body of opinion doubted the wisdom of this policy. For some, transportation was simply a cheap form of punishment. The convicts atoned for their crimes, and their suffering supposedly acted as a deterrent for others. Transportation could also be defended as a scheme for rehabilitation. In a new social setting, it was possible that some of them would start afresh and be-

Map 4. Africa in the Late Eighteenth Century

come useful members of society. There was also an economic argument. The convicts were a source of labor, and it was better to use
their labor in some part of the King's dominions where labor was
scarce. But for most people, the real advantage of transportation was
the simple fact that it removed undesirable people from Britain.

For a number of reasons, Africa seemed to provide a suitable alternative to America. If it were a question of removing undesirables,
the African "climate" would make quick work of them. With potential riches in a region where Europeans might not go of their own
will, convict labor seemed an easy solution. Convicts would be especially useful during the assumed dangerous period at the beginning
of any settlement, before clearing and cultivation had improved the

"climate." At the same time, Africa was something of a land of opportunity. It was still possible that some of the convicts sent there would reform and find an honorable place in a colonial society.

Small-scale convict shipments to West Africa had begun during the American War itself, thus creating a precedent, however unhappy. The Home Office had provided involuntary convict recruits to the military forces both in the royal colony of Senegambia and the forts controlled by the African Committee, but the scheme was not a success. Out of 350 men sent to the Gold Coast in 1782, only seven were alive and on duty in 1785. The rest had either gone over to the Dutch, escaped and turned pirate, or died of disease—mostly the latter.[1]

But further requests for convicts came from the officials in Africa. In 1776, Governor MacNamara of the Senegambia recommended Bintang on the Gambia as a desirable place for convict settlement. Others suggested a point further up the river at Nyanimaru.[2] At the end of the war, Chief Justice Morse sent in a more elaborate scheme with an emphasis on economic development. In his opinion, "The River Gambia is universally allowed to be the richest spot in Africa. It produces Bees Wax, Ivory, Gold, Rice, Castor Oil, Dye Woods, Mahogany equal to that of Jamaica, Sugar Canes, Indigo, Cotton, Balsam, Tobacco, and many other articles; Indian and Guinea Corn of various sorts and variety; the Vine, Coffee, Cocoa, Ginger, and Aloe. . . ."

Surely, here was wealth worth developing, and Morse thought it could be done in a way that met the problems posed by the post-war situation in Europe and America. He hoped to develop the Gambia as a route into the interior. New posts at Nyanimaru and Fattatenda would reach into the hinterland otherwise served by a French post in Galam, thus destroying the value of the Senegal, returned to French control in 1783. Development along the Gambia itself could concentrate on indigo and rice to replace the old supplies from South Carolina and Georgia. Timber, slaves, and plantation provisions from the Gambia would also shore up the West Indian economy and replace North America's functions in the South Atlantic System. The convicts were needed to man the posts and plant the new crops, but

1. Evidence given the Parliamentary Committee on Transportation, 1785, *Commons Journals*, XL, 959.
2. J. M. Gray, *A History of the Gambia* (Cambridge, 1940), p. 277.

they were not to be under punishment after they arrived. Instead, Morse hoped to settle a select group of convicts mixed with free immigrants in ordinary civil society, thus creating a true colony of Britons in Africa.[3]

The home government began to move in 1784. It first obtained an Act of Parliament giving the Crown authority to select a place overseas for the reception of convicts.[4] The initial plan was to use the Gambia, though not quite as Morse had suggested. It was a mixture of dumping, pure and simple, along with some hope for the development of tropical agriculture. John Barnes, an Africa merchant, supplied the detailed suggestion and urged the Gambia partly to keep undesirable convicts away from the other centers of African trade.

As developed further at the Home Office, the plan took on some curious utopian overtones. Lemain Island (later MacCarthy Island) was selected as the best site, situated as it was about 125 air miles inland from the coast. A first contingent of about 200 convicts were to be left there with tools and six-months' provisions. The guards would then retire downstream to Nyanimaru, where they could live aboard an armed ship and prevent escape by river. The convicts themselves would be left on their own, under an elected chief and council, to form their government and fare as they could. It was assumed that a great many would die, but new contingents could be landed from time to time until the island reached its estimated potential population of 4,000.[5] As a result, agriculture would flourish and soon Britain would have a rich trade. Nor were the possibilities of rehabilitation discounted. As the Home Office memorandum put it: "in a very few years they would become Planters, and take those who might be sent out hereafter into their Service—as they grow rich they naturally grow honest."[6]

A preparatory mission was sent up the river to negotiate with the African authorities. In February 1785, it purchased Lemain Island for Britain at a total cost of £579 in bribes and gifts and the promise of a future annual tribute.[7]

3. "Sketch of a Plan for Erecting a Colony in the Territory Belonging to the River Gambia in Africa," enclosed in Edward Morse to Lord Sydney, 26 April 1784, CO 267/8.

4. 24 George III, c. 56.

5. In fact, the population of MacCarthy Island only reached 1,786 at the census of 31 December 1960.

6. Undated memorandum, enclosed with Lord Sydney to Lords of the Treasury, 9 February 1785. HO 35/1.

7. Gray, *Gambia*, p. 278.

Map 5. Senegambia in the 1780's

In the early part of 1785, however, the Gambia scheme began to
meet difficulties in Britain. Criticism built up from two different
sources. On the one hand, enthusiasts for other parts of Africa began
to enter their claims. Edward Thompson, the naval commander in
West African waters, disliked the site and thought São Thomé should
be purchased from Portugal in its place.[8] His first plan was not accepted, but he followed it with a glowing report of the coast of
South West Africa near the mouth of the Orange River. Here the
promise of wealth was held to be greater even than at the Gambia,
and the "climate" was so good that voluntary European settlers could
be easily recruited.[9]

Thompson had never been to South West Africa, but his report
fell in with a flurry of European excitement about the prospects of
settlement north of the Cape and south of Angola. The Portuguese
governor at Luanda sought to push south with European settlement
in what is now southern Angola. From the Dutch side, Henrik Hop
had travelled north of the Orange in 1761–62 and investigated the
copper of Namaqualand. François le Vaillant explored to the north
of the Dutch settlements in the early 1780's, and published in 1790
an extravagant and partly fictitious account of what he found there.
He returned to Europe in 1784, and it is possible that some of his
exaggerations had become common knowledge.[10] Whatever the
source of the information, the British government shifted its interest
to South West Africa, but it kept that interest a secret for the time
being.

The second source of criticism directed at the Gambia scheme came
from Parliament. Edmund Burke protested in April 1785 that sending convicts to the Gambia meant imposing the death penalty, "after
a mock display of mercy."[11] In May a Committee of the House of
Commons began to hear evidence. Some was humanitarian. Some was
the *ex parte* testimony of the West Africa traders, afraid of a convict
settlement near their posts. The stream of expert witnesses agreed,
however, that the Gambia was too unhealthy for settlement, that

8. Edward Thompson to Secretary of State, 15 February 1785, CO 267/9.
9. "Some Account of the Country on the West Coast of Africa between 20° and 30°
of South Latitude, well calculated for the reception of the loyal Americans and where
Convicts of Britain may be made useful to the State," 9 March 1785, CO 267/9.
10. F. C. C. Egerton, *Angola in Perspective* (London, 1957), pp. 50–51; H.
Vedder, *South West Africa in Early Times* (London, 1938), pp. 21, 31.
11. *Cobbett's Parliamentary History*, XXV, 431.

Europeans could never work in the tropics and survive, that the Africans would kill any settlers the "climate" spared.[12] The virtues of South West Africa were also expounded, and Sir Joseph Banks, who had been to Australia with Cook, suggested still another possibility—Botany Bay in New South Wales.[13]

The Committee's conclusion was anti-Gambia and against the scheme of letting convicts run their own government while some were becoming rich and honest. It approved the substance of Thompson's report and recommended South West Africa as the best site, especially since it might serve for the relocation of North American loyalists as well as British criminals.[14] All that remained was to send a survey party to examine the coast itself. After some delay *Nautilus* sloop returned with a discouraging account—the entire coast from 15° to 33° South Latitude was barren and sandy. It was, in fact, the Namib Desert. With this, the South West Africa boom collapsed. The Home Office gave up all thought of Africa and ordered a fleet prepared for Botany Bay instead.[15] Thus the first post-war effort to develop West Africa ended in the foundation of Australia.

In spite of the final outcome, the Gambia project has some interest as an indication of British official thinking in the 1780's. The picture of tropical wealth had been accepted without question, and even the terrible mortality was not enough to rule out West Africa as a possible site for a colony. A certain carelessness with the selection of a distant place on scant or uncertain information was also evident. If responsible and practical officials like Lord Sydney and Commodore Thompson could indulge in thoughtless and optimistic planning of this kind, others, less practical and more enthusiastic, might find support for utopian settlements.

Two outlines for a project in West Africa emerged in the year of the peace, and in time they merged to serve as the basis for an actual attempt at settlement. One was the work of Henry Smeathman, the naturalist. When he returned from his collecting trip in the Banana Islands, he was anxious to help the African people, and in 1783 he wrote to a prominent Quaker, offering his services to the Society of Friends. He saw an opening for humanitarian good works in the po-

12. *Commons Journals*, XL, 954–59.
13. Minutes of Evidence in HO 7/1.
14. *Commons Journals*, XL, 1163–64.
15. Unsigned draft addressed to Lords of Treasury, 18 August 1786, HO 35/1.

litical order then prevalent on the Windward Coast around Sierra
Leone. The African nations in this region had only a rudimentary
political organization. The way had long since been open for European slave dealers and their mulatto descendents to create virtually
sovereign enclaves. Armed with guns, any man who could gather a
few hundred followers and slaves was a law to himself. The Banana
Islands, where Smeathman had lived so happily, were ruled in
this way by the Afro-English Caulker family. Smeathman sensed
that if a state could be founded by an ill-educated slave dealer it
could also be done by an educated European. A properly sponsored
and conducted expedition might found a "true commonwealth" on
the African coast, beyond the sovereignty of any European power.

The scheme was backed by the economic calculation already publicized by Postlethwayt and others. With the potential wealth of
African agriculture, tropical products could be supplied more cheaply
with free labor in Africa than with slave labor in America. By founding a settlement in Africa, Smeathman believed the West Indies could
be driven from their place in world markets. They would lose their
supply of slaves, since a demand for labor in Africa would raise the
cost of slaves to prohibitive levels. African labor would stay in Africa,
and the whole South Atlantic System would collapse of its own inefficiency. Furthermore, the promoters would gain wealth for themselves
in return for their good deeds.[16] It was a combination of ideas based
squarely on the accepted British beliefs about West Africa, and it
lived on to become the basis for countless projects in later decades.

Smeathman's original project had a social as well as an economic
program. He was consciously interested in creating a new and better
society, but he reasoned that such could not be founded with men
already set in their ways, especially if they were drawn from a single
culture. European settlers would merely create a little Europe. He
hoped, therefore, to begin with men intentionally chosen for the
variety of their cultural background. Poor Negroes stranded in England in the aftermath of the war, British artisans, slaves purchased in
Senegal, and volunteer settlers from the Canaries and Madeira would
be amalgamated together with slaves and voluntary recruits from the
immediate vicinity of the new colony. With such a mixture, there
would be no established institutions to combat, and a truly new society

16. Smeathman to Knowles, 21 July 1783, printed in *New Jerusalem Magazine*,
I, 179, 281–93 (1790).

Map 6. Part of the Windward Coast

could be molded under the forms of democratic liberalism. Political freedom, elective office, and a color-blind constitution would attract still more settlers, and a true commonwealth could grow. "In short, if a community of 2 or 300 persons were to be associated on such principles as constitute the prosperity of civilized nations, such are the fertility of the soil, and the value of its products, and the advantage of such an establishment, that it must, with the blessing of the Almighty, increase with a rapidity beyond all example; and in all probability extend its saving influence in 30 or 40 years, wider than even *American Independence.*"[17]

The second sketch of an African utopia prepared in 1783 came from the hand of Granville Sharp, for more than a decade past the unofficial protector of Negroes in Britain. Sharp was a man with

17. Smeathman to Knowles, 21 July 1783, *New Jerusalem Magazine,* I, 293.

broad connections throughout the world of British philanthropy, with the Quakers, the anti-slave-trade people, and especially with the "Clapham Sect." The latter was a loosely knit group of friends and neighbours in Clapham who formed, during the 1780's and 1790's, the core of the Evangelical party among the laymen of the Church of England. In one way or another, they dominated a wide range of humanitarian causes. At the center of the group were Henry Thornton, James Stephen the elder, Henry and John Venn, and William Wilberforce, but its ramifications and connections were much wider, extending through Wilberforce's political activity to the government itself.

It was only natural that any colonization project would be shown to Sharp, as the known defender of the Africans. His own earliest recorded response took the form of a memorandum dated 1 August 1783, commenting on the outlines of a project he had seen, probably the Smeathman plan. In any event, Sharp's document took up where Smeathman left off and outlined more detailed constitutional and legal provisions to be followed at the new settlement.[18]

Between 1783 and 1786, plans were maturing in several directions at once. Smeathman continued to agitate his project. In London, the problem of the stranded Negro Americans, and other "black poor," became more severe. A noted philanthropist, James Hanway, organized a Committee for the Relief of the Black Poor, including among its members some of Sharp's Evangelical friends. Sharp both supported the organization and continued his private patronage of Negro clients. Early in 1786, Smeathman's project had been taken up by Sharp and the Committee and shifted slightly to become that of a colony principally, but not exclusively, for the purpose of settling the "black poor" in Africa. A Prospectus was issued over Smeathman's signature. It offered the privilege of enrolling for the sum of £5 to, "Any person desirous of a permanent and comfortable establishment, in a most pleasant and fertile climate, near SIERRA LEONE, where land may be purchased at a small expense, . . ."

Emigrants were to receive all the land they could cultivate, passage to Sierra Leone, and supplies for three months after landing. A clergyman for their spiritual comfort, a schoolmaster for their children, and a "physician skilled in tropical medicine" were to accom-

18. Memorandum of 1 August 1783. printed in Prince Hoare, *Memoirs of Granville Sharp,* 2nd ed., 2 vols. (London, 1828), II, 11-15.

pany the party.[19] The government also contributed a subsidy of £12 for each settler. By the early part of 1786, the expedition was preparing to leave under Smeathman's direction, but with varied support from other individuals and groups.[20]

At this juncture, Smeathman died. The project passed definitively into the hands of Granville Sharp and the Committee for the Black Poor, though Sharp assumed the principal responsibility. After a hurried reorganization, an expedition actually sailed early in 1787 with 411 passengers under the command of Captain T. Boulden Thompson of the Navy. In May, it arrived in Africa and founded the "Province of Freedom," under circumstances that made it one of the oddest of all efforts to create human happiness in Africa.

Captain Thompson bought a tract of land from the African authorities in the King's name—not on the Banana Islands as Smeathman had planned, but on the Sierra Leone peninsula near by. Most of the settlers were "black poor" recruited in London, though about sixty English prostitutes were also recruited to provide wives for the settlers. Thompson's command of the expedition was simply a temporary expedient. Once the settlers were landed, he withdrew and left them to govern themselves.[21] The motives of the principal sponsors were clearly humanitarian and altruistic, but others simply wished to rid England of people they thought undesirable. At this level, there was an element of similarity to the Gambia convict project.

Sharp's own intention was quite different. He wanted not only to help the black poor but to experiment in social engineering. He equipped the expedition with an elaborate code of regulations, built on Smeathman's scheme and modified by ideas Sharp himself had been maturing since 1783. The constitution of the new state was modelled on what Sharp understood to have been that of ancient Israel, modified by that of medieval England. Ultimate power in political affairs was given to a common council, made up of all house-

19. Henry Smeathman, *Plan of a Settlement to be made near Sierra Leone* (London, 1786).

20. See C. Fyfe, *A History of Sierra Leone* (London, 1962) for the authoritative account of the Sierra Leone settlement. Fyfe (pp. 14–15) gives a slightly less favorable view of Smeathman's project and character.

21. The legal status of the colony was not precisely defined, but it was clearly not sovereign British territory at this stage, nor do the settlers appear to have been considered British subjects. In English law, the colony itself might have been held to be a sovereign entity, or, more likely, under the authority of Naimbana, the King of the Koya Temne. See Fyfe, *Sierra Leone*, pp. 16, 19–20, and 24–25.

holders gathered together. Actual administration was left to elected magistrates—"tythingmen" elected by each twelve householders and "hundredors" to represent each eight tythings, or ninety-six households. All males between sixteen and sixty years of age were to serve in rotation as a militia for defense and police.

In spite of its representative government, the Province of Freedom was not designed to be a classless society. The householders were to be a kind of yeoman class with two inferior groups. One of these was a class of indented servants, serving up to five years for adults or eleven for children before they attained equality of rank. Still lower on the social scale, slaves purchased in neighboring countries might be introduced into the colony. Slave-holding was prohibited for individuals, but slaves were permitted as state property under an arrangement that allowed them to earn their redemption by five years' labor at public works.[22]

Sharp's regulations also called for some radical economic experiments. He began with the proposition that, "HUMAN *Labour* is more essential and valuable than any other article in new settlements, which chiefly depend on the cultivation and produce of the earth for their subsistence and commercial profit."[23] Hence the medium of exchange should be based on labor rather than gold or silver. The device chosen was a labor tax, due from each male citizen at the rate of 62 days a year, or 20 per cent of each man's working time. At the first of each year, each man was to sign a series of labor indentures in favor of the government, in denominations of five, ten, or more days of work. These indentures were transferable. As the government sold them, they became a circulating medium, based on an article of real value. Taxation was also progressive. "Gentlemen" were to pay triple taxes and skilled workers double, though their actual service would be done by unskilled deputies.[24]

Land values were also tied to the system of labor-currency. The original settlers had been promised free land, but later settlers or young men coming of age would have to purchase an allotment with four years' service to the state, paid in the form of labor-currency indentures. The scheme of allotments also tried to take account of

22. Granville Sharp, *Short Sketch of Temporary Regulations . . . for the Intended Settlement on the Grain Coast of Africa, near Sierra Leone* (London, 1786), pp 1–11, 22–32.
23. Sharp, *Temporary Regulations*, p. 13.
24. Sharp, *Temporary Regulations*, pp. 13–15, 56–67.

Adam Smith's recent discussion of rents. Each householder was to receive a town lot plus a farm, the farms varying in size according to distance from town, 20 acres if it were only three miles from town, up to 200 acres twelve miles away.

Finally, an element of state enterprise was added. Sharp intended the government to keep 30 per cent of the land in its own hands, to be worked through the "investment" of part of the labor tax. Income from both its own farms and the labor tax should have provided very generously for financing education and other government services.[25]

On the whole, it was an ingenious plan, foreshadowing utopian socialism and based squarely on the eighteenth-century faith that rational planning could produce a "good society" on earth—so much so that some of Sharp's close friends and admirers thought he had gone too far.[26] In retrospect they were certainly correct, and Sharp appears exceedingly naive to have expected utopia from human material drawn so largely from the outcasts of London slums. In fact, Sharp did not intend to create quite the kind of colony that took shape. He hoped to form a multi-racial settlement and to send out a broader cross section of English society. European settlers were especially encouraged by large land grants, and some individuals were to be given free land in return for their special contribution of skill or intellect. Early in 1788, lots were reserved for Thomas Clarkson, the anti-slavery leader, his brother John, then a naval officer, and twelve Swedenborgians anxious to reach the interior of Africa.[27]

Sharp himself was well pleased with his regulations, and he wrote some months after the expedition sailed: "The Code of Regulations which I drew up for the settlement, not being objected to by the Government, was adopted by the Settlers before they sailed: and, if they would be careful to maintain it, they would become the freest and happiest people on earth; because the poor are effectually provided for, and their rights secured. . . ."[28]

In practice, the regulations were not applied, but the failure was not so much Sharp's utopianism as the more basic errors he shared

25. Sharp, *Temporary Regulations,* pp. 32–53, 56–73.
26. G. Sharp to inhabitants of the Providence of Freedom, 16 May 1788, printed in Hoare, *Memoirs of Granville Sharp,* II, 104.
27. Hoare, *Memoirs of Granville Sharp,* II, 11.
28. G. Sharp to a New York Lady, 12 January 1788, printed in Hoare, *Memoirs of Granville Sharp,* II, 85.

with other Britons of his time. The soil was poor, and the crops failed. Mortality was well within the range that should have been expected. Even though the settlers were mainly Negro, half died between May 1787 and November 1789.[29] At the end of 1789 a minor chief attacked and dispersed the settlers in retaliation for injuries done him by other Europeans. By then the Province of Freedom was already a failure.

While plans for the Province of Freedom were maturing in humanitarian quarters, other outlines and projects had been advanced. Many of them came to nothing, but they indicate some of the vast possibility open to European activity—ranging from the Province of Freedom on one hand to the Gambia convict scheme on the other. One scheme, proposed in a private letter to William Pitt in 1785, centered on the Gold Coast. Its author, a Lt. Clarke of the Army, was concerned about the need to recover from the American losses in the late war. He saw the golden opportunity where there were already British trading forts. All that was needed was to shift from commerce to agriculture. The land was "rich beyond conception," given proper organization and manpower. The organization, according to Clarke's scheme, would come with the appointment of Crown Commissioners to replace the African Committee. Two hundred soldiers could protect the settlement, while three hundred convicts could be sent out as settlers. Other manpower would come through the institution of forced labor for Africans, though limited to six hours each day. Still more labor could be obtained from slaves, and Clarke thought slaves would be available in large numbers if the export slave trade to America were forbidden. Thus the accustomed slave trade from the interior would be held and used on the Gold Coast itself.[30]

Still other plans were laid for the vicinity of Sierra Leone. One centered on Smeathman's chosen Banana Islands, hoping to make them into another and more successful plantation colony on the West Indian model.[31] Another chose the Sierra Leone mainland.[32] Some of the slave merchants in the Sierra Leone River actually began about this time to grow plantation crops on Tasso Island as a side line to

29. See Appendix.
30. Lt. Clarke to W. Pitt, 17 March 1785, PRO 30/8/363.
31. W. H. [William Halton?] to Duncan Campbell, undated, CO 267/10.
32. J. Matthews, *A Voyage to the River Sierra-Leone* . . . (London, 1788), pp. 21–23, 52–59, and 63.

their commercial operations. Still other projects kept to the European-managed plantation as the expected economic form, but incorporated some of the anti-slavery aspects of the Smeathman scheme.[33] Many of these plans were sketchy and perhaps only half serious. Others were not only seriously projected but were brought forward again and again over a decade or more in the face of real discouragement.

One of the most energetic, if erratic, of the colonial enthusiasts was Carl Berns Wadström, a Swedish explorer and promoter who first made his appearance in England in 1788. He was an engineer by profession, a Swedenborgian by religion, and he came to England with an interest in colonization that dated back to 1779. His original idea was to set up a utopian community of Swedenborgians somewhere in Europe, but he and his supporters soon shifted the scene of their project to Africa—in part, certainly, because of Swedenborg's African doctrines.[34] Their plans were held up at first by the American War. Then, after they had obtained a charter from the Swedish Crown and had begun to organize a Swedish colony in West Africa, religious dissension broke out in the group. Wadström himself, who had been president of the Swedish colonization society, left Sweden in 1787. His first objective was to explore Africa and find a site for the colony he might sometime found. He therefore joined Sparrman and Arrhenius on their unsuccessful reconnaissance expedition to Gorée. On his return to Europe, Wadström made for England where the growing anti-slavery movement, the launching of the Province of Freedom, and the rise of interest in Africa suggested that he might find backing for a new effort. Further Swedish support was out of the question in any case, not only because of his old Swedenborgian quarrels but also because of the outbreak of war with Russia.

Once in England, Wadström got in touch with Thomas Clarkson, gave information about the slave trade, and talked with Granville Sharp about the possibility of merging the Swedenborgian venture with the Province of Freedom. It was then that he got permission for himself and eleven other Swedenborgians to sail with the relief ship due to leave in the summer of 1788. Something went wrong, as things usually did with Wadström's schemes, and the ship sailed

33. Henry Gandy to C. B. Wadström, 17 August 1788, printed in *New Jerusalem Magazine*, I, 165 (1790).

34. See obituary by Helen Maria Williams, *Monthly Magazine*, VII, 462–65 (1799); C. B. Wadström, *An Essay on Colonization, Particularly Applied to the Western Coast of Africa . . .* 2 vols. (London, 1794–1795), II, 179–181.

without them. After this break with Granville Sharp, he turned to other sources of help and obtained permission to sail again for Africa on a British naval vessel. This time the ship was ordered off on other duty following the Nootka Sound crisis, and Wadström was still left stranded in England.[35]

He swallowed his disappointment and settled down as a publicist and colonial projector. With the aid of Augustus Nordenskiold, a friend and supporter in the old Swedenborgian quarrels, he gathered a group of English Swedenborgians, and together they published a prospectus for a new West African colony. It was to be located at Cape Mesurado, where Monrovia now stands, entirely under Swedenborgian religious control, and beyond the sovereign power of any European state. The goal was still much the same as that of the original Swedish group—escape from Europe as it was. Africa offered itself as a "place out of the bounds of Europe, where the natives shall be found in a simple state of nature, comparatively innocent, because uncorrupted with the vices which have hitherto sprung from a disordered circulation."[36]

The design for this particular utopia was partly based on the pseudo-ethnography of the "noble savage," and partly on Swedenborgian theology. The political constitution, unlike that of the Province of Freedom, was calculated not to free men from the trammels of an old society, but to protect the faithful from deviation. All office holders were to be members of the Church of the New Jerusalem, and a complex set of regulations assured a Swedenborgian theocracy.

But the new society was not projected for Swedenborgians alone, nor exclusively for Europeans. Europeans, according to Wadström were morally bound to invite Africans into the settlement. In his view, human cultures were divided into the civilized and the uncivilized. In civilized society, understanding is elevated above will and passion. In uncivilized societies, will and passion dominate. This

35. Wadström, *Colonization*, II, 185–95, 399; R. L. Tafel, *Documents Concerning the Life and Character of Emanuel Swedenborg*, 2 vols. (London, 1875–1877), I, 640; T. Clarkson, *History of the Rise, Progress, and Accomplishment of the Abolition of the African Slave Trade by the British Parliament*, 2 vols. (London, 1808), I, 488.

36. *Plan for a Free Community Upon the Coast of Africa Under the Protection of Great Britain, but Entirely Independent of All European Laws and Government* (London, 1789), p. 43. See also C. B. Wadström, "Letters of a Voyage to Africa," *New Jerusalem Magazine*, I, 70–73, 125–32, 157–74 (1790).

situation could and should be corrected through education. Just as the individual is morally committed to educate his children, civilized people are morally committed to promote the "happiness of the barbarous and uncivilized."

The moral obligation also carried concomitant rights. Among these, Wadström found the right of European peoples to rule over the Africans: "If the tutelage of children be regarded as a period of slavery, I allow that civilized nations have some right to exercise a certain dominion over the uncivilized, provided that this happy dominion be confined as a paternal yoke, and that the duration do not exceed the period of a child's maturity."[37]

It followed therefore that Africans would be recognized as fundamentally equal to the European settlers; but initially they would have to accept a status of "gentle servitude," from which they could gradually redeem themselves by work and education. Ultimately they would advance to full membership in society and intermarry with the colonists from Europe.[38]

As might be expected from the narrowly exclusive religious base, nothing came of the Mesurado project. There were very few Swedenborgians in England. Wadström had nevertheless detailed a version of Christian paternalism that was uncommon in eighteenth-century England, though basic to many nineteenth-century concepts of the proper relations between differing societies. His intellectual justification, however, was not completely new: much the same kind of thing had been said again and again in sixteenth-century Spain.

Wadström would be heard from again. Meanwhile he drifted off to Manchester, ostensibly to learn the textile industry so that he could introduce it into his new colony whenever it should be established. He was quiet for a time after 1790. Those of his followers who were determined to reach Africa went there under other auspices.

The most significant colonization project of 1789 and 1790 came, instead, from Granville Sharp's Evangelical and humanitarian friends. "The Province of Freedom" was clearly a failure, as Sharp himself recognized by the middle of 1789. It was necessary to save what might be saved, but Sharp, who had put nearly £2,000 of his own money into it, was not able to carry on alone. The potential profits

37. C. B. Wadström, *Observations on the Slave Trade* . . . (London, 1789), pp. 58–61; p. 60 for quotation.
38. *Plan for a Free Country.* esp. p. 50.

of legitimate commerce were well advertised. He therefore appealed
to friends with business connections, hoping to use the Province of
Freedom as a base for commercial operations.[39] Through William
Wilberforce, he appealed to the government for a charter. At the
end of 1789, with the aid of Henry Thornton, the Evangelical banker,
the St. George's Bay Association was formed. By then, the original
settlers had been dispersed, but plans went forward and the Association received a Parliamentary charter in July 1790 as the Sierra Leone
Company.

In sharp contrast to the other African projects of the period, the
Sierra Leone Company began without a blueprint for utopia, or even
a very clear idea of what should be done. It appears that Sharp only
intended to add a commercial adjunct to the utopian colony, but in
fact he lost control altogether. His financial interest in the new firm
was that of a minor stockholder along with two thousand others.
While he was given a place on the committee, control passed to
Henry Thornton as chairman. The Sierra Leone Company gradually
abandoned the goals of the Province of Freedom, and Sharp became
a somewhat embittered critic watching from the sidelines.[40]

The Company was given control of the land originally purchased
in Sierra Leone for Sharp's settlement, to be used as a trading post.
In the words of the charter, it was to serve as a place "where they
may form a Factory or Settlement for their Servants, a secure De-
pository for their Goods and Merchandize, and a safe Harbour for
their Shipping."[41] The principal goal was clear enough. It was to
work in the spirit of Wilberforce's belief that Africa should be
civilized through the influence of "legitimate trade," not colonization
for its own sake.

Before an expedition could be launched, however, the scope and
nature of the project began to change. A secure profit from trade
depended on the grant of a Parliamentary monopoly excluding other
British merchants from the Sierra Leone River and its hinterland.
When the Company's request for such privilege failed—as it did at
an early stage through the opposition of the Company of Merchants

39. Hoare, *Memoirs of Granville Sharp*, II, 124, 136–40.
40. [G. Sharp], *Free English Territory in Africa. An Account of the District Purchased for the Settlement at Sierra Leone* (London, 1790); Hoare, *Memoirs of Granville Sharp*, II, 82, 157–59, 172–82.
41. 31 George III, c. 55.

Trading to Africa—the promoters were forced to consider other alternatives.[42] The idea of free-labor plantations came naturally to mind. Lt. John Matthews' glorious picture of tropical luxuriance at Sierra Leone gave a nudge in this direction.[43] Through the latter part of 1790 and early 1791 the Company thought in terms of sending out "a hundred or so enterprising Englishmen" to lay out plantations worked by local African labor. Lt. Henry Hew Dalrymple was engaged to lead the expedition. He was a warm advocate of the plantation form of enterprise, and he had served at Gorée during the American War. The Company still planned to engage in trade on its own account, and it hoped for a *de facto* monopoly over the trade of its own settlement; but the principal revenue was to come from land rents. This was the second phase of the project.

Toward the middle of 1791 the plan again changed. Dalrymple was a difficult man to deal with, both on grounds of personality and of policy. The Company requested his resignation, and with it many of his associates also resigned. The directors were also disappointed with the would-be European settlers who were often men without capital, character, or experience. The Company learned, about this time, that several thousand Negro loyalists from the thirteen lost colonies were stranded in Nova Scotia and might be willing to emigrate to Africa.[44] The project was hurriedly readjusted. White settlers were now discouraged, and the Company's servants were to be the only Europeans allowed in the colony. The Company still intended to run plantations of their own, but the economic base would be peasant cultivation by the "Nova Scotians."[45] Plans went ahead on this basis. About 100 Europeans went direct from England to organize a settlement. They were joined in March 1792 by 1131 Negroes from Nova Scotia and later on by some 64 survivors of the Province of Freedom, who had been living precariously in the vicinity.

The political constitution of the new colony carried remnants of

42. Williams to Schoolbred, 23 April 1790; Schoolbred to Williams, 28 April 1790, BT 6/8.

43. *Sierra-Leone*, 21–23, 52–59, and 63.

44. For the earlier history of these loyalist refugees, see B. Quarles, *The Negro in the American Revolution* (Chapel Hill, 1961), esp. pp. 158–181.

45. H. Thornton to John Clarkson (Private), 30 December 1791, Ad. Mss. 41262A. Sierra Leone Company, *Report of the Court of Directors of the Sierra Leone Company to the General Court*, 7 vols. (title varies) (London, 1791–1808), I (1791), 21–28.

all the planning stages through which it had passed, and a good deal of continuing uncertainty as well. As Henry Thornton later wrote: "Who were to be the governed party at Sierra Leone, we knew not—whether many or few, blacks or whites, whether natives who might migrate thither, or Nova Scotians, or Europeans in general, or British, and if British, whether servants of the Company or independent settlers of all ranks, and degrees.—Nothing in the world could be more uncertain than the speculation; who were to be the governed part of the new colony, at the time it became necessary for us to fix some government."[46]

The directors therefore began with a Governor and Council of eight members, modelled on that of the East India Company in the time of Warren Hastings. The powers of the councillors were independent of the governor. It was a system designed for governors in whom the home authorities had little confidence—in short, for H. H. Dalrymple. In fact, the first Governor was John Clarkson, brother of the anti-slavery leader and much closer to the directors than anyone else in the colony. He thus began with uncertain authority, and political squabbles among the Council made a clear line of action difficult.

In time, the directors straightened out the upper reaches of the constitution, giving John Clarkson full authority as Governor along with authority to settle constitutional details on the spot. The final shape of the political and economic structure was therefore hammered out in Sierra Leone itself, based on official advice from Henry Thornton and unofficial suggestions from the Clapham Sect and their friends.

Thornton himself had no strong views on the government of colonies, though he was a Tory in politics and distrusted the Nova Scotians as a possible electorate. Thomas Clarkson and Granville Sharp, on the other hand, wanted to preserve the radical democracy of the Province of Freedom. The result was a compromise. The offices of Tythingman and Hundredor were retained, but without their old function as a magistracy. They were merely constables with the power to advise the government on matters of common concern. Executive and judicial power remained with the Company's servants, but with safeguards such as trial by jury and a guarantee of equal

46. H. Thornton to J. Clarkson, 14 September 1792, Ad. Mss. 41262A, f. 166.

rights regardless of race. Sharp and his friends had managed to salvage the representative forms, but little else.[47]

There were equivalent cross currents of opinion about what ends these political means should serve. Thornton was anxious to recover some of the stockholders' investment by the collection of rents. Sharp wanted to recreate as much as possible of his old utopia. Thomas Clarkson was anxious to use Sierra Leone as an outpost in the battle against the slave trade. He had little faith in the efficacy of "legitimate trade," or any other kind of trade, in civilizing Africa. Instead, he thought of the colony as a kind of bridgehead on the African continent, from which "civilization" could be extended by persuasion. To this end, he urged his brother to create three committees of council. One was to work at persuading African kings to give up the slave trade and shift to agricultural production. A second was to work for the abolition of African slavery by persuasion and by "ransoming" young slaves to serve on the Company's plantations. The third was to work for the eradication of "superstition."[48]

William Wilberforce meanwhile kept up pressure for his own panacea of "legitimate trade," and especially trade into the distant interior where the existence of "considerable towns" was known or suspected. He had the support of Henry Thornton and the possibility of working with the African Association, which also hoped to open up the trade of the interior through exploration. A trading post on the Gambia was planned in co-operation with the government and the African Association, but the plans never materialized. In the end, the African Association acted alone and sent a single explorer, Mungo Park, inland from the Gambia in 1795.[49]

An even more promising prospect opened briefly in the spring of 1792, when it appeared that the abolition of the slave trade might well pass the House of Commons. Pitt intimated privately that, with abolition, all British West African posts might be turned over to the

---

47. H. Thornton to J. Clarkson, 14 September 1792; T. Clarkson to J. Clarkson, 17 July 1792; G. Sharp to J. Clarkson, 24 July 1792, Ad. Mss. 41262A. Sierra Leone Company, *Account of the Colony of Sierra Leone From its First Establishment in [sic] 1793 . . .* (London, 1795), pp. 74–76.

48. T. Clarkson to J. Clarkson, 28 August 1791 and January 1792, Ad. Mss. 41262A.

49. W. Wilberforce to J. Clarkson, 28 December 1791 and 27 April 1792; H. Thornton to J. Clarkson, 6 June 1792, Ad. Mss. 41262A. Undated draft of instructions to James Willis, CO 267/10. Association for Promoting the Discovery of the Interior Parts of Africa, *Proceedings* (London, 1790), p. 204; Gray, *Gambia*, p. 283.

Sierra Leone Company, along with the £13,000 annual subsidy for their upkeep.[50] With this support, the Company could have returned to its original commercial basis, but abolition failed in Parliament. The beginning of the new war with France early in 1793 ended further opportunities for extension. Sierra Leone then settled down to live its life as the turn of events had created it—a settlement of Negroes under a Chartered Company, which also participated in trade.

Even before the Sierra Leone expedition had left England, the very fact that a colony was to be established in Africa, and with substantial support from commerce and government, encouraged other projectors. Among those left out of the Sierra Leone venture were the associates of H. H. Dalrymple, displaced from the Company toward the middle of 1791. Many were half-pay officers from the forces, and the most active of these was Lt. Philip Beaver, a former shipmate of John Clarkson and a man of liberal views. Dalrymple and his friends formed their own colonization committee and gained a little support in the City, notably from Paul Le Mesurier, then a Member of Parliament and later Lord Mayor of London. C. B. Wadström took an interest in the scheme, bringing in further support from Manchester and from Swedenborgians generally. By the end of 1791 this ill-assorted group of speculators and philanthropists formed the Bulama Island Association, with the intention of founding a colony on what is now Bolama Island in Portuguese Guinea.[51]

The essential elements of the project were those cast aside by the Sierra Leone Company at the time of Dalrymple's dismissal. It was to be a colony of European settlers operating plantations of sugar and other tropical staples in competition with the West Indies. The main purpose was to make the settlers rich, but the group had other philanthropic objects for the Africans: "To purchase land in their country, to cultivate it by free natives hired for the purpose; and thereby to induce in them habits of labour and industry, it was thought might eventually lead to the introduction of letters, Religion, and civilization, into the very heart of Africa."[52]

The object was clearly to be agriculture and not commerce (though

50. H. Thornton to J. Clarkson, 3 May 1792, Ad. Mss. 41262A.
51. Philip Beaver, *African Memoranda* (London, 1805), pp. xiii–xiv; Wadström, *Colonization*, II, 133–34.
52. Beaver, *African Memoranda*, p. 3.

some of the individual settlers hoped for commercial profits as well).
Instead of selling shares, the Association sold land—at the rate of
£30 for each 500 acres to actual settlers, and £60 per 500 acres to
absentees. These were generous and attractive terms, as well they
might be for land the promoters did not own and had never seen.
The scale was designed for large plantations, and some absentee
subscribers took up 2000 acres or more.[53]

In other respects the project fell short of its first hopes. Some of
the subscribers, being self-chosen as colonists, were badly chosen.
William Bant, a Quaker who had an unsavory reputation in the City,
alienated some of the potential financial support. The powerful interests of the Sierra Leone Company and the West Indian planters were
equally opposed, and the Government seems to have concluded that
the Association was under-capitalized at a mere £7,000, where
£25,000 or more would have been realistic.[54] Whatever the inspira-
tion, the Government refused its recognition and support. The Association nevertheless went ahead with its plans and mounted an
expedition. Two hundred and sixty-nine settlers including women and
children sailed from England in April 1792 in two parties commanded by Dalrymple and Beaver respectively.

The legal problem of non-incorporation and the lack of any authority to found a colony were settled after departure by drawing up
a written constitution in radical democratic terms. Sovereignty was
held to reside with the people, represented in a thirteen-member
legislative council, elected annually by adult male suffrage, and subject to impeachment and recall by the voters. The legislative council
in turn elected the president or governor. Slavery, the slave trade, and
a public debt were equally prohibited. The liberties of the individual
were guaranteed, with trial by jury and the rights of free assembly,
consultation, address, petition, and remonstrance. The only defense
force was to be a militia of all able-bodied males who had no religious objections against military service, and the militia officers
were to be elected.[55]

When the settlers arrived on the Coast in June 1792, they had a
brief military encounter with the African owners of their prospective

53. H. H. Dalrymple, Memorandum of 2 November 1791, CO 267/9; Wadström,
Colonization, II, 359–62.
54. Unsigned, undated memorandum in CO 267/9.
55. "Memorandum of Agreement," 9 March 1792, CO 267/9. Also printed in
Beaver, *African Memoranda*, pp. 425–32.

territory. After a slight delay, however, they managed to buy Bulama Island twice over from different claimants. The discomfort of the rainly season and a series of personal quarrels further discouraged many of the party. Their actual mortality was exceptionally low, with only nineteen dead by the middle of July, but even this was more than they had expected. Dalrymple and about 150 of the would-be colonists abandoned the project and sailed for Sierre Leone, where a third of them died of fever during the six weeks their ship lay in harbor waiting to leave for England.

Philip Beaver and 91 others remained on Bulama to salvage what they could of the original plan. They set to work with hired African labor to build a blockhouse for protection and clear the ground for planting. The following sixteen months were an epic of achievement in the face of obstacles, but it ended in failure. The blockhouse was built, the ground cleared and planted, but two-third of the settlers died of fever and others deserted or returned to England. At the end of November 1793, only Philip Beaver and eight others remained, and they decided they were too few to carry on alone.[56]

Beaver's enforced return to England was discouraging enough. In addition, war with France had begun in January 1793, and Beaver was recalled to the Navy. The original investment had been dissipated. By 1794 the Association's resources were reduced to something less than £1,000 in credits of doubtful value. But there was still a fund of optimism among some of the original promoters, not least with Beaver himself. They tried again to raise a public subscription, this time £10,000, but without any evident success. They continued nevertheless to memoralize the government, asking for a charter, and as late as 1796 were still pleading for government support in the reestablishment of their colony.[57]

Instead of retiring from their advanced political views, as might be expected in these years of the Jacobin fear in England, the new Bulama project of 1794–95 was, if anything, more utopian than the first. C. B. Wadström, who had been merely a peripheral supporter

---

56. Beaver's journal for his period in command is reproduced in *African Memoranda*, pp. 89–283. There are slight variations in different accounts of the number of settlers present at any time.

57. Wadström, *Colonization*, II, 168; Bulama Association to Dundas, 27 January 1794; Paul Le Mesurier to John King, 16 August 1796, CO 267/10; Andrew Johansen, *Description of Bulama Island* (London, 1794).

now became a principal publicist for the Association. His two fat
volumes on the history and theory of African colonization reviewed
the past attempts and put forward his outline for another try.

If earlier projects can be divided according to emphasis on commerce or agriculture, Wadström's new plan was far over toward the
side of agriculture. His theoretical defense was based on the arguments of the physiocrats—"Commercial colonies tend to slavery, agricultural to liberty." There were, according to Wadström, two kinds
of commerce. Good commerce was "commission commerce," where
goods and monetary metals move freely according to their "natural"
values. "Speculation commerce," on the other hand was dangerous.
Under this form, paper money, coined metals circulating as fiat
money, and monopolies open the way to the anti-social greed of the
merchants, speculators, and money-jobbers. Speculation commerce
was therefore to be controlled in the new colony by adopting Sharp's
labor-currency, ending imprisonment for debt, allowing the free coin-
age of monetary metals and avoiding a monopolized trade in the
hands of the company itself. Land tenure also followed Sharp's
scheme, as adjusted by Paul Le Mesurier to favor large planters rather
than peasant proprietors. The basic division was a district of 50,000
acres, subdivided into tythings of 5,000 acres, and lots of 500 acres
each.[58]

The dominance of agriculture was to be further assured by political
safeguards. Colonists were divided into three estates according to
economic function. In the first estate were the producers of raw materials; in the second, manufacturers; and in the third, merchants.
Producers alone would have the right to vote, and a system of progressive taxation would fall most lightly on planters, somewhat more
heavily on manufacturers, and more heavily still on merchants. The
strictly Swedenborgian aspects of Wadström's earlier plan were
quietly dropped, and the colonists were promised full religious freedom, except for Roman Catholics, whose belief in a celibate clergy
ran counter to the Swedenborgian emphasis on "conjugal love."[59]

It was futile to hope that government or private capitalists would
support a scheme of this kind, much less in wartime, and less still
after a destructive French raid on Sierra Leone in September 1794.

58. Wadström, *Colonization*, I, 66–72, 85–92, 103–05, 117.
59. Wadström, *Colonization*, I, 95–96, 118–19.

Wadström himself gave up the effort to secure support in England and skipped across the Channel in 1795, leaving a debt of £126 to the man who helped him compile his *Essay on Colonization*.

The last four years of Wadström's life were spent in France, and they form an illuminating postscript to his ubiquitous activities as a colonial promoter. In this phase, he began to work out suggestions for an international trusteeship over the "uncivilized" peoples of Africa. In one proposal to the Directory he suggested that France and Britain should join together when the war ended and found a new international association for the civilization of Africa and the end of slavery and the slave trade. Member states would reform their own colonial systems and then bring pressure to bear on non-members, mainly through an international naval squadron blockading the West African coast. Each of the associated states would also indicate some part of the African coast as its own sphere of influence and responsibility for civilizing Africa, and slavery would be prohibited in all African colonies. Sierra Leone and Bulama, as humanitarian colonies, were to be given a special status, including neutrality in war time.[60] It was an odd twist of fate that these suggestions, unrealistic as they were in their own time and place, prefigured more that was actually to happen during the coming century than any of Wadström's other projects.

Even as a colonial projector, Wadström was more warmly received in France than he had been in England. A commission of the Assembly reported favorably in 1798 on his last colonial blueprint, the only one of his many projects that was ever attempted. By the time it materialized, however, Wadström was dead, and the project was altered beyond recognition. Its setting was shifted from West Africa to Egypt, where it took the form of Napoleon's drive to the east.[61]

By the later 1790's the first scramble for Africa was over. The brakes were first applied at the beginning of the Anglo-French war

60. C. B. Wadström, *Adresse au Corps législatif et au Directoire exécutif de la République française* (Paris, 1795). There was other interest in African colonization from France in these same years, including one project to revive the Bulama idea under French sponsorship. See Charles Le Clerc de Montlinot, *Essai sur la transportation comme recompense et la deportation comme peine* (Paris, 1797).

61. C. L. Lokke, *France and the Colonial Question: A Study of Contemporary French Opinion, 1763–1801* (New York, 1932), pp. 174–82; Eschasseriaux, aîné, *Rapport au nom de la commission chargée d'examiner l'ouvrage présenté au Conseil par le citoyen Wastrom* [*sic*] ... (Paris, 1798).

in 1793. For a year or so the movement ground along under its own
momentum. By 1795 it had come to a stop. Only Britain had un-
restricted access to West Africa, and any British resources that could
be diverted from the European war would go to the seizure of existing French and Dutch colonies, not to doubtful projects for founding
new ones.

Examining the dozen or so British projects for West Africa during
the decade of peace, their outstanding characteristic is the apparent
lack of contact with reality, at least with African reality. They were
based firmly enough on the European attitudes and theories of the
day, but the actual setting was something of a dream world. In spite
of the Europeans' detailed knowledge of the coast, sites were selected
with an amazing nonchalance. Two of the expeditions planned for
West Africa ended in Australia and Egypt respectively. Other locations were picked for superficial appearance, or on information long
out of date. Sierra Leone attracted attention by its spectacular terrain.
(The mountains of the peninsula stand alone like a high island barely
attached to a flat shore, the most impressive landmark along the
whole coast from the Senegal to the Cameroons.) It satisfied the romantic love of natural beauty, but its value for agriculture was slight.
Dalrymple and his associates selected Bulama Island sight unseen
from a description written ninety years earlier by Sieur de la Brue.
Wadsröm picked Cape Mesurado from a similar description by Des
Marchais. Even the Swedenborgian myth of the interior and the centuries-old Arab accounts of the Western Sudan played a role in drawing some optimistic planners toward the commercial penetration of
the interior.

Ethnographic information was either ignored or buried under
largely imaginary concepts of man-in-general, "the barbarian," or
"the savage." Specific customs of specific peoples counted for much
less than their cultural difference from Europeans. For all the projectors, Africa was barbarism confronted by civilization. Some may
have chosen Africa because of its reputation for untapped wealth,
but the utopian planners were also attracted by the lack of "civilization." They followed the unconscious assumption of popular
culture theory that a lack of civilization meant a lack of culture.
African society therefore lay there, a *tabula rasa* ready and waiting
for the utopian inscription. All planners, utopian and otherwise, took
it for granted that Africans had little but unskilled labor to offer the

new settlements. Many assumed what Wadström made explicit—that the absolute superiority of Western culture implied a moral obligation to change African culture. This obligation in turn gave a moral sanction to colonization, which was contested only by the West Indian planters and the slave traders. Even these opponents often accepted the ideal of the culture bearer as a moral goal. They merely thought the job was too difficult to be worth trying, or else impossible on account of the irremediable "racial inferiority" of the Africans.

Compared with their opponents—or with most nineteenth-century advocates of African colonization—the eighteenth-century projectors were remarkably free of overt racism. With the exception of those who simply wanted to set up West Indian slave plantations in West Africa, they accepted the goal of an integrated and multi-racial society; but, for most, the equality of races was potential and not actual. Even the Province of Freedom discriminated by giving larger land grants to Europeans. Almost all the projectors assumed a racial division of labor even when it was not explicitly stated: the blacks would do the work and the whites would supervise. This had been the pattern of tropical colonization in the past, and it was the teaching of medicine that Europeans could not do field work in the tropics. Only Smeathman clearly had in mind a multi-racial society where whites might be found at all social levels, but he alone believed in hard work as the best way to keep alive in West Africa.

Another curious element, perhaps connected with a degree of latent racism, was a common tolerance for some form of forced labor. This appears in projects ostensibly tied to the anti-slavery movement and utopian in their political forms. Only Philip Beaver believed unreservedly in free labor for wages, with no other form of control than the market price. Wadström's early project ordained a "gentle servitude" for Africans. Sharp allowed a class of indented laborers and another of ex-slave redemptionists in state service. Smeathman also allowed temporary slavery as a means of redemption. The Sierra Leone Company enjoyed its own kind of dominance as the only sizeable employer of labor and set wage rates as it chose. It is uncertain how far this pattern merely reflected customary relations between masters and servants in eighteenth-century England, and how much it may have drawn on the expectation of laziness caused by tropical exuberance.

All the projectors believed in tropical exuberance. It was the basis for their dreams of wealth. They mainly differed in their ideas of how that wealth should be tapped. One division of opinion was clearly that between an emphasis on trade and African proprietorship, as against one on European-managed agriculture. Both sides had the support of a considerable body of theory. Wilberforce and other followers of the commercial ideal could draw on social theory that glorified the "commercial stage" of civilization. They could also find economic justification in Adam Smith's belief that the division of labor was the key to economic progress: exchange was therefore the key to economic development. On the other side, Wadström and the agriculturalists in general could draw on the popular *mystique* of land as the only real source of wealth, fully developed in theoretical form by the physiocrats.

In other respects, the projectors were curiously fuzzy in their economic thinking. Adam Smith had pointed out in *The Wealth of Nations* that land is cheap in new countries and labor is dear. Sharp's labor-currency was, indeed, a recognition of this principle. But the Sierra Leone Company, the original Bulama project, and Wadström's project of 1794 all put their faith in a prospective inflation of land values. They bought land from the Africans for very little, and then hoped to sell it immediately at many times the price they had paid. Having given less than £100 for Bulama Island, the Association was trying in 1794 to raise subscriptions of £100 for a mere 400 acres.[62] If the promotors themselves had not been the principal subscribers, one would suspect them of fraud. As a more probable explanation, they were accustomed to thinking of land in English terms, as intrinsically valuable, not merely subject to the market like other commodities.

Still another carelessly handled subject was the question of sovereignty and international law. Some might, like Wadström, try to prove the Europeans' moral right to dominion in Africa. Or they could do as Smeathman did, and simply observe that *de facto* petty Afro-European states had been created on the coast. If it had been done before, it could be done again. But the land purchases at Sierra Leone, Bulama, and Lemain Island were made in a way that confused property rights with sovereign political dominion. It is extremely unlikely that any of the African sellers had a legal right to sell sovereignty over the ceded territory, or that they understood the treaty in these

terms.[63] In effect, sovereign control was acquired as Smeathman had
said it could be done—by *de facto* usurpation in a social setting where
the European concept of sovereignty simply had no meaning.

But the handling of sovereignty was curious even in relation to Europe. The convict colony at Lemain Island and the Province of Freedom were both to be recognized in some vague sense as British territory, but in fact the government had not the slightest intention of
carrying out the normal obligations of a sovereign in either of them.
Though chartered, the Sierra Leone Company had no legal right to
the judicial functions its officers carried out on an *ad hoc* basis from
1792 to 1800. More anomalous still, Beaver's Bulama settlement,
Smeathman's project, and Wadström's Swedenborgian project would
have been new states founded by men already subject to recognized
European rulers. Yet none of these writers seemed to be seriously
concerned about the problems this might raise. In fact, though not
in theory, European international law did not fully extend to tropical
Africa.

Compared with their unconcern with external relations, the projectors were deeply concerned about the political constitutions appropriate to new settlements. The American Revolution and the Parliamentary reform movement had already popularized the tenets of
political liberalism, with a special stress on representative government
and written constitutions. Some projects clearly reflected this influence,
but not all projects were democratic or even liberal. They can, indeed,
be arranged along a spectrum from complete democracy at one end
to complete autocracy at the other. On the side of democracy, the
extreme form of primitive democracy foreseen for the Lemain Island
convicts would have to be counted the most radical of all. The Province of Freedom was hardly less democratic, but its democracy was
guarded by a constitution protecting the rights of the individual.
Wadström's projects ran to oligarchy, either of "producers" as in the
1794 version, or of Swedenborgians in that of 1789. The Bulama
constitution of 1792 was also an oligarchy of European planters, since

63. The custom along most of the Coast had been for slave dealers to make regular payments to the African authorities, which might have been interpreted either as
tribute or rent. In most cases, the Africans seem to have assumed, on the precedent of
earlier dealings with Europeans, that they were now entering into a similar arrangement. The Sierra Leone settlement, for example, rested on two treaties of 1787 and
1788, neither of which was legally sound. (Fyfe, *Sierra Leone,* pp. 19–20, 22, and
24–25.)

no representation was planned for the African workers attracted to the settlement.

Toward the other end of the spectrum, Smeathman's scheme called for enlightened despotism, but with liberal institutions and freedom for all. The Sierra Leone Company was, in fact, a despotism in the hands of the company's officers, but controlled from above by the Directors in London, and capable of being checked from below by elected minor officials. Finally, at the extreme of despotism, the convict settlement destined for South West Africa (and actually founded in New South Wales) was an autocracy on the spot, even though it might be controlled by the ultimate power of the British Parliament. If any field of thought was neglected in planning for human happiness in Africa, it was certainly not political theory.

In fact, no important body of European theory was left out of account. The failures were not failures in theory, but in practice based on wrong or incomplete information. Some information—anything, for example, that might have corrected the belief in tropical exuberance—was simply not available at the time. Other information was available but not used. This was most serious in regard to health precautions. Lind and others with experience on the coast had made the dangers abundantly clear, but they were either disregarded or passed over in the hope that clearing and cultivation would "improve the climate." The utopian plans would probably have failed in any case, but they had no chance. Mortality alone was enough to ruin the Province of Freedom and the Bulama settlement, and it very nearly ruined Sierra Leone as well. But Sierra Leone was not ruined. For a decade, when more grandiose projects were impossible, it continued unhappily as the first true British colony on the Coast. It was, therefore, a base for gathering new information and experience to serve a new generation of policy-makers—and perhaps to bring success where lack of knowledge had so clearly brought failure.

PART II

*The Age of Exploration
and Disappointment*
1795–1830

5

SIERRA LEONE:

THE

LESSONS OF EXPERIENCE

The world-wide strategy of British affairs began to alter markedly in the mid 1790's. As the possibility of a quick victory over Revolutionary France faded, the global strategy of the eighteenth-century wars for empire was re-established. Where, in the decade of peace from 1783 to 1793, undeveloped regions like West Africa seemed at least potentially valuable, they were now pushed into the background. Old settlements of known value were available for the taking, and their capture could be justified as part of the military effort against France. French colonies in the West Indies and India, Dutch colonies at the Cape of Good Hope and Java—these were the principal objectives. The minimum requirement for West Africa was the protection of the British slave-trade factories and the interception of French shipping. Resources could be diverted to the capture of the French posts or the exploration of the interior only when other circumstances permitted.

In this situation Sierra Leone remained as the one permanent product of the earlier African enthusiasm, and that enthusiasm was fading. It was pushed aside, on one hand, by the rally of British conservatism and the hysterical fear of "red Jacobinism" in 1793 and 1794. In addition, it was simply overshadowed by other and more pressing concerns.

But Sierra Leone, unlike the other posts, was a miniature society with a resident population of African descent, however small. As such, it continued to serve as the sole enduring example by which to measure any and all of the utopian projects of the 1780's. It was mainly coincidence that the least single-minded and theoretically planned of these projects should be the one to stand the test of maintaining itself. The Bulama experiment was too short-lived to prove much. The Province of Freedom was forgotten or absorbed, in popular view, by its more permanent successor.

Sierra Leone, however, was neither a just example of the other projects, nor a fair test of the Directors' original intentions. The wars themselves changed the objective conditions on which the Sierra Leone Company had based their hopes. They had anticipated high trading profits, partly because they expected the slave trade to be made illegal for British subjects. Abolition had, indeed, been carried in principle in the House of Commons in April 1792, only to be lost through the delaying action of the House of Lords. With the growing impact of revolution in France, war in Europe, and slave revolt in Saint Domingue, the marginal supporters of abolition fell away and the measure was delayed till 1807. The Company was therefore forced to operate in direct competition with the slave trade.

They were also forced to operate under wartime conditions, and this was probably the more serious disadvantage. Insurance rates went up, and the Royal Navy was unable to provide constant protection against commerce raiders. A hit-and-run raid on the colony itself by a small French fleet in September and October 1794 was nearly fatal. During a fortnight's stay in the Sierra Leone River, the French destroyed or removed the buildings, furniture, equipment, and trade goods that could not be carried away into the forest for safety. The Company set their losses at almost a quarter of their capital. They were undercapitalized in any case, and the raid forced a policy of retrenchment, inhibiting any real effort to carry out the original plans for development.

Whatever their other motives, the Directors were running a commercial concern. However much they intended to help humanity, their first obligation was to achieve financial success. Otherwise they could only admit failure and liquidate. Even before the French raid, it was obvious that their calculations of agricultural production had been over-optimistic. At least in Sierra Leone, the expected wealth burgeoning from the tropical soil was simply not forthcoming. The Directors admitted in 1794 that they had been misinformed in this respect, and they placed the blame on Lt. Matthews of the Navy, whose report they had trusted. (This was, perhaps, a little sly on their part, since Matthews' was not the only report they trusted; but he was a pro-slavery man, and thus a political opponent.) One early lesson was, therefore, a revision of emphasis. Freetown, the new capital of the colony, was again thought of principally as a commercial station, supplemented by the agriculture of its environs.[1]

The Directors were thus thrown back to their initial plan to civilize Africa through "legitimate trade." Most supporters of the Company at any time would have agreed with their Chairman, that "trade is the great engine by which towns are made to rise up, and industry excited in all civilized countries."[2] The expected competitive relation of their trade to the slave trade, however, was not always clear in the Company's early statements. Their first and most optimistic hope appears to have been that legitimate trade would prove more economic than the slave trade, driving it out like a commercial Gresham's law in reverse. But this optimism was not universal, even before the founding of Sierra Leone. Another school of thought held that legitimate trade could not compete without help. It needed either government suppression of the slave trade, or else its own plantations from which to draw African products.

In the event, legitimate trade in the hands of the Sierra Leone Company was not a success. Whether the French wars, the slave trade, mismanagement, or some other factor was the principal cause, the Company placed the blame squarely on the slave trade. This view was most useful. It excused the Directors for their original over-optimism, and it could serve their immediate political needs. Even though the slave trade was an important branch of British commerce,

1. Sierra Leone Company, *Report of the Court of Directors of the Sierra Leone Company to the General Court*, 7 vols. (title varies) (London, 1791–1808), II (1794), 15. The most authoritative general history of Sierra Leone is C. Fyfe, *A History of Sierra Leone* (London, 1962).

2. H. Thornton to J. Clarkson, 14 September 1792, Ad. Mss. 41262A, f. 177.

Map 7. Sierra Leone and Vicinity

they could claim that the African trade would be even larger if it were abolished. The promise of wealth through trade could still be upheld.

Meanwhile, other avenues were not abandoned. Even the plantation alternative associated with the second, or Dalrymple, phase of planning was retained. The original site on the Sierra Leone peninsula was clearly not suited to plantation agriculture, but other locations were possible on the Bullom shore, across the river from Freetown and still under African sovereignty. The Company first set up a plantation of its own, but without success. Toward the end of the century they turned it over to Major Peregrine Francis Thorne, recently retired from the Army. Thorne looked into the possibilities; but he thought the labor supply was undependable, and he feared that a plantation beyond the area of British control would not be sufficiently secure. In 1800 he gave up and went home. Governor Ludlam also tried briefly to start a plantation of his own in the higher mountains of the peninsula, but this too failed. The only European plantation with a reasonably continuous history in the whole region was on Tasso Island, worked as an appendage to the slave-trade post at Bance Island and worked by slave labor.[3]

Several different conclusions could be drawn from the failure of planting under the Company's auspices. Philip Beaver retained his old faith in plantations, but he thought that Sierra Leone was the wrong place on the right continent: "On the Bullom shore, the soil is very poor, but on the Sierra Leone side there is scarcely any soil at all; and when they make a hogshead of sugar there, I will engage to do the same at Charing Cross."[4]

He thought the Company had also been guilty of mismanagement, both in running the plantation and in their relations with the neighboring African authorities. Without the cooperation of the chiefs, there could be no steady supply of labor for hire. For Beaver, therefore, the Sierra Leone experiments were no fair test, and his dream of an African bonanza remained undefiled.[5]

Other critics of the Company's plantation effort also tended to stress the question of labor supply. J. B. L. Durand, a French observer, argued that the "natural and invincible indolence" of the Africans was too great for a successful wage labor system. Plantations could only be successful under some form of labor coercion. His suggestion was to buy the labor of slaves from nearby African chiefs, just as a West Indian planter might buy the labor of a jobbing gang from another slave owner. Once the slaves had become disciplined plantation workers, they might safely be purchased from their owners and given their freedom.[6]

3. Sierra Leone Council Minutes, 1 May 1800, CO 270/4, pp. 34–37; Report of the Directors of the Sierra Leone Company, 1802, in PP, 1803–1804, v (24), pp. 18, 27–28; Sierra Leone Company, *Report* (1801), pp. 27–29.
4. Philip Beaver, *African Memoranda* (London, 1805), p. 305 n.
5. Beaver, *African Memoranda*, pp. 305 and 386.
6. J. B. L. Durand, *A Voyage to Senegal* (London, 1806), pp. 83–88. First published, Paris, 1802.

Such a device had its appeal, even in anti-slavery circles. Both Granville Sharp and Thomas Clarkson had thought of using "redeemed" slaves to work the Company's land. Coercion was, indeed, used by the Crown administration of the colony after 1808, though not for plantations. By that time, numbers of "liberated Africans" were being landed from the slavers captured by the Royal Navy, and their forced labor was made available to the earlier settlers through a system of "apprenticeship." For itself, the Company stayed clear of forced labor, though their public statements occasionally returned to the problem of labor supply, which remained a serious concern. In 1802, Henry Thornton blamed the scarcity of labor on the local Temne people and their opposition to the Company; but in later years the matter was dropped, and Thornton finally claimed in 1807 that the "natives" had been willing to work as free laborers, and at reasonable rates.[7]

In fact, the Company quietly dropped their plantation experiments after 1800 and based their agricultural hopes on the smaller plots of the peasantry. This alternative had been dominant from 1791, even though it was not part of the original plan. The Nova Scotian settlers had been added only fortuitously and at the last moment, but the Company thought of them as a source of revenue in two different ways. They were expected to grow exportable produce, which would then pass through the Company's hands at a profit before being sold in Europe. At the same time, the Company set the prices of European goods in the settlement so as to make a net profit of 10 per cent on turnover. "Legitimate trade" of this kind was limited to their own bailiwick, and it was only partly free of competition from the slave trade. It might well have been profitable, if it were not for military and administrative expenses.[8] The second source of revenue was taxation of the settlers, principally taxes on commerce and quitrents on the land granted out to peasant proprietors.

Before either source of profit could become substantial, it was essential to produce crops for export. The Company's principal device

7. Sierra Leone Company Directors, in PP, 1803–1804, v (24), pp. 27–28; Henry Thornton, Commons, 29 July 1807, H 9, c. 1005.

8. Practical limits to the Company's selling monopoly were set by the presence of a French post at Gambia Island until 1794 and an English post at Bance Island. There were, in addition, a half dozen other merchants in the slave trade within a day's canoe travel of the settlement, and many of these would have been willing to sell European goods in return for food or other produce.

for achieving this end was a system of premiums and subsidies. In the first years, they offered competitive prizes, designed to reduce the colony's dependence on imported food. They began by offering £100 in various awards to the settlers who raised the greatest quantities of rice, yams, plantains, eddoes, cabbages, maize, and cotton.

As time passed, the objectives changed. In 1794 and 1795, settlers were encouraged by prize money to build houses on their land and to cultivate land in the hills at some distance from the shore, rather than live in Freetown. The new emphasis also fell on export items, with tobacco, camwood, and ivory added to the list of encouraged products. By 1798 food crops had been dropped, and only cattle and export crops were on the list. The nature of the award was also shifted from a competitive prize to subsidies payable to any farmer who reached the production quotas set in advance by the government.[9] The system continued till the end of the Company's administration in 1808, and even afterwards it was taken over briefly by the African Institution.

While the Company's administrators clearly considered incentive payments a useful device, the practical results were far below expectations. By 1800, only about 180 of the 300 heads-of-family among the settlers seem to have been engaged in any farming at all, and land under cultivation averaged only about 3.5 acres per family. Only a third of those who did farm grew crops for export, and then only in small quantities.[10]

If the attempt to encourage export agriculture was a failure, the attempt to collect direct taxation was a disaster, and one that followed from the Company's initial errors. They believed that Sierra Leone would be infinitely productive with very little work. It followed that some of the productivity might be fairly drawn off in the form of taxes. The over-estimate of land values extended even to the Company's opponents, one of whom set a value of four to five million pounds on the undeveloped concession.[11] It was only natural that the

9. Sierra Leone Company, *Account of the Colony of Sierra Leone from its First Establishment in* [*sic*] *1793* . . . (London, 1795), pp. 70–72. Sierra Leone Council Minutes, 7 January and 8 May 1794, CO 270/2, pp. 139 and 162; 19 May 1795, CO 270/3, p. 155; 5 February 1798 and 1 December 1799, CO 270/4, pp. 191–93 and 317; 20 January 1801, CO 270/5, p. 142.

10. Sierra Leone Council Minutes, 1 May 1800, CO 270/4; Z. Macaulay, Evidence before Select Committee on Sierra Leone, PP, 1803–1804, v (24), p. 54.

11. [Campbel], *Reasons Against Giving a Territorial Grant to a Company of Merchants to Colonize and Cultivate the Peninsula of Sierra Leone* . . . (London, 1791), pp. 8–9.

Company should sooner or later try to realize something from this asset.

The Company began, however, without a clear land policy. The Nova Scotians were promised in Nova Scotia that they would receive land in Sierra Leone "free of expense" at the rate of twenty acres for each male settler, plus an additional ten acres for a wife and five for each child. A family with two children might thus expect to receive a grant of forty acres.[12] In practice, the promise could not be kept. The Company in England thought of the grant as measuring about 250,000 acres—about twenty miles along the northern shore of the Sierra Leone peninsula and about twenty miles inland. As it turned out the actual concession measured less than ten miles along the shore of the Sierra Leone River. The Sierra Leone peninsula was not twenty miles wide, so that part of the concession was the water of the Atlantic Ocean. The area was also a parallelogram rather than a rectangle, as supposed. The southern shore of the peninsula was unsafe from European or African raids. The interior was mountainous and unfit in large part for agriculture, and much of the north coast was occupied by Temne villages. The villagers did not understand that their land had been sold, and to save quarrels, Governor Clarkson was forced to confirm their claims to the land they actually occupied.[13]

Initial allotments in 1792 and 1793 therefore averaged only about five acres per family, ranging from two acres up to eleven. The Company's failure to keep its promise became an immediate cause of discontent among the settlers, and the discontent was multiplied when the Company made the tenures conditional. They were to be withdrawn if one-third of the area were not cleared and cultivated at the end of two years, and two-thirds by the end of three years.

By the time the settlers had actually arrived in Sierra Leone, the Company emerged from its original indecision about the finer points of land policy and decided to impose a quitrent. The rate was set at one shilling an acre during the first two years, changing then to a variable assessment based on the gross annual produce of the land,

12. For the Company's policy on land and taxation see N. A. Cox-George, "Direct Taxation in the Early History of Sierra Leone," *Sierra Leone Studies*, II (n.s.), 20–35 (December, 1955) and *Finance and Development in West Africa. The Sierra Leone Experience* (London, 1961), pp. 38–52.
13. Fyfe, *Sierra Leone*, p. 47.

and rising gradually until it reached the rate of 7 per cent by 1797.[14] These rates reveal something of the Company's expectations. The initial annual quitrent was set at a figure higher than the original purchase price, only £150 in trade goods for the entire concession.[15] To ask for any payment seemed, to the settlers, to contradict the promise that land would be given them "free of expense." They took the position that a quitrent was a rent, presumably out of ignorance of the legal niceties. Their interpretation, however, was more nearly correct than that of the Company. A quitrent in English law is a permanent obligation, not subject to variation in amount at the will of either party. By tradition the quitrents in royal colonies during the eighteenth century had been set at a very low rate. They were in fact merely token payments. Both in level and variability, the quitrent demanded in Sierra Leone was not a quitrent in the ordinary sense. It was partly a property tax and partly an income tax.[16] More serious still from a practical rather than a legal point of view, the rate of 4 to 7 per cent of gross product was higher than the full economic rent on the land. Any settler seriously interested in farming could have found land much more cheaply, merely by applying to the African authorities outside of the Company's jurisdiction.

The quitrent policy caused more trouble than any other aspect of the Company's administration, in spite of the fact that quitrents were not generally collected. The first attempt was abandoned after the French attack of 1794. A second in 1797 led only to a bitter resistance on the part of the settlers and helped to cause a revolt against the Company's rule in 1800. A final effort in 1801 and 1803 failed as well, and the net result was a serious dampening of economic development. Even when quitrents were not actively collected, settlers were unwilling to take up land while the threat remained, and they might someday be asked for unpaid arrears plus interest.

In retrospect, one lesson to be drawn from the quitrent controversy is clear enough: cheap land cannot be made valuable by putting a high price on it. The Directors never admitted their original miscalculation. Only Granville Sharp, whom the others often considered a utopian dreamer, tried to get to the bottom of the land problem. In 1792, he returned to his favorite occupation of drawing up proj-

14. Sierra Leone Council Minutes, 22 August 1797, CO 270/4.
15. Fyfe, *Sierra Leone*, p. 22.
16. Cox-George, *Finance and Development*, pp. 45–48.

ects—in this case a project for making cheap land valuable by changing the economic environment. In form, the scheme was a plan for
the allocation of land and the layout of townships in a newly founded
colony. He held that after each township has been surveyed, part of
the land should be granted free of charge to settlers, while the proprietors held the rest. Once the settlers had established a thriving
community, the reserved lots would begin to take on a scarcity value,
based on their location near a bustling economic center. They might
then be sold, to the profit of the proprietors. Sharp sent an outline of
this plan to John Clarkson in Sierra Leone, but it was not accepted;
and he finally worked it out in more detail as a pamphlet project for
possible application elsewhere.[17]

A second lesson might have been drawn, and was drawn by some—
Sierra Leone, and perhaps all of West Africa, was simply not a land
of agricultural wealth. While the Sierra Leone Company admitted
its initial disappointment, Henry Thornton still argued as late as 1807
that Sierra Leone had fine soil for agriculture, though he must have
done so with less conviction than he had shown fifteen years earlier.[18]
Others were less optimistic, and the skeptics had Sierra Leone as a
living example.

It was an example of political failure as well. The political constitution of the colony was confused from the beginning, torn as it
was between the radical democracy of Granville Sharp and the Tory-
ism of William Wilberforce and Henry Thornton. Both groups,
however, counted on being able to impose whatever political forms
they chose. They made no allowance for the wishes of the settlers
themselves, assuming the Nova Scotians would be grateful to bene-
factors who had made it possible for them to settle again in the
land of their ancestors—that in their gratitude, the settlers would be
willing to accept advice and direction.

John Clarkson, who recruited the settlers in Nova Scotia and came
with them to Africa, knew they were not the pliant and unformed
human material of the British mental image. Instead, they were
men and women whose background first as slaves and then as displaced persons made them especially suspicious of "arbitrary proceed-

17. G. Sharp to J. Clarkson, 24 July 1792, Ad. Mss. 41262A, f. 153; G. Sharp,
*A General Plan for Laying out Towns and Townships, of the New-Acquired Lands
in the East Indies, America, and Elsewhere . . .*, 2nd ed. (London, 1804), esp.
pp. 5–6. First published 1794.
18. Henry Thornton, Commons, 29 July 1807, H 9, c. 1005.

ings." As he wrote in his diary, kept as a semi-public record for the use of the Directors,

The people have been deceived through life and have scarcely ever had a promise made that was performed; they have been removed from America in the hopes of bettering their condition and of improving the black character, under the protecting laws of the British Constitution. A person likely to be of benefit here must be very circumspect in his conduct to the blacks—he must bear with their ignorance, make allowances for their change of situation, and must not be hasty with them always keeping in mind, that the success of the Colony and the civilization of Africa will greatly depend upon the management of the Nova Scotians.[19]

Unfortunately, the warning was not taken to heart by Directors in London—nor by William Dawes and Zachary Macaulay, who acted as Governor in rotation between 1792 and 1799. Dawes was moderately popular at times, but the Company's administration soon lost the confidence of the settlers. There was an organized strike in 1793 against the Company's rate of wages. The land grievance appeared, and later in the same year settlers circulated a petition and sent two representatives to England to protest against the Sierra Leone authorities—specifically against the lack of full land distribution, against the prices charged for European goods, and against the general nonfulfillment of the promises made them in Nova Scotia. The strike and the deputation were followed by riots and another deputation shortly before the French attack in 1794.[20]

The raid was followed by a year of relative peace and joint rebuilding, but political relations between the government and the settlers deteriorated again in 1796. In addition to old grievances new issues appeared—racial discrimination, land distribution, quitrents, and a sectarian quarrel between the Company's Anglican officials and the settlers, who were mainly Dissenters. Mutual confidence declined rapidly from 1797 through the year 1799.

On the government side, Zachary Macaulay tended to take an increasingly self-righteous attitude. He was given to issuing proclamations, exhorting the settlers to be grateful to himself and members of council, who had come out to "an unhealthy climate, and among a murmering people" in order to raise up "God's Temple" in Sierra

19. "Diary of Lieutenant J. Clarkson, R.N., Governor, 1792," *Sierra Leone Studies*, VIII. 31 (1927), entry for 29 August 1792.
20. CO 270/2, ff. 178–88.

Leone.[21] He kept himself aloof as a matter of policy, but the policy led to resentment instead of the intended respect for his person and office. On the matter of the quitrent, the settlers certainly had a legitimate grievance, and one on which compromise might have been possible. Macaulay, however, was intransigent. When, in 1797, the settlers presented a letter of protest, he answered in these terms: "I will be bold to say, that this letter has been sent to me not because there is anything hard, or unfair, or unreasonable in your paying a Quit Rent; but because there is in 'some' of you, a spirit of opposition, contradiction, dishonesty, and discontent, which, because there is no real ground for complaint, labours to create strife, and contention, by means however unjust and falsehoods however gross."[22]

The settlers became more suspicious than ever, and the more radical among them prepared for resistance. They seized on the embryonic representative institutions provided by the elective offices of tythingman and hundredor. In theory, the tythingmen and hundredors had very limited responsibility. They were supposed to maintain the peace within their respective tythings and hundreds and generally to help the administration as minor executive officers. They had some authority over the police in the town, executed the warrants of the Governor-in-Council, and examined grievances, reporting just grievances to the government. Their independent authority was restricted to minor regulatory functions such as setting the price of bread or conditions for the retail sale of meat.[23]

In this restricted form, representative democracy appears to have worked fairly well during the first five years of the colony. Especially in the era of good feelings around 1795, it met the approval of both Macaulay and Dawes. At that time, Macaulay praised the efforts of the tythingmen and hundredors and told them their activities promised that "a future house of Commons might arise to give Laws to Africa . . . were they to prove themselves worthy [of] the privileges that had been extended to them."[24]

21. "Proclamation of the Council to the People of Sierra Leone," 25 June 1794, Council Minutes, CO 270/2. See also speech to the tythingmen and hundredors, 4 March 1795, CO 270/3, p. 52; and CO 270/4, esp. pp. 159 ff. (1797).

22. "Address to the Settlers," 21 August 1797, CO 270/4, f. 162. See also Z. Macaulay's journal entry for 24 November 1794, printed in M. J. Holland, Vicountess Knutsford, *Life and Letters of Zachary Macaulay* (London, 1900), p. 83.

23. Sierra Leone Council Minutes, 2 March and 9 June 1795, CO 270/3, ff. 78–79 and 175.

24. Sierra Leone Council Minutes, 4 March 1795, CO 270/3, f. 62; Dawes to Court of Directors, 13 July 1795, CO 268/5, ff. 78–79.

After 1797 the more radical settlers began to see the institution not as a privilege, but a means of asserting rights. As they did so, friction increased, and government benevolence waned. In 1799, the hundredors and tythingmen tried to increase their own power by petitioning for elected justices of the peace. The request was refused but they kept up pressure by voting a tax on the white settlers the government was then trying to introduce. The government attitude hardened still more, and the Governor tried to set aside the election of undesirable representatives. Having failed, he appealed to London for greater authority. The Directors then stiffened their constitutional position by obtaining a Parliamentary "Charter of Justice," in order to regularize the judicial power of the Company's executive officers. They also sent out a small force of European soldiers. In short, the Company's reaction to assertive democracy was first to shore up its legal authority, and then to increase its physical power to enforce its will.[25]

As the government appealed for outside aid from England, the radical settlers appealed to the Temne chiefs. The showdown came in September 1800. The radical leaders called for open rebellion, and only a minority of the settlers was willing to stand by the government. Three days after the outbreak of fighting, and before the issue was decided, transports arrived in the harbor in the proverbial nick of time. They brought not only the new garrison of European soldiers but also a new group of Negro settlers, who, in the event, were willing to fight on the side of the government. The result was rapid military defeat for the rebels. Two of the leaders were executed and others deported to Gorée, though some also managed to escape to the safety of neighboring African states.[26]

The combination of rebellion and reinforcement drastically changed the position of the government. The new settlers were a body of about 550 Maroon Negroes, also from Nova Scotia. They had originally lived in the mountains of Jamaica as escaped slaves maintaining their own communities beyond the area of British administration. In the Maroon War of 1795–96, they had been defeated by the forces of the Jamaican government, and many had been deported to Nova Scotia. Now they were moved again to Sierra Leone. In spite of their earlier record of resistance to British rule, they settled down in the colony as a separate element in the population, more amenable to government influence than the earlier group of

25. See CO 270/4, *passim;* Sierra Leone Company, *Report* (1801), pp. 3–7.
26. See CO 270/5, *passim.*

Negro Americans had been. As a result, the government was internally very much stronger, and the threat of rebellion died away.

At the same time, the external relations of the colony deteriorated. The Temnes were increasingly fearful of the growing power of the colony. They had, therefore, helped the rebels of 1800 and had received dissident refugees after the defeat. The result was an emigré-Temne alliance which attacked the colony in 1801 as the first engagement in a war that was to last, off and on, until 1807. The wars further inhibited rational planning for colonial development. The Company had to meet extraordinary expenses for fortifications and military expeditions. Agriculture at a distance from Freetown and its defenses became virtually impossible. The only compensating advantages to the Company were slight. They annexed the western tip of the Sierra Leone peninsula as part of the ultimate peace settlement, and they received some financial help from the British government, begining with an annual parliamentary grant of £4,000 in 1800, later increased to £10,000 a year.

By the early years of the nineteenth century, it was clear that the Sierra Leone Company was not a financial success and would never be one. Parliamentary committees considered the problem in 1802 and again in 1804. On their recommendation, the subsidies were continued and increased, but the Directors were increasingly eager to lay down their responsibilities. On January 1, 1808, Sierra Leone passed from Company hands and became a Crown Colony.

Political and military problems overshadowed all other concerns during the last decade of the Company's administration. Foreign wars and internal rebellion could be used as a sufficient excuse for economic failure, but the Directors were merely forced back from one kind of explanation to another. In the main, they blamed the settlers and excused the errors of their own administration. As a result, they revised their earlier ideas about the nature and capabilities of the human material they had dealt with.

They had begun by saying the Nova Scotians were "superior to the generality of people of the same order in this country," even though they seemed ungrateful for favors done them. The native Africans near Sierra Leone were also relatively well thought of in the be-beginning. No Christian could, of course, approve of Temne religion, and the Company thought the Africans were "superstitious to the highest degree" and far gone in savagery. But they also seemed to be reclaimable. They were more grateful for favors than the Nova Scotians, and they were eager for Christian knowledge and improvement. The Company at first reserved complete disapproval for those Africans who lived near the slave factories. They were found to be "much given to liquor, . . . suspicious of white men, crafty, and deceitful, as well as savage and ferocious: they are said likewise to be selfish, unreasonable, and encroaching." These faults, however, were blamed on contact with slave traders and might be corrected in time.[27]

While these views were by no means completely favorable to Africans, the Company's attitude hardened still more as time passed. After 1800, the Directors accepted Zachary Macaulay's analysis of Sierra Leone politics. They blamed the troubles on the "idle, turbulent, and unreasonable" settlers, whose behavior was one of the chief obstacles to progress.[28] As for the Temnes, according to the Directors' report to the Parliamentary Committee of 1802: "The Timmaneys have the general character of being remarkably indolent, faithless, and ferocious; and their Chiefs, who were also the principals of the late attack on the Settlement, have proved to be rapacious, drunken, and deceitful; easily impressed by Artifice and Misrepresentation, and ready to promote any Design, however flagitious, which promised to gratify their Avarice or Passions."[29]

The Company, in short, needed a scapegoat: the Temnes and settlers were the most convenient ones available. The pro-slave-trade publicists had already helped to prepare the public with an image of savage Africa. The Company's new views fitted well into the existing preconceptions. At the same time, there appeared to be no danger of aiding the cause of the slave trade. The failings of the Temnes, as friends and allies of the slave dealers, and of the settlers, as ex-slaves, could both be traced back as the evil results of the South Atlantic System.[30] The intermediate African scapegoats could be made to appear as a creature of the ultimate scapegoat—the institution of slavery itself.

One conclusion that followed from the sterner appraisal of African

27. Sierra Leone Company, *Account of the Colony*, pp. 80–82, 86–87, 201–03.
28. Sierra Leone Company, *Report* (1801), p. 8; Sierra Leone Company Directors. Report (1802), PP, 1803–1804, v (24), p. 22.
29. PP, 1803–1804, v (24), pp. 22–23.
30. See arguments of Henry Thornton and William Wilberforce, Commons, 3 April 1798, *Parliamentary Register*, V (new series), 526 and 546–48.

or Creole culture was a modified constitutional policy in the colony. After the rebellion of 1800, the Company no longer talked of representative institutions leading to an African parliament. For them, the hundredors and tythingmen had been "more often ready to patronize the unjust pretentions of the settlers, and to join in their unreasonable clamours, than to enforce the authority of the laws."[31] The offices were abolished in 1800. The sin of the elected representatives was to have chosen to represent the interests of the electorate, rather than serve as prefects for the government. The lesson was applied in arrangements for the Maroons. The obligations of the new settlers were made known in advance, and nothing was said about any rights to land or other favors. Stress was laid instead on the necessity for "subordination and industry."[32]

The humanitarians had come a long way from the radical democracy of Smeathman and Sharp. In the last year of Company administration, the most glowing claim of the African Institution was merely to say "that free Negroes are capable of being governed by mild laws, and require neither whips nor chains to enforce their submission to civil authority."[33]

This assessment of political capabilities was fully in line with the new humanitarian assessment of Africans in general. There had always been an ambivalence between Christian acceptance of spiritual equality, and the obviously unchristian state of African culture. Disappointment in the Sierra Leone experiment shifted the emphasis. Humanitarians seldom defended African culture after 1800, as they had occasionally done in the 1790's. But the Company's final statement of *potential* equality was still uncompromising in 1808: "It is now proved beyond reach of controversy, and this Company have been the chief instruments in establishing the point, that the African does not labour under the intellectual inferiority, which had been so long imputed to him; that he is capable of comprehending and fulfilling every civil and social obligation; and that he can feel with the same

31. Sierra Leone Company, *Report* (1801), pp. 3-4.
32. Sierra Leone Company, *Report* (1801), especially p. 24; Governor and Council to Directors of the Sierra Leone Company, undated, enclosed with Governor and Council to Duke of Portland, 10 June 1799, CO 267/10.
33. African Institution, *Reports of the Committee of the African Institution.* 18 vols. (London, 1807-1824), I (1807), 51.

force as the Europeans, the considerations by which Christianity exalts the mind of man."[34]

This was a fine ringing statement, but it has to be read in the light of their other belief that Africans had a very long way to go before they could realize this potential. The shift in humanitarian attitude between 1788 and 1808 was from one point of view only a subtle shift in the balance of opinion, but its consequences were more serious. One of the few groups in Britain that had ever made an effort to understand and defend African culture had gone into opposition. The remaining guarantee of spiritual equality was not enough to prevent a broader swing of British opinion in non-humanitarian circles, where the promise and implication of spiritual equality was not given so much weight.

34. Sierra Leone Company, *Report* (1808), p. 13.

6

WEST AFRICA

IN THE NEW CENTURY:

A

PATTERN OF DISCOVERY

During the fifteen years in which the Sierra Leone Company unhappily carried out its experiments with colonization and legitimate trade, the British Empire was almost constantly at war, and the fortunes of war profoundly changed the British outlook on the world. Britain and the Allies were unable to hold Napoleon at bay in Europe, but the French were gradually deprived of all the most valuable parts of their tropical empire. Saint Domingue, in chronic civil war since 1791, was permanently lost when the Haitians defeated a French expeditionary force in 1802–03. Disorders in the other French West Indian colonies, combined with interruptions of maritime contact, broke the French segment of the South Atlantic System, at least for the time being. For the British West India interest, a French loss was as good as a British victory. The British sugar islands now held a sellers' monopoly in tropical staples, and there was less reason than ever to break that monopoly by opening new plantations in Africa.

Elsewhere, the change in Britain's position in the tropical world was equally impressive. Coastal Ceylon was seized from the Dutch

in 1795–96 and made a Crown Colony in 1802. On the Indian mainland during the 1780's and 1790's, the British East India Company
slowly made themselves the ruler of the sub-continent. By 1805 the
area of British India had doubled, and the Company increasingly
exerted a vague though substantial power within the Indian states
beyond their immediate sphere. As long as this remained a private
empire, protected by the Company's legal monopoly over trade between Britain and the East, private traders had to look elsewhere
for tropical markets and sources of supply. When, in 1813, the
Company lost their monopoly over the India trade, their sphere of
sovereignty and influence promised the independent British merchant
a great deal more than he was likely to find on the uncertain and
fever-ridden coast of West Africa.

After 1808 there were also greater opportunities in South America.
With Napoleon's invasion of Spain, the Spanish-American empire
fell to pieces, never to be restored in its old form. British traders
could now exploit legally and openly the trade they had been gradually building up through encroachment, smuggling, and the gradual
relaxation of Spanish commercial controls. The situation was more
favorable still in Portuguese America. Portugal was an ally with
ancient commercial ties to Britain. In the face of the French threat
to the metropolis, the Portuguese court was carried to Brazil by a
British fleet, and it remained there during the French occupation of
Portugal. Unlike Spanish America, Brazil had no civil wars to dis-
turb trade, and the Strangford Treaty of 1810 gave British goods a
special place in Brazilian markets.

By contrast, West Africa had little to offer for the time being.
The failure of Sierra Leone, at least in a financial sense, was fully
recognized by 1802, and this was one straw in the wind, casting
doubts on the future of "legitimate trade." The really significant
African trade was still in slaves until 1807, when Parliament made
the trans-Atlantic slave trade illegal for British subjects. From 1808,
Anglo-African commerce was permanently changed. In the first instance, it was reduced to a fraction of its earlier value, but the place
of West Africa in the pattern of British economic interests changed
too. The West Indians and their commercial associates in Britain
no longer cared about maintaining West African posts for the sake
of their labor supply. For them, West Africa was out of bounds,
and any British activity there was a threat to their own position in

British markets. British slave traders were forced into a period of difficult readjustment. For all the advertised wealth to be had from legitimate trade, Africa merchants found no immediate alternative to the slaves traditionally exchanged for British goods. Some of the ex-slave traders held on and did what business they could on the Coast, but others turned away from West Africa and found more profitable commerce elsewhere.

For all of these reasons, British interest which had begun to shift away from West Africa about 1794—initially on account of wartime pressures—never fully returned. (Even during the great "scramble for Africa" after 1880, West Africa followed well behind the Nile Valley or South Africa on the list of British priorities.) The new trend of the nineteenth century was clearly visible in its first decade, and it was reinforced after the victory over France in 1815. In a sense, the pattern of the 1780's was now reversed: as British fortunes rose, British interest in West Africa declined. The new situation was underlined by a lack of public interest in Africa or African affairs. The press, the reviews, and Parliament preferred to talk and write about other and more promising subjects. The first British scramble for Africa was finished.

Even the old generation of African enthusiasts gradually responded to new conditions and new opportunities. Granville Sharp reworked the utopian project he had designed for Sierra Leone and published it for use in India, where he hoped that properly laid out townships, with tythingmen and hundredors, would help to break down caste lines and undermine Hindu law and religion.[1] From the later 1790's the Clapham Sect, which had worked together in the Sierra Leone Company, also worked together to help found the Church Missionary Society, the British and Foreign Bible Society, and other philanthropic enterprises. For any of these organizations, West Africa was only one concern among many. Even the African Institution, founded in 1807 to keep up the humanitarian objectives of the Sierra Leone Company, soon shifted away from its first and narrowly African focus. The suppression of the non-British slave trade took priority, and the Institution moved on to help improve the lot of

_____

1. G. Sharp, *A General Plan for Laying out Towns and Townships, of the New-Acquired Lands in the East Indies, America, and Elsewhere* . . . , 2nd ed. (London, 1804), especially pp. 17–24.

slaves in the British West Indies. West Africa in general, and even
Sierra Leone, soon dropped to secondary importance, though the
Institution itself continued until 1826.[2]

Along with this increasing breadth of world interest, there came
a second major change in the British attitude of the early nineteenth
century. This was a new note of confidence, even of arrogance. It was
too gradual and pervasive to be pinpointed in time or origin. In
essence, the British arrived at a different assessment of the heights
to which British "civilization" had come. They saw, by contrast, a
wider gap between their own achievements and those of other peoples.

Some roots of the change lay in the self-confidence of a victorious
power after a long war—not merely the war beginning in 1793,
though this was victory enough. In the longer run, it was victory
over France in a struggle that went back a century and a half. British
power had never stood higher within the European state system. Still
another important factor was the rise of Evangelical religion and a
new consciousness of Britain as a moral and Christian country—in
certain respects *the* Christian country, in contrast with popish error
across the Channel and heathen error further overseas. But most of
all the new attitude rested on the facts of material achievement.

By the first decade of the new century, Britain had passed through
the most critical phase on the way to full industrialization. This
phase can be called the "industrial revolution" and traced back
into the mid-eighteenth century, or more narrowly defined in
W. W. Rostow's terms, as a period of "take-off" toward sustained
economic growth. Rostow locates "take-off" for Britain in approxi-
mately the period 1783–1802. After 1802, industrialization spread
more widely into new sectors of the economy, but the crucial beginning had already been made.[3] Even before the end of the Napoleonic
Wars, there was a new awareness of material growth, and it continued in the face of post-war depression, increasing and changing
in subtle ways. Whatever the voices of doom, Malthusian or otherwise, the new canals and the flow of cheap cotton textiles were an
outward and visible sign of changes running deep within the body

2. African Institution, *Reports of the Committee of the African Institution,* 18
vols. (London, 1807–1824).
3. W. W. Rostow, *The Stages of Economic Growth* (Cambridge, 1960), pp. 38–40.

economic. Self-satisfaction was already building toward its mid-century pinnacle of the early railway age.

The new economic base also helped to prevent an even more thoroughgoing withdrawal of British interest in West Africa. As economic growth continued, it came to be expected, and it was clear that present commercial outlets would not satisfy future needs. West Africa might be without immediate promise, but future prospects were another matter. The Africa boom of the 1780's had collapsed before its most grandiose claims of great wealth in the far interior had even been investigated, and the failures of coastal colonizers were beside the point in this context. The death of so many explorers was paradoxically a cause for continued optimism: the veil of African mystery still hid the promise of possible wealth, as well as knowledge to be gained for its own sake.

In spite of the difficulties of the 1790's, exploration had continued on a modified scale. The Sierra Leone Company sent James Watt and Matthew Winterbottom, the brother of their physician, into the hinterland during the period of Company activity before the French raid.[4] The explorers visited Timbo and Labe in the substantial Islamic state of Futa Jallon, about 300 miles from Sierra Leone and 150 from the coast. This success did something to revive the promise of still greater discoveries, but the real impetus for a thorough exploration of the interior came from another direction. In 1797 Mungo Park re-emerged on the Gambia after almost two years in the interior between the upper Gambia and the upper Niger. He brought back the first solid and recent information about the Western Sudan, including an eye-witness account of the fabled River Niger previously known only through ancient or Arabic texts. From Park's descriptions of populous agricultural villages and commercial centers, a whole range of new possibilities opened to European speculations. With the publication of his *Travels in the Interior Districts of Africa* in 1799, the information became available throughout Europe.[5] It "opened" the Western Sudan to Western penetration and it opened the classic age of European exploration in West

4. A manuscript journal of James Watt's trip to Timbo is preserved at Rhodes House, Oxford.

5. Mungo Park, *Travels in the Interior Districts of Africa* (London, 1799). See also A. A. Boahen, "British Penetration of North-West Africa and the Western Sudan 1788–1861" (Unpublished Ph.D. thesis, London, 1959), pp. 65–68, J. M. Gray, *A History of the Gambia* (Cambridge, 1940), p. 283.

Map 8. West Africa, c. 1800

145

Africa. The first phase naturally centered on the course and destination of West Africa's greatest river which Park "discovered," and it ended only in 1830, when Richard and John Lander emerged at the mouth after having explored the lower course through modern Nigeria.

But the progress of exploration was fitful and interlocked with other events. Little could be done during the war years immediately after Park's return, though the African Association followed up immediately with a new effort from the east. Frederick Hornemar set out from Cairo toward the Western Sudan. During 1797–1800 he was able to send back reports of his journey as far as Fezzan, but he died somewhere beyond Murzuk on the way to Bornu and the Niger.

The signature of the Peace of Amiens in 1801, however, brough a spate of new projects. The wartime rivalry between France and England was still fresh, and enthusiasts in each were afraid the other might act first. In France, three different authors published elaborate works in 1802 and 1803, calling French attention to West Africa. Pierre Labarthe gathered the reports of French naval officer and others, weaving them into two separate geographical account of Senegal and the Windward Coast. J. B. L. Durand, a Director of the Senegal Company before the Revolution, began to petition the government for the charter of a new company to exploit the Senegal trade, and he too published an elaborate two-volume work to help whip up public support. The most ambitious project of al came from S. M. X. de Golbéry. It called for a French protectorate over all West Africa from Cape Blanc to Cape Palmas and eastward to the upper waters of the Niger. The project included the establishment of a line of posts along the coast, and another leading into the interior by way of the Senegal River.[6]

None of these projects was likely to find much support with the French government. The Consul had already initiated another project that of reconquering Saint Domingue. He was unlikely to risk renewing the war with England for a prize as questionable as West

6. P. Labarthe, *Voyage en Sénégal pendant les anées 1784 et 1785, d'après l mémoires de Lajaille* (Paris, 1802); P. Labarthe, *Voyage à la côte de Guinée* (Paris 1803); J. B. L. Durand, *Voyage au Sénégal*, 2 vols. (Paris, 1802); S. M. X. Golberry [S. M. X. de Golbéry], *Travels in Africa Performed during the Years 178 1786, and 1787*, 2 vols. (London, 1803). See also P. Cultru, *Histoire du Sénégal du x siècle à 1870* (Paris, 1910), pp. 295–96.

Map 9. British Exploration, 1795–1805

Africa. In addition, the French position in West Africa was extremely weak. They had lost Gorée to the English in 1800, and their only remaining post was Saint Louis, at the mouth of the Senegal. Saint Louis itself was garrisoned by less than a hundred soldiers, and they rebelled against the Governor in 1802, forcing him to take refuge with the English on Gorée. Whatever might be published in Paris, there was no new French activity on the Senegal, and no likelihood of French activity.[7]

The main weight of the French projects was felt instead in Eng-

7. Cultru, *Sénégal*, pp. 282 ff.

land. Golbéry's work was translated and published in 1803, where
it fell in neatly with the needs of the British projectors—if only as
a red flag to wave in the face of the government. The British
Africanists were already on the move. In 1799 the African Associa-
tion had passed a resolution in favor of a British occupation of the
Gambia Valley and the intervening country as far as the upper Niger.
This was, of course, a reversion to a much older concept of West
African commercial strategy, repeated by Chief Justice Morse as re-
cently as 1783. It was now merely extended to the recently discovered
Niger.

Sir Joseph Banks himself went further still in a proposal of 1799
—in effect a British equivalent of the Golbery project—for annexation of the whole coast from Arguin to Sierra Leone, seizure of the
Senegal Valley, and formation of a chartered company to carry the
march of empire into the interior. After the outbreak of peace,
Banks was joined by Zachary Macaulay and Philip Beaver, among
others, each with his own strategic and institutional suggestions but
all with the same goal. The object was to establish a defensible
route between the coast and the navigable upper Niger that Park
had visited, aiming for a point near the modern city of Bamako.[8]

These projects raised issues of political and commercial strategy
that were to be hotly debated for a half century and more. The
object was agreed, but the route was not; and it was far from easy
to select the best point of entry with the information then available.
The choice involved a consideration of the topography and political
geography of the whole Western Sudan and the hinterland of the
western Guinea coast. The only recent information came from the
French publications, from Watt and Winterbottom's penetration to
Futa Jallon, and from Park himself. It was little to go on, but the
self-appointed authorities went to work, selecting a route over mountains none of them had seen, along rivers of speculative navigability,
and through conjectured kingdoms.

Four routes came under active consideration during the Peace of
Amiens. One was the Senegal River, temporarily out of the question because of the French base at its mouth, but still in the background. A second was the Gambia. A third was the valley of the
Rio Grande, which flows into the Atlantic opposite Bulama Island

8. Banks to Lord Liverpool, 8 June 1799; Z. Macaulay's memorandum of 4 September 1802; Capt. Philip Beaver's memorandum of 13 August 1802, CO 2/1.

Map 10. The Strategy of Western Approaches to the Upper Niger, 1799–1805

149

A fourth led to Port Loko on the Sierra Leone River, then to Timbo and on to the upper Niger. The possibility of entry by way of the rivers Pongas, Nunez, or Mesurado was also considered, but less seriously than the others.

By curious coincidence, each of the principal advocates of a particular route favored one that began at whatever point on the coast he knew best. Sir Joseph Banks, Mungo Park, and the military commander at Gorée, all believed the best entry was up the Gambia. Philip Beaver wanted to use the Rio Grande and base the enterprise on Bulama Island. Zachary Macaulay preferred Sierra Leone.[9]

A plan was ultimately drawn up by the government, coordinating all of these suggestions. In its most elaborate version, it called for a four-pronged attack, with military expeditions moving inland simultaneously from Sierra Leone, Bulama, the Gambia, and directly across country from Gorée to the upper Senegal. This latter force was to capture Fort Saint Joseph from the French. The other three were to solidify the British hold on the Gambia and move on to the Niger, exploring the country along the way. The effort was to take place in 1803, but a series of postponements and modifications intervened. The war in Europe began again. Perhaps the government discovered that there were, in fact, no French posts on the upper Senegal for them to attack. In any case, the residual legatee of all this planning was a small military force, hardly more than an escort, led by Mungo Park along the familiar route he had pioneered from the Gambia to the Niger. The purpose was changed from an impressive show of force to a mere exploration of routes and commercial conditions along the Niger.

Even so, it was not a success. Park marched from the Gambia to the Niger in 1805, sending back a series of reports, but most of the escort died of disease on the first leg of the trip. Park's last report came from Sansanding, hardly further than his earlier penetration. He and the few survivors who were able to descend the Niger by canoe were killed near Bussa in Northern Nigeria, and the expedition ended as a spectacular failure which added very little to existing knowledge.

The Park expedition of 1805 was nevertheless a new kind of ex

9. Z. Macaulay to Lord Hobart, printed in Macaulay, *A Letter to His Highness th Duke of Gloucester* . . . (London, 1815), appendix, pp. 23–30; Philip Beaver, *African Memoranda* (London, 1805), pp. 403–10; Gray, *Gambia,* pp. 287–89; Boahen, "Britis⊩ Penetration of North-West Africa," pp. 108–32; and CO 2/1, *passim.*

pedition. It marked the beginning of government sponsorship of
African exploration, and it marked the beginning of a new emphasis.
The enlightened travellers of an earlier generation had been confined to the coast, where they necessarily concentrated on a detailed
study of peoples and plants. The new generation beginning with
Park went into the far interior, where they saw more, but in less
detail. They were now interested in roads, rivers, and the potential
returns of trade, coupled with a growing interest in putting down
the African slave trade.

The African Association still sent occasional expeditions, but
they never repeated the great success of Park's first expedition.
Horneman's death in 1800 was one source of discouragement. Another of the Association's explorers died in Calabar in 1805, before
he had even moved from the coast. They later sent two explorers to
attempt the approach from Egypt, but neither one reached West
Africa. Sir Joseph Banks, the moving spirit, died in 1820 and the
Association became less active. In 1831, it merged with the Royal
Geographical Society.

The new phase of government-sponsored exploration nevertheless
retained its links with the earlier period. The principal figure to
replace Banks and the Association was John Barrow, who had himself been one of the enlightened travellers in South Africa during
the 1790's. As Under-Secretary of State at the Admiralty from 1805
to 1845, he was in a position to send out expeditions to many different parts of the world and to help explorers secure sponsorship
from other government departments. As a founder of the Royal
Geographical Society, he was also active in the cause of geographical
scholarship.[10]

In spite of Barrow's interest, the renewal of the war and the death
of Mungo Park effectively ended all serious thought of further
African activity for a decade after 1805, and after Waterloo the
nature of British commercial interests in West Africa had changed
beyond recognition. The abolition of the British slave trade and the
transfer of Sierra Leone to the Crown forced the government to re-
consider the role of the Company of Merchants Trading to Africa.
The Company had been created and supported specifically to control
the slave-trade forts on the Gold Coast and elsewhere. Their initial

10. Boahen, "British Penetration of North-West Africa," pp. 102–6, 137–42. A. A.
Boahen, "The African Association, 1788–1805," *Transactions of the Historical Society of Ghana*, V, 43–64 (1961).

reason for being disappeared with the slave trade. In the new situation, it seemed logical either to abandon the posts altogether or to take them under royal administration. To meet either threat, the African Committee made a serious effort to change with changing times. They accepted the end of the slave trade and tried to adjust to the new possibilities of "legitimate trade." George Torrane was sent out as Governor in 1805 to reform the administration and strengthen the Company against the coming transition.[11]

This assignment was difficult for reasons quite unconnected with events in Europe. The region now including Ghana, Togo, Dahomey, and Nigeria was passing through its own period of revolutionary political change in the first decades of the nineteenth century.

On the Gold Coast, the major alteration was the emergence of Ashanti. Most of the hinterland of the Gold Coast forts was Akan in language and culture, organized in a multitude of petty states. Larger confederations had been formed from time to time in the past, such as the Akwamu Empire which flourished in the hinterland of Accra in the later seventeenth century. By the eighteenth century, the most important larger confederation had come to be Ashanti, founded about 1700 and centered on Kumasi, 100 miles inland from Cape Coast. Ashanti had followed a course of aggressive expansion during a great part of the eighteenth century. The Dutch, Danish, and English authorities had watched from a distance and maintained occasional diplomatic contact with the Asantehene's court. There were, however, a number of smaller states separating the forts from direct contact with the center of Ashanti power. From the British point of view, the most important of these were the Fante states, forming a belt from a point slightly west of Cape Coast to a few miles west of Accra. The Fantes were the principal trade partners and, in a sense, the political allies of the British at most times. Their territory was by no means a British "protectorate," rather the reverse. The British were allowed *de facto* sovereignty within the forts, but they paid ground rent and minor tribute for the right to be there. The prosperity of the Fantes and the Europeans alike rested on the slave trade with the interior. Ashanti also depended both economically and politically on the slave trade, exporting slaves

11. E. C. Martin, *The British West African Settlements, 1750–1821* (London 1927), pp. 147–51.

Map 11. The Fulani Empire and Its Neighbors, c. 1830

153

toward the coast in return for firearms and European manufactures.[12]

From the point of view of Ashanti, the Fante, and other coastal peoples were mere middlemen, exacting a profit that might be avoided if Ashanti could deal directly with the forts. The Fante states were turbulent toward the end of the eighteenth century. Their political disorganization was a constant cause of friction with Kumasi, and it was bad for trade. Some coastal people recognized a rather vague Ashanti claim to suzerainty, but Ashanti armies appeared on the coast itself only in the early nineteenth century. In an apparent attempt to subdue disorder on their southern frontier, the Ashanti armies drove through to the coast and appeared in the vicinity of the forts in 1806–07, 1809–11, and 1814–16, defeating a coastal alliance and breaking Fante military power in the process. It is doubtful that Ashanti intended to conquer and rule the coastal states, but in 1816 they tightened their indirect suzerainty over a corridor leading to the sea.[13]

From the British point of view, the rise of Ashanti power raised a problem that was not effectively settled on a permanent basis for almost a century. Either of two clear policies might have been chosen —providing always that the British were unwilling or unable to carry a full conquest of all that is now southern Ghana. One was to form an alliance with the Fante and other coastal peoples and attempt to build a military force strong enough to keep Ashanti at bay. The other was to maintain a genuine neutrality, coupled with a willingness to deal with whatever African power effectively occupied the hinterland of the forts. In practice, the British followed neither of these policies but practiced instead a vacillating alternation between the two. Governor Torrane, the African Committee's new broom, began by first trying to defend the remnant of a defeated Fante army at Anomabu fort in 1806. Then he surrendered a number of his Fante quasi-allies in order to save the fort itself. In 1807 he had swung over to a pro-Ashanti position and suggested using an Ashanti alliance as means of pushing British trade into the interior—first to

12. M. Priestley, "The Ashanti Question and the British: Eighteenth-Century Origins," *Journal of African History*, II (1), pp. 35–59 (1961); Ivor Wilks, "The Rise of the Akwamu Empire, 1650–1710," *Transactions of the Historical Society of Ghana*, III, 99–136 (1957).

13. For a general account of Anglo-Ashanti relations see W. E. F. Ward, *A History of the Gold Coast* (London, 1948), especially pp. 130–54.

Kumasi and then on north as far as Timbuctu and the sources of the Niger.[14] In short, for Torrane and some of the other Gold Coast officials, the rise of Ashanti opened a new possibility of penetration toward the eldorado of the Western Sudan trade.

To the east of Ashanti, there were other political changes of even greater importance, and these also contributed to the new look of African politics. Toward the end of the eighteenth century two strong African states were located, as Ashanti was, on the northern fringe of the forest. These were Dahomey, centered on Abomey, and Oyo, centered at Old Oyo or Katunga in the far north of what is now Western Nigeria. Dahomey had conquered its own road to the sea even earlier than Ashanti, though Oyo still dealt with the Europeans through coastal middlemen based on the trading cities of Lagos, Badagri, and Porto Novo. Still further north, in the Hausa-speaking part of Northern Nigeria, the relatively dense agricultural population was organized around a series of walled cities. Each of them was a political power of considerable local importance, but the group as a whole was not united as a single Hausa state. They had, therefore, less weight in international affairs than their wealth and population might indicate.

Of these three—Dahomey, Oyo, and the Hausa states—Oyo was by far the most powerful in the later eighteenth century, exacting tribute at times from Dahomey and raiding northward across the Niger into Nupe and the fringes of Hausa. But at the turn of the eighteenth century there was a revolutionary shift in the locus of political and military power. The Alafins (or kings) of Oyo were clearly over extended, with more tributary peoples than their popular following or military power could effectively control. Even in the Yoruba-speaking core area, there were elements of dissidence, and the strength of Oyo was fragile. About 1800 an internal revolt broke out against the Alafin in power. He was overthrown, and no successor could re-establish the old dominance. The Oyo state began to disintegrate. In some areas power was re-established on a more local level, but in general the former Oyo territories fell into a condition of quasi-anarchy, lasting in its most serious form throughout the first three decades of the nineteenth century.

The disintegration of Oyo was made still worse by the simul-

14. G. Torrane to African Committee, 20 July 1807, T 70/35, ff. 66–67.

taneous rise of a new power to the north. In addition to the Hausa
peasants and townsmen, the Hausa kingdoms contained sizeable
minorities of Fulani or Fulbe peoples.[15] These were migrants from
further west, who had been drifting into Hausa over the past several
centuries. Some of them were cattle-keeping people, who lived sym-
biotically with the Hausa farmers. Others were urban, Muslim, and
partly integrated into the dominant culture of the Hausa cities. At
the end of the eighteenth century the urban Fulani had begun to
respond to the winds of religious change blowing through the
Muslim world. Under the leadership of Usuman dan Fodio, some of
them organized a military revolt in the name of religious purity
and preached a *jihad* against the rulers of the Hausa states. Between
1804 and about 1810, the Fulani purists had conquered all of Hausa
and Usuman dan Fodio established his domination from a capital at
Sokoto. Individual Hausa states were put in charge of Fulani Emirs,
ultimately owing political and religious allegiance to the Sultan at
Sokoto.

Once Hausa had been conquered, the Fulani were free to carry
their conquests to the surrounding non-Hausa areas; and the dis-
integrating Empire of Oyo was a relatively easy target. Different
Yoruba authorities could be played off against one another. Katunga
itself was attacked and later deserted by the Yoruba, many of whom
moved southward into the protection of the forest. Ilorin, formerly
near the core area of Oyo, became the seat of a Fulani Emirate, and
the center of gravity of Yoruba power shifted to new centers like
Ibadan and Abeokuta. Gradually about 1830 some order emerged
from Yoruba anarchy. The military drive from Ilorin was stopped
and a new series of smaller states sprang up within the Oyo empire.
It was only a relative recovery, however, and the remainder of the
nineteenth century was marked by frequent wars between the various
Yoruba states themselves.[16]

15. The accepted English-language terminology for these people is in a state of
confusion. In Nigeria they are called Fulani, as the Hausa called them. In Gambia
and Sierra Leone, they are called Fula, a Bambara word. The French call them by the
Wolof term, Peuls. Their own name for themselves is Fulbe (sing. Pullo). (D. J.
Stenning, *Savanna Nomads* [London, 1959], p. 2.) For purposes of this book, I shall
use the term, Fulbe, for the people as a whole, reserving the more familiar "Fulani"
for the Fulbe of Northern Nigeria, who raised a large state in the nineteenth century.

16. The account of Yoruba history given here and below is based on J. D. Fage,
An Introduction to the History of West Africa (Cambridge, 1955); Samuel Johnson,
The History of the Yorubas (Lagos, 1921); S. O. Biobaku, *The Egba and their
Neighbours, 1842–1872* (London, 1957).

These events were only dimly perceived in Europe before the mid-1820's, but some of their consequences were more immediately apparent. The fall of Oyo and the rise of Fulani power moved the center of the slave trade to the Bight of Benin, between the mouths of the Volta and the Niger, especially to the ports of Ouidah, Lagos, Porto Novo, and Badagri which were in a position to draw in prisoners captured during the Yoruba wars. The presence of slaves for sale brought European slave dealers, after 1807 principally Spanish, Portuguese, and Brazilian. This was not a part of Africa where British merchants were especially strongly entrenched—less so, for example, than in the Niger Delta or the Bight of Biafra further east. The only official British post was a small factory at Ouidah, and the anarchy inland rendered the area less promising for legitimate trade than it had been for the slave trade. In time, however, British attention would necessarily shift to the Bights of Benin and Biafra, led on in part by the activities of the foreign slave traders.

Meanwhile, what little attention could be spared for coastal West Africa during the later years of the Napoleonic Wars went to the Sierra Leone and the Gold Coast, where the British were already committed. The principal problem of creating a new administration suitable to a post-slave-trade era was not met head on. Instead, the government responded as it was pushed by various pressure groups. The two most important between 1808 and 1815 were the African Institution and the African Committee. The Institution, in spite of its primary concern with the suppression of the foreign slave trade, maintained a watching brief for Sierra Leone. It gathered and disseminated information, provided a little aid to African education, and a little encouragement for African exploration (though this was still the special sphere of the African Association). It was especially anxious to have the government use Sierra Leone as its principal base on the African coast, mainly for the suppression of the slave trade but also for the more general object of diffusing Western culture throughout Africa. Zachary Macaulay was by now a man of some influence, and he became the principal spokesman for the Institution. It was partly on his advice that a Vice-Admiralty Court was established at Sierra Leone, and slave ships captured by the Royal Navy were brought there for adjudication. Since there was no easy way of returning the captured slaves to their homes, they were liberated in

Sierra Leone and became in a short time the majority of the population.

The Navy also became an important factor in coastal affairs. Its
long-term interest in the suppression of the foreign slave trade began
almost by accident, certainly without any foreknowledge that the
work would continue for the next sixty years. The Navy was automatically responsible for enforcing the British abolition act on the
high seas. During the war years, it was a normal naval function to
capture enemy ships, whether carrying slaves or not. Since the enemy
initially included France, Holland, and Spain, suppression of a fair
portion of the foreign slave trade was also a legitimate goal. Since the
slave trade was also illegal for Danish and United States ships, the
Royal Navy took it upon themselves (with doubtful legality) to
search these ships for slaves as well. After 1810 Portuguese (including Brazilian) ships were also stopped, since the Strangford Treaty
prohibited the slave trade, except that between parts of the Portuguese Empire. In effect, the Navy had a free hand in West Africa
to capture slavers of all nations, except Portuguese ships sailing between Portuguese ports.

In the concluding years of the war, the Foreign Office worked
through diplomatic channels to continue the Navy's wartime work.
It was successful to the extent of inserting an anti-slavery declaration
in the final act of the Congress of Vienna, but the declaration was
valueless without enforcement; and other powers were unwilling
either to enforce it themselves or to allow the British to do so freely
against their ships. Further legal complications arose in 1817 when
British courts held, in the case of Le Louis, that the Navy could
not legally seize or search foreign slavers in peacetime.[17]

After the peace, anti-slavery sentiment was still strong in Britain;
and it was reinforced by the material interests of the West Indian
planters, who could hardly stand by with their own labor supply
cut off and see their foreign competitors receiving a steady stream
of manpower from Africa. Under both kinds of pressure, the government entered into direct negotiations with Portugal and Spain.
They obtained a treaty with each in 1817, limiting the legal slave
trade to the region south of the equator, giving the Royal Navy a
right of search and a right of capture if slaves were actually found

17. African Institution, *Reports,* esp. I, 69–71.

on board. The captured slavers were to be taken for adjudication to a Court of Mixed Commission, of which three were created—one in Havana, one in Brazil, and one at Sierra Leone. When Brazil became independent, the Portuguese treaty applied to Brazil as well. The treaties were extended and modified in various ways over the years, beginning what was to become a very elaborate network of bilateral treaties, all of them to be enforced by the Royal Navy and enforced in very large part by cruisers stationed off the coast of West Africa.[18] Thus the conduct and administration of the naval blockade was added to the problem of administering the West African posts.

A decision on the future of these posts was slow in coming. There were first the unsettled wartime conditions, and later the continuing cross current of strategic interest—the African Institution and the humanitarians generally favoring more activity centered on Sierra Leone, while the African Committee wanted to develop their caretaking function over the Gold Coast forts into something more substantial. Three Commissioners—Thomas Ludlam and William Dawes, both former Governors of Sierra Leone, and Captain E. H. Columbine, the current Governor—were asked to report on conditions from the Gambia to the Gold Coast, but their report was not presented until 1811.

The four years' wait between abolition and the Commissioners' report left room for a flurry of new suggestions for an African policy. Governor George Torrane of the Gold Coast had his pet project for commercial penetration through an Ashanti alliance, and it was generally supported by the African Committee. Most of the others returned to the strategic thinking common during the Peace of Amiens. Joseph Corry published a new variant of the basic scheme proposed by Sir Joseph Banks and by Golbéry. Like its predecessors, it called for a wholesale declaration of a protectorate, from Cape Palmas westward along the coast and northward to the desert. It was to be backed by fortified strongpoints along the coast and a chain of forts running into the interior from Sierra Leone to Timbo, beyond to the navigable Niger, and downstream to Timbuctu. As with the Banks' proposal of 1799, the whole operation was to be controlled by a chartered company operating under a parliamentary

18. For the British suppression of the foreign slave trade see C. Lloyd, *The Navy and the Slave Trade* (London, 1949) and W. L. Mathieson, *Great Britain and the Slave Trade, 1839–1865* (London, 1929).

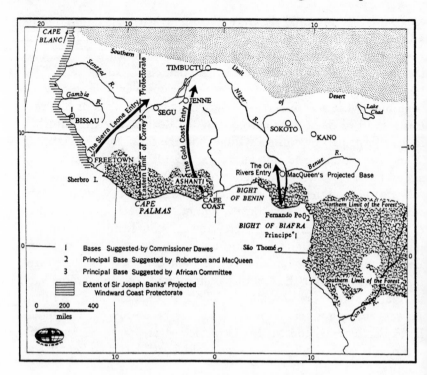

Map 12. Post-War Strategic Plans

monopoly.[19] The basic concept could be varied to taste. Governor
T. Perronet Thompson of Sierra Leone suggested a similar plan of
attack, with military rather than commercial control—he was a military man—and with the coastal factories omitted. He offered himself
as a volunteer to lead an expedition to Timbo as the first stage of
the operation.[20]

When the Commissioners finally reported, they disagreed among
themselves. All were cautious about plans for inland penetration.
They concentrated on the suppression of the slave trade, and the
majority report, principally the work of Captain Columbine, wanted
to continue the strategic emphasis on the Windward Coast. It argued
that anti-slavery patrols could not police the whole coast. Therefore
they should concentrate on the vicinity of Sierra Leone and let the

19. J. Corry, *Observations upon the Windward Coast of Africa . . . made in the
Years 1805–1806* (London, 1807), pp. 85–89.
20. P. Thompson to C. Jenkins, 6 June 1810, CO 267/28.

rest go for the time being. Even the Gold Coast establishment should be reduced to three forts, and the African Committee should be reorganized.

Dawes disagreed with the windward emphasis and presented a minority report in which he claimed (quite correctly) that the slavers were most common in the Bight of Benin, and the cruisers ought to be there too. He followed with a more detailed proposal for the whole coast, suggesting three bases—Bissau for the far west, Sierra Leone for the center, and the island of Principe to cover the Bights. Dawes thought that Britain ought to buy out the Dutch and Danish forts on the Gold Coast, but his was otherwise an anti-Gold Coast view. He would have kept only three forts in active service. The rest could either be dismantled or sold to private British firms. Neither Dawes's nor any other plan was adopted, but Dawes's was the first official response to the new slave trade drawn from the Yoruba wars. The strategic claims of the Bights of Benin and Biafra were now given a hearing along with those of Sierra Leone, Senegambia, and the Gold Coast.[21]

For ten more years, from 1811 to 1821, the question of future strategy in West Africa was undecided. Public discussions in Britain drew diverse threads into a complex net, in which the obvious rivalry between the African Institution and the African Committee had an important part. The proper form of administration was another element—chartered company or royal colony, and if a company, what company? The issue of West Indian slavery was also involved. Pro-slavery writers saw the possibility of scoring a point against the emancipators if they could show free Africans in Africa to be nearly incapable of "advance" without coercion. Thus an attack on the Sierra Leone experiment was a defence for the West Indian planters.

The West African question was again before Parliament in 1816 and 1817, when Select Committees were appointed to look into it. It remained before the public until 1821, with the debate roughly divided according to two alliances of factions. The cause of African Institution was combined with the strategic claims of Sierra Leone and the Windward Coast, opposition to West Indian slavery, and administration of the West African posts by a royal government. The pro-slavery people, on the other hand, preferred company ad-

21. Report of the Commissioners, PP, 1812, x (101) and (180); William Dawes, Memorandum of 27 August 1811, CO 267/29.

162 Age of Exploration

ministration and a strategic emphasis on Cape Coast; and they launched a bitter public attack on the Sierra Leone experiment.[22]

Other strategic suggestions called for a principal base still further east. G. A. Robertson, a Liverpool merchant with African experience, repeated in 1819 most elements of the Dawes report of 1811, and in a way that sought to compromise with the existing interests on the Coast. The desires of the Sierra Leone group were to be met by reviving the idea of a Windward Coast protectorate, this time stretching from the Gambia to the Sherbro. The African Committee was to be protected by an effort to drive trade inland through Ashanti, but Robertson's main interest centered on the Bights. He suggested Fernando Po (in place of Dawes's choice of Principe) as the principal base, and it was to be more than a convenient coastal base near the most active slaving area. Robertson brought out evidence that the Oil Rivers were in fact the mouths of the Niger. Thus Fernando Po lay opposite a navigable entry into the heart of Africa: commerce and humanity both demanded an eastern focus and an eastern base. But Robertson's ideas on commercial organization were thoroughly traditional. He still thought in terms of the older system of the slave trade, where African middlemen alone went into the interior and British merchants stayed on the coast.[23]

James MacQueen took up where Robertson left off, adding an anti-Sierra Leone and pro-West Indian element to his case. He supported the Oil Rivers theory about the Niger mouth, and he went to the Admiralty in 1820 with a suggestion for thorough exploration up the rivers. In 1821 he published a geographical survey, reconstructing the course of the Niger from known information. He also spelled out an elaborate plan for the penetration of Africa. As a first step, Sierra Leone should be evacuated. It was useless as a stepping stone into the interior; and it was a bad center for landing captured slaves, since most slavers were captured in the Bights. His preferred coastal base was also Fernando Po, but only as an entry to a second major base in the interior. Without the aid of direct evidence, MacQueen deduced that a second river joined the main branch of the Niger near the point where the Niger turns southward toward

22. See, for example, Joseph Marryat, Commons, 19 March 1819, 1 H 34, cc. 1105–10.

23. G. A. Robertson, *Notes on Africa . . . with Hints for the Melioration of the Whole African Population* (London, 1819), especially pp. 12–13, 21–23, 132–45, 210–13, and 297–98.

the coast. He was, of course, correct, and the second river was the Benue. His projected inland base was to be located at the confluence, where the town of Lokoja now stands, and linked to Fernando Po by steamboat.[24] Decades later he was justified, and the principal British inland station grew up at the point he had selected sight unseen.

The difference between Robertson and MacQueen reflected a second basic division in strategic thought—the difference between a coastal strategy and one aimed mainly at the penetration of the interior. It was superimposed on the other quarrel over the best point for a coastal base; and it had hardly been raised by the eighteenth-century projectors, who took it for granted that a coastal base would lead to closer contact with the hinterland. With the 1810's, however, the lines of argument were more closely drawn, and a controversy was born which was to have an active life for a half century and more. The disappointments on the coast themselves helped to bring it on. On one hand, it could be argued that commercial failure on the coast had proved nothing, since the valuable trade of West Africa was to be found in the interior. On the other, the clear and increasing evidence of high European mortality suggested that the number of Europeans present in West Africa must be strictly limited, and this in turn implied a limitation to a very few coastal points, leaving the interior trade to African middlemen.

The medical problem influenced other details of strategic planning. Principe and Fernando Po were favored because they were offshore islands, presumably less dangerous than the mainland. Captain John Adams, formerly the master of a slaver, suggested an eastern base at the town of Malemba, now in Cabinda, just north of the Congo mouth. At this point the coast is dry during a part of the year and backed by savanna rather than the forest usual along most of Upper Guinea. The absence of dense vegetation suggested the absence of fevers.[25]

Another recurrent hope was to reach the interior by some route that avoided the Guinea coast altogether. One possibility was to use the desert route from the north. James Grey Jackson, who had been

24. James MacQueen, *Geographical and Commercial View of Northern Central Africa Containing a Particular Account of the Course and Termination of the Great River Niger in the Atlantic Ocean* (Edinburgh, 1821), pp. 169–207.

25. John Adams, *Remarks on the Country Extending from Cape Palmas to the River Congo* (London, 1823), pp. 155–59.

a resident in Morocco for several years, gathered together and published in 1809 whatever he could find out there about the trans-
Sahara caravans and the trade of the Western Sudan. Later on, he
used this information as the basis of an elaborate project, calling
for a large chartered company to organize the trade of the Western
Sudan and bring it into British hands. His chosen route avoided both
the dangers of Guinea and the political problems of dealing with
the Muslim powers of the Maghrib. It began with a base on the
desert coast north of the Senegal and south of Morocco. From that
point the British-managed caravans could move directly inland to
Timbuctu on the Niger bend.[26] An even more far-fetched suggestion
called for an entry from the Red Sea to Timbuctu. The base was to
be at Massawa, from which point trade could be driven inland into
Ethiopia, across the Nile valley, and westward through Darfur,
Bornu, and Kano.[27]

Against this background of suggestion, and while the decision
about coastal administration was still hanging fire, the eldorado of
the Western Sudan was by no means forgotten. Exploration had
stopped between the death of Mungo Park in 1805 and the end of
the wars in 1815, but new information about the interior kept alive
the prospect of marvels still to be found. Some came from the
Maghrib, like that furnished by J. G. Jackson. The prominent pressure groups exploited every opening for publicity. In 1815, the
African Institution published Mungo Park's last journals and letters along with a glowing account of the riches to be won in the
interior by British commerce. In 1816, the African Committee sponsored another, and more suspect, account of the Western Sudan.
Robert Adams, the author of this narrative, was a sailor wrecked on
the Sahara coast near Cape Blanc. He claimed to have been taken
inland to Timbuctu by his Moorish captors before making his way
across the desert to Morocco. A second and similar sailor's tale
appeared in 1821. Whether the shipwrecked sailors were merely
mistaken about where they had been, or deliberately falsified their

26. James Grey Jackson, *Account of the Empire of Morocco* (London, 1809); Vasco
de Gama [Pseud. for J. G. Jackson], *Blackwood's Magazine,* IV, 652–53 (March,
1819); J. G. Jackson, *Account of Timbuctoo and Houssa* (London, 1820), esp.
pp. 247–71.
27. Poplicola [Pseud.], *Letter the Second to Lord Liverpool on the Political and
Commercial Importance of Africa to Great Britain . . .* (Manchester, 1815).

narratives, the interest their stories aroused indicates the continuing fascination of Timbuctu the mysterious.[28]

With the coming of peace, the Government fell in with the enthusiasm for further exploration. Two coordinate efforts were launched to take up the unfinished work of Mungo Park. A Colonial Office expedition under Major Peddie was ordered to make an entry from the Windward Coast and strike the Niger near the scene of Park's original discovery. For the five years, 1816–21, the expedition tried successively to penetrate by way of the Senegal, the Gambia, and the Nunez, meeting the usual problem of high mortality and political difficulties with the African authorities. Peddie died. His successor, Captain Campbell, also died. The expedition was finally commanded by Major William Gray. He and Staff-Surgeon Dorchard were able to traverse a good deal of the country lying between the upper Gambia, the Upper Niger, and Sierra Leone, but only with small parties. The expedition as a whole was finally withdrawn without having accomplished its main objectives.[29]

A second expedition under Admiralty sponsorship was sent to examine the rivers around the Bight of Biafra, to see if one of them might turn out to be the mouth of the Niger. It was elaborately organized with a staff of scientists under the general command of Captain Tuckey, R.N. The first objective was the Congo, with the Rio del Rey and the Formosa also on the agenda. In fact, the Formosa was a mouth of the Niger, but the expedition never reached it. It went inland about 150 miles along the course of the Congo

28. Jackson, *Morocco;* Robert Adams, *The Narrative of R. Adams, A Sailor who was Wrecked on the West Coast of Africa in . . . 1810* (London, 1816); T. S. Traill, "Account of the Captivity of Alexander Scott among Wandering Arabs of the Great African Desert," *The Edinburgh Philosophical Journal,* IV, 38–54, 225–34 (January and April, 1821). Another, similar tale was so specious as to be not merely a hoax, but a parody on the earlier hoaxes. See "Specimens of Timbuctoo Anthology," *New Monthly Magazine,* XI, 22–28 (1824).

29. William Gray, *Travels in Western Africa in the Years 1818, 19, 20, and 21* (London, 1825). In imagining these and other European "explorations" of West Africa, it is necessary to avoid the tendency to see too close a resemblance to European explorations in North America or Australia. In contrast to those other two continents, this part of Africa was relatively densely populated and had its own commercial system with a network of trade routes stretching from the desert to the Guinea coast. African commercial travellers regularly moved about with a security roughly comparable to that of twelfth-century Europe. African exploration was difficult and dangerous for Europeans, mainly on account of disease, but, for all that, they were merely outsiders investigating an alien society—not by any means the first men to march or ride over their long routes.

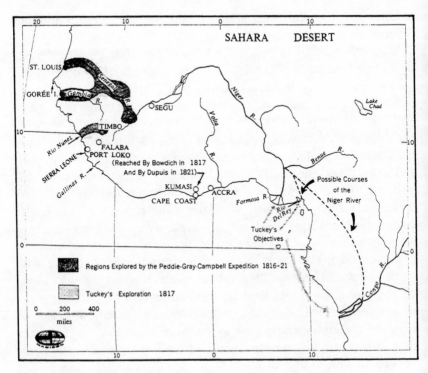

Map 13. Post-War Explorations, 1815–1821

in 1816–17, but Tuckey and all of the scientists died. The survivors were withdrawn before they could attempt any of the other rivers.[30]

A third possible approach also appeared in the post-war years. This was to enter West Africa along the caravan routes from the Maghrib. One such route was especially inviting in the later 1810's and it was called to the Government's attention by a series of widely separated events. In Tripoli, Yusuf Caramanli (1795–1830) was Pasha, theoretically under the suzerainty of Turkey but effectively an independent ruler. In the early nineteenth century he began to strengthen his control over the hinterland, subduing Fezzan by 1811. Traffic could then move safely southward from Tripoli to the oases lying on the route to Bornu and Lake Chad or further west to the Hausa states. At the southern end of the caravan route, the Hausa states had been seriously disturbed in the first decade of the century by the Fulani rising, and Bornu had had its own troubles with the

30. Boahen, "British Penetration of North-West Africa," pp. 132–50.

Fulani *jihad*. By 1814, however, Bornu had responded with a religious and political resurgence of its own, led by Mohammed el-Amin el-Kanemi, himself a religious leader like Shehu Usuman dan Fodio. He was able to contain the military threat on his western frontiers by 1814. The Mai of Bornu returned to power in his own kingdom, but with El-Kanemi as *de facto* ruler until his death in 1835. Internal peace was thus re-established at the southern terminus of the route from Tripoli, and El-Kanemi also established an entente with Tripoli as a makeweight against the Fulani Empire. Thus the caravan road was held at either end by a strong power, and these powers were on friendly terms with each other.

The possibilities thus opened were brought to British attention by the combined efforts of Col. G. H. Warrington and Captain William Henry Smyth, R.N. Warrington served as H. M. Vice-Consul in Tripoli from 1814 to 1846, and he was initially on close personal terms with the Pasha. Smyth had served with Philip Beaver in the Indian Ocean during the later phases of the Napoleonic Wars. He was infected with Beaver's enthusiasm for African colonization and later became Beaver's biographer. In 1815 he was appointed to survey the coasts of Sicily and the nearby shores of Africa and Italy, and he took this assignment as an excuse for travelling south from Tripoli. On the basis of his reconaissance, he showed that a full-scale expedition could be sent toward the Western Sudan. The suggestion was seconded by Warrington, who also obtained the Pasha's consent and support. As a result, Joseph Ritchie was appointed Vice-Consul for Fezzan and posted to Murzuk, with orders to obtain scientific and commercial information and to travel overland to Timbuctu if possible. Ritchie and his party actually reached Murzuk in 1818, but he died there and his two companions returned to England. One of them, George Francis Lyon, wrote an account of their travels, though it did little to modify the earlier reports from Murzuk by Hormeman and Lucas.[31] Thus all three of the post-war government expeditions ended in failure and the death of their leaders.

A fourth effort in these same years met with more success. The African Committee were interested in showing their competence to handle British affairs on the Gold Coast. They also wanted to dem-

31. Boahen, "British Penetration of North-West Africa," pp. 164–81; G. F. Lyon, *A Narrative of Travels in Northern Africa in the Years 1818, 19, and 20* (London, 1821); Heinrich Barth, *Travels and Discoveries in North and Central Africa,* 5 vols. (London, 1857–1858), I, xiii.

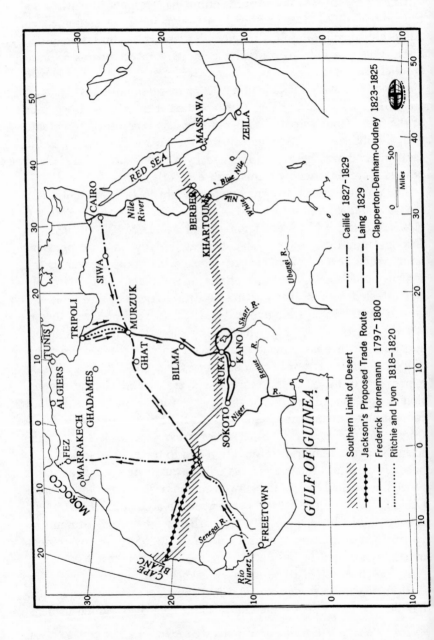

		· · · · · ·	Caillié 1827–1829		
		— — —	Laing 1829		
		——	Clapperton-Denham-Oudney 1823–1825		

Southern Limit of Desert

●●●● Jackson's Proposed Trade Route

Frederick Hornemann 1797–1800

—··—··— Ritchie and Lyon 1818–1820

Miles
500

onstrate the potential value of their forts as a base for inland trade. In 1817, they sent an expedition to Kumasi to open direct negotiations with the Asantehene. Although the original leader was Frederick James, the Company's governor of Accra fort, one of the members was Thomas Edward Bowdich, an amateur naturalist and ethnographer, and a writer in the service of the Company. Bowdich ultimately assumed command, and in 1819 he published an account that went far beyond the original orders to report on political and commercial conditions.

His glowing description of Ashanti society caught the public imagination at a time when other expeditions were ending in failure. His reports of hearsay evidence about the trade routes still further into the interior indicated, quite correctly, that Kumasi was one of the way points on a major route leading from the coast to the Fulani Empire. He therefore recommended a commercial and political alliance with Ashanti (reminiscent of Torrane's Ashanti policy a decade earlier). British trade could then be carried directly into the interior, first to the great market at Salaga and ultimately still further to Yendi, Wawa, and Hausa.[32]

The main line of Bowdich's suggestion was accepted by the Government, but not in a form the African Committee could approve.[33] Joseph Dupuis was sent to Kumasi in 1820 as a resident British representative reporting directly to the Foreign Office. He signed a new agreement with Osei Bonsu, the Asantehene. For reasons partly personal and partly political it was opposed by the Company's officials on the coast, and the treaty failed ratification in England.

The Dupuis mission took place at a time when the government was finally reaching a decision about the future administration of the West African posts. By an act of Parliament in 1821, the Company of Merchants Trading to Africa was disbanded. Their forts were turned over to the Crown to be placed, along with the new post at Bathurst on the Gambia, under a single West African government at Sierra Leone. The implications for coastal strategy were clear. It was a defeat for the advocates of more activity in the Bights of Benin and Biafra, a defeat for the African Committee, and a victory for the Sierra Leone faction. The failure of Dupuis' treaty with

32. T. E. Bowdich, *Mission from Cape Coast Castle to Ashantee* . . . (London, 1819), esp. pp. 341–43, 453–60.
33. Arbuthnot to African Committee, 3 September 1818, T 70/36.

Ashanti was also a defeat for those who hoped for diplomatic aid in pushing British trade inland. After fourteen years of uncertainty some kind of decision had finally been reached.

The decision implied only limited activity—and that centered on the Windward Coast. It was soon reinforced by further events on the Gold Coast. Sir Charles MacCarthy, whose Governorship of Sierra Leone now included command of the Gold Coast forts, was soon embroiled in a war with Ashanti, in alliance with the Fante and other coastal peoples. He himself was killed in a skirmish with the Ashanti army in 1824. The coastal alliance retrieved the defeat with a decisive victory at Dodowa in 1826, but there was no formal peace until 1831. Hence there was no possibility of penetration by way of Ashanti. MacCarthy's death, furthermore, made a strong public impression at home and went far to erase the high hopes Bowdich had aroused. The cost of the war made an even stronger impression on the Treasury, and no further schemes based on the Gold Coast would be favorably received in high places for some time to come.[34]

Meanwhile, men-on-the-spot in Sierra Leone worked unofficially for an opening toward their own hinterland, much as Bowdich had done from the Gold Coast. The home government had been thoroughly discouraged by the failure of the Peddie-Campbell-Gray expedition of 1816–21; but enthusiasts could rest their continued optimism on the successful journey of Gaspard Théodore Mollien, who travelled overland in 1818 from St. Louis to Timbo and then down to the coast in what is now Portuguese Guinea. His report was translated into English by T. E. Bowdich and published in 1820.[35] The Sierra Leone government also kept up the rather tenuous relations established with the Almami of Futa Jallon and the Bambara King of Segu by the expedition of the later twenties. Embassies went up from Sierra Leone to Timbo in 1821 and again in 1822. The second of these was led by Captain Alexander Gordon Laing, later the first European to reach Timbuctu in the nineteenth century. Laing followed his trip to Timbo with a suggestion for establishing close relations with selected African states, his own choice being Sulima in the vicinity of Falaba.[36]

In 1825 and 1826 even more ambitious plans for diplomatic ac-

34. See Ward, *Gold Coast*, pp. 169–82.
35. G. T. Mollien, *Travels in the Interior of Africa* (London, 1820).
36. A. G. Laing, *Travels in the Timanee, Kooranko, and Soolima Countries in Western Africa* (London, 1825), pp. 387–98.

tion were taken up by General Charles Turner, the Governor of
Sierra Leone. During his short governorship he bombarded the Colonial Office with projects representing an extreme version of the
Windward Coast strategy. Among other things, he wanted two small
steamers to patrol the coast from the Gambia to the Gallinas, plus
small military posts located so as to command the river mouths.
Britain could then control the trade with the interior. The power to
cut off trade would give control without the necessity of using large
forces inland. Peaceful commercial penetration could proceed with
the aid of a British resident at Timbo, pushing down the trade routes
to the Niger and on to Segu and Timbuctu.[37]

The idea itself was simply a revival of the project for a Windward Coast protectorate, but Turner followed ideas with action. He
signed treaties taking Sherbro Island and other coastal territory under
the protection of Sierra Leone. He led two small military and naval
expeditions to the south and another to Port Loko on the Sierra
Leone River. Then he died. His work was left unfinished—not only
unfinished but undone by the Colonial Office, which refused to accept most of his annexations.[38]

After so many failures and the death of so many of its officers,
the British government was less and less inclined by the mid-1820's
to look with favor on increased commitments in Guinea. The Colonial Office had a vastly increased body of commitments elsewhere.[39]
It rejected Turner's plans for expansion from Sierra Leone, but it
fell in easily enough with his suggestion that Britain should with-
draw from the Gold Coast. A first decision, shortly after MacCarthy's
death, was to evacuate all but Accra and Cape Coast.[40] In 1826 it
was changed to complete withdrawal from the Gold Coast.

Not only had the Guinea coast produced one disappointment after

37. See Turner's despatches of 22 February 1825, 9 April 1825, 25 June 1825,
20 July 1825, and 20 December 1825, in CO 267/65 and 267/66.
38. Relevant despatches are in CO 267/65 and 267/66. See also J. J. Crooks, *A
History of the Colony of Sierra Leone Western Africa* (London, 1903), pp. 117–29.
39. It would, however, be a mistake to underestimate the official concern with West
Africa in the mid-1820's. In 1806 the Secretary of State had sent out only 209 despatches to all colonies. At that time in West Africa, only Gorée was directly under
Crown government, and it received only four of these communications. By 1824, the
total number of outgoing dispatches rose to 3,460, of which 324 went to Sierra Leone
and the other West African posts. By this measure, at least, West Africa now bulked
larger than all colonial business had done in 1806. The volume of West African business in 1824 was also larger than that of the Cape of Good Hope, the only other part
of sub-Saharan Africa then within the British sphere. (D. M. Young, *The Colonial
Office in the Early Nineteenth Century* [London, 1961], pp. 248–49.)
40. See Minute of 2 July 1825 on Turner to Bathurst, 9 April 1825, CO 267/65.

another, it now appeared that better routes to the Western Sudan were available. In 1825 an expedition returned to Tripoli, having made a successful round-trip crossing of the Sahara and a detailed survey of what is now Northern Nigeria. It was the first really successful British expedition to the interior of West Africa since Mungo Park's first journey, in the 1790's.

In spite of Ritchie's death, the effort to open the Tripoli-Bornu route had been continuous from 1818 onward. The expedition that ultimately succeeded had been mounted in 1821, through the cooperation of the Colonial Office and John Barrow at the Admiralty. The staff consisted of Dr. Walter Oudney, a medical man with an interest in natural history, Hugh Clapperton of the Navy, and Dixon Denham of the Army. They were ordered to penetrate to Bornu and carry out the scientific and commercial investigations originally assigned to Ritchie. After crossing the desert they moved about widely between 1822 and 1824, often in separate parties. Denham explored to the south and east of Lake Chad, while Clapperton travelled west to Hausa, visiting Kano and Sokoto, where he made contact with Sultan Bello. Even though Dr. Oudney died, the results were extremely encouraging.[41]

New efforts in the same direction began at once, attempting to exploit both the Tripoli opening and the new contact with the Fulani Empire. In a pair of simultaneous expeditions, Major Laing was sent toward Timbuctu by way of Tripoli, while Clapperton was sent to try a southern approach to the Fulani Empire from Badagri on the Bight of Benin. He travelled up from the coast, keeping just to the west of the most disturbed parts of Yoruba, and crossed the Niger at Bussa, near the point where Mungo Park had been killed. Most of the Europeans in the party died before the expedition crossed the Niger, but Clapperton continued with his personal servant, Richard Lemon Lander, going on into Hausa through Zaria and Kano, until he ultimately arrived once again at Sokoto. His luck held no further. Sultan Bello declined to sign the hoped-for treaty of commerce and friendship with Britain, and Clapperton himself died in

41. Dixon Denham and Hugh Clapperton, *Narrative of Travels and Discoveries in Northern and Central Africa in the Years 1822, 1823, and 1824*, 2 vols. (London, 1826). See also Boahen, "British Penetration of North-West Africa," pp. 190–98, 249–55.

Labels: Lake Chad, KUKA, ZINDER, KANO, SOKOTO, GWANDU, ZARIA, YOLA, Benue, Niger, BUSSA, ILORIN, OLD OYO, ABEOKUTA, ABOMEY, OUIDAH, PORTO NOVO, BADAGRI, LAGOS, BRASS, Fernando Po, ACCRA, CAPE COAST.

Legend:
Clapperton And R. L. Lander 1825-1827
R. L. Lander Alone 1827-1828
R. L. And John Lander 1830

Scale: 0 100 200 Miles

Caption: Map 15. Clapperton, Lander, and the Lower Niger

Page number 173.

10, 0, 10.

Map 15. Clapperton, Lander, and the Lower Niger

173

Sokoto. Lander, however, made his way back to the coast, retracing the overland route to Badagri.[42]

Meanwhile, Laing had left Tripoli and reached Timbuctu in August 1826, the same month Clapperton arrived at Sokoto. His misfortunes also began after he had reached his objective. On leaving Timbuctu, Laing was killed, and his papers disappeared, though one of his servants lived to bring word to Tripoli. The repercussions were more far reaching than the mere death of another explorer, a common enough occurrence. The difficulty came from the fact that René Caillié, a free-lance French explorer, reached Timbuctu two years later, following a route inland from the River Nunez near Sierra Leone, along the valley of the upper Niger, then home across the desert by way of Fez and Tangier. When Caillié's report was published, Consul Warrington in Tripoli believed it was a fabrication —that it was, in fact, based on Laing's journal which he presumed to have been stolen and sold to the French. Among other things, Warrington accused the Pasha of Tripoli of bad faith, and the affair of Laing's papers ended good relations between Britain and the Caramanlis. The British government withdrew its support of the dynasty. Revolts broke out in both Tripoli and Fezzan. After 1831 the Tripoli route was no longer open to British travellers. In 1834 Yusuf Caramanli was forced to abdicate. The Ottoman Empire, previously only the most distant suzerain, intervened and began to re-establish order; but it was a long process, and the roads south from Tripoli were unsafe for more than a decade.[43]

For the time being, therefore, the only useful way to reach the Fulani Empire (or solve the Niger problem) was the route from Badagri opened by Clapperton and Lander. By 1829, most geographical authorities had come to believe that the Oil Rivers were the Niger mouth, but there was still no conclusive proof. On the strength of Lander's book and experience, and in spite of his social origins, he was given a commission from the Colonial Office to return and explore the lower Niger. He set out with his brother John

42. Hugh Clapperton, *Journal of a Second Expedition into the Interior of Africa, from the Bight of Benin to Soccatoo* (London, 1829); R. L. Lander, *Records of Captain Clapperton's Last Expedition to Africa . . . with Subsequent Adventures of the Author*, 2 vols. (London, 1830).

43. René Caillié, *Travels Through Central Africa to Timbuctoo*, 2 vols. (London, 1830); Boahen, "British Penetration of North-West Africa," pp. 270–92.

in 1830 over the familiar route overland to Bussa. On reaching the Niger, they returned to the coast by canoe.[44]

This final evidence of the Niger's lower course did more than settle an academic puzzle. It showed without question that an all-water route into the interior existed. The claims of Sierra Leone as the principal focus of British interest were now decisively ended, and the Niger was to dominate British strategic thought for the next quarter century.

But the Landers' exploration was not alone in producing this result, and there was no immediate revival of interest in West Africa. The home government had been increasingly disappointed with all its operations on the Coast. The decision of 1826 to evacuate the Gold Coast was an early sign, though the evacuation never took place. It was only barely prevented by the protests of British merchants who traded there. As a compromise, the government withdrew in 1828 as the administering authority, turning the forts over to a committee of merchants sitting in London. Local control was vested in a President and Council at Cape Coast, with limited jurisdiction and a government subsidy of only £4,000 a year.

The value of Sierra Leone was again called into question in these same years. A new set of royal commissioners, James Rowan and Henry Wellington, were sent to survey the West African settlements, and their report was far from favorable. The commissioners' report was presented to Parliament, and another Select Committee of the House of Commons considered West African policy in 1830.

The Committee followed the main lines of the Commissioners' report. The Sierra Leone peninsula was to be kept, but with European staff reduced to a bare minimum. If it were not for the fact that Sierra Leone had a Westernized population, settled there through British agency, it too would have been evacuated. The main base for the anti-slavery patrols and the headquarters of the Court of Mixed Commission was to be moved to Fernando Po.[45] In preparation for the move, the island was occupied by a British naval expedition from 1827 to 1832, but there was a problem of sovereignty. Spain

44. Richard and John Lander, *Journal of an Expedition to Explore the Course and Termination of the Niger* . . . 2 vols., Rev. ed. (New York, 1858). First published in 3 vols., London, 1832.

45. Report of the Commissioners, PP, 1826–1827, vii (312) and (552).

still had a highly theoretical title to the island, and she refused to sell except at a price the British considered prohibitively expensive. In the end, therefore, Sierra Leone continued to be the seat of British government on the Coast, and the principal naval base—but only on suffrance.

In spite of a few short bursts of excitement, the trend of British thinking about West Africa was one of steadily increasing pessimism throughout the first three decades of the nineteenth century. The 1830 Committee marked the nadir, both for West Africa in general and Sierra Leone as a British colony.[46] The only hope for the future lay in the incorrigible optimism of an small group of enthusiasts, many of whom had served on the Coast—and on the still untried promise of the Niger as an all-water route into the interior.

46. Report of the Committee, PP, 1830, x (661), pp. 1–5.

7

THE

PROBLEM OF SURVIVAL

During the whole of the nineteenth century, the most important problem for Europeans in West Africa was simply that of keeping alive. Until the 1840's the essential facts about the "climate" remained what they had been in the eighteenth century. Any European activity exacted an appalling price. Every assignment of missionaries or officials, every journey of exploration, every trading voyage or anti-slavery patrol took its toll. Unlike the situation of the later eighteenth century, when men could plan in optimistic ignorance, the facts were now more broadly publicized. Lind and some others had spoken out earlier, but the coastal experiments of the 1790's brought the image of West Africa as "the white man's grave" into new focus. The initial death rate for Europeans sent to the Province of Freedom had been 46 per cent. The Sierra Leone Company lost 49 per cent of its European staff, and the Bulama Island Association lost 61 per cent in the first year.[1] These figures were not far out of line with the eighteenth-

1. See Appendix.

century expectation of a 20 per cent loss from the crew on a slaving
voyage to the Coast, but they were something to ponder.

Even so, the full implications were only gradually recognized.
The projectors of the 1790's were very much disturbed when the
death rate was known, but their public reaction was to explain it
away and hope for something better in the future. They pointed to
the reduced mortality in the second and later years at any settlement
(which we would now expect in the light of modern malariology)
and they sensed correctly that the "seasoning sickness" was the serious hurdle to be passed. They fell back, this time incorrectly, on
their own prediction that Sierra Leone could be made healthy if it
was cleared and cultivated. Some of the more religious humanitarians
also saw the high death rates as a form of retributive justice. Granville Sharp blamed the drunkenness of the settlers for the mortality
at the Province of Freedom. A rapid death had been their punishment, but better conduct from future settlers might solve the problem. Other consolation could be sought in the continued hope of
finding a healthy place on the coast or a better climate inland. An
undertone of continuing optimism was therefore still possible, even
after the mid-1790's.[2]

This remaining optimism was only gradually eroded away during
the quarter century after 1792. Even the African enthusiasts in the
first years of the nineteenth century were not quite so enthusiastic
about the health prospects as their predecessors had been. Golbéry
chose the ancient personification of Africa as a woman holding a
cornucopia and a scorpion. The one was a "just symbol of the treas-
ures hidden in the bowels of this auriferous country, and the riches
which its inexhaustible fecundity offers to Europe," the other a
symbol of "all the diseases and dangers of a burning climate."[3] The

2. Sierra Leone Company, *Report of the Court of Directors of the Sierra Leone
Company to the General Court,* 7 vols. (title varies) (London, 1791–1808), I (1791),
11: H. Thornton to J. Clarkson, 14 September 1792, Ad. Mss. 41262A, f. 179; Sierra
Leone Company, *Account of the Colony of Sierra Leone from its First Establishment
in [sic] 1793* . . . (London, 1795), p. 53; C. B. Wadström, *An Essay on Colonization,
Particularly Applied to the Western Coast of Africa* . . . , 2 vols. (London, 1794–
1795), I, 39; Philip Beaver, *African Memoranda* (London, 1805), pp. 365–66; G.
Sharp to a New York Lady, 12 January 1788, quoted in Prince Hoare, *Memoirs of
Granville Sharp,* 2nd ed., 2 vols. (London, 1828), II, 84; J. Corry, *Observations upon
the Windward Coast of Africa* . . . *Made in the Years 1805–1806* (London, 1807),
pp. 100–101.

3. S. M. X. Golberry [S. M. X. de Golbéry], *Travels in Africa Performed during
the Years 1785, 1786, and 1787,* 2 vols. (London, 1803), II, 209.

price to be paid was now recognized, even though the reward might justify the cost.

By the 1820's the cost seemed to rise in the eyes of the British public. It was in this decade that Sierra Leone received its reputation as the "white man's grave" *par excellence.*[4] The high mortality among new arrivals continued. It seemed, indeed, to be worse than ever, and there were political reasons for giving the facts full publicity. The opponents of Sierra Leone could and did point out that all of the full Governors of the colony between 1810 and 1830, with the single exception of Col. C. W. Maxwell, died either in Africa or on the way home. But the full force of gubernational mortality was not felt until after 1827. The entire period, 1816-1824, was taken up with the long Governorship of Sir Charles MacCarthy, and he was finally killed by the Ashanti, not by the "climate." Between 1826 and 1830, however, precisely when the future strategy for West Africa was under discussion in the press and Parliament, MacCarthy's three successors died in three successive years—Charles Turner in 1826, Sir Neil Campbell in 1827, and Lt. Col. Dixon Denham in 1828. During these years the image of the "white man's grave" was set in the public mind.[5]

It was supported by abundant statistical evidence furnished by the investigation of Commissioners Wellington and Rowan, sent out in 1826. They looked into the mortality figures reaching back to the foundation of Sierra Leone, and they circulated a questionnaire to the medical officers then on duty. The answers were universally unfavorable, and the Commissioners' conclusions were even more damaging. They called attention for the first time to the apparent death rates for Sierra Leone Negroes. These figures had been largely ignored, even though the published data showed an initial death rate of 39 per cent for the "black poor" who settled the Province of Freedom, and at least 17 per cent for the Nova Scotian settlers at Sierra Leone a few years later. The Commissioners' new data showed that the Nova Scotians and their descendants had continued to de-

4. To my knowledge, the earliest use of the phrase in print occurs in J. C. de Figaniere e Morao, *Descripçao de Serra Leon* (Lisboa, 1822), p. 38, where he refers to the colony as the "sepulcro dos Europêos." (C. Fyfe, *A History of Sierra Leone* [London, 1962], p. 151.)

5. See, for example, *John Bull,* 22 April and 30 April 1827 and 30 August 1829; *The Times,* 17 November 1827; Joseph Hume, Commons, 15 June 1830, 2 H 25, cc. 394-99; *Quarterly Review.* XXXIX. 180-83 (January, 1829).

cline in numbers ever since, dropping from 1,131 in 1792, to 722 in 1822, and 578 in 1826. Even the Maroon population had declined for a time before it began slowly to rise again. Over the whole period from 1787 to 1826, some 22,000 non-European settlers had entered the colony, but the population in 1826 was only 13,000.

The Commissioners drew no explicit medical conclusion from these data, but a conclusion was clearly implied. Sierra Leone was not simply the white man's grave. It was everyman's grave. In fact, the high mortality of the "black poor" is explicable enough. Though Negro in race, they had been absent from regions of endemic malaria for decades or generations. Their mortality in Sierra Leone was therefore within the range that might have been expected for European settlers. Roughly the same pattern would be expected of the Nova Scotians, and even the Maroons from Jamaica had not known hyperendemic *falciparum* malaria before. By far the largest number of settlers in Sierra Leone by 1826, however, were "liberated Africans" and the sharp decrease in their numbers cannot be explained on medical grounds. In this case, the Commissioners apparently made a mistake. There is known to have been a considerable emigration from Sierra Leone into the hinterland, partly for trade and partly by the return of some "liberated Africans" to homes not far away. The Commissioners made no allowance for this.[6]

In other respects as well, they tried to undermine the props that had shored up optimism about the West African "climate." They held, as Lind had done, that mortality was not accountable to the "misconduct" of individuals. Nor was there any evidence that one part of the Coast was more healthy than another. In the long run, it was all unhealthy, though mortality varied in the short run with the appearance of epidemics. They could find no evidence that either clearing, cultivation, or sanitary regulations brought an improvement. In all these matters they were correct. It was a thoroughly damning report, and a thoroughly realistic one.[7] The only remaining cause for hope was the prospect of a better "climate" in the interior, and on this point there was still insufficient evidence. The later 1820's and early 1830's thus marked the nadir of pessimism about the Afri-

6. R. R. Kuczynski, *Demographic Survey of the British Colonial Empire, Volume I: West Africa* (London, 1948), p. 71.

7. Report of Commissioners, PP, 1826–1827, vii (312), pp. 12–13, 20, and 104–9. For answers to medical questionnaire see PP, 1830, xxi (57), pp. 63 ff.

can "climate" and the possibility of European activity on the Guinea coast.

It is not easy to explain, for this period or any other, why so many Europeans were willing to go to West Africa in the face of the known facts about the "climate." The dreams of untold wealth or the special religious zeal of the missionaries must be counted as part of the answer. And again, most Europeans who went to West Africa before 1830 did not, in fact, go voluntarily. The European soldiers of the Royal African Corps were recruited by allowing them to serve on the Coast in commutation of punishment in Britain.[8] The others, the voluntary travellers with no intention either to save souls or grow rich, seem to have been sustained by a strain of personal optimism. For the veterans, optimism was natural, once they themselves had safely passed the seasoning sickness. Those with most experience in Africa were often the most optimistic. Mungo Park, after losing more than three-quarters of his men on the overland stage of his last expedition, still wrote back that health conditions had not been so bad. He thought he could do it again with a loss of only 6 or 8 per cent, if only he had chosen the right season for the march.[9] Almost any explanation was more satisfying than the truth— that virtually everyone would come down with "fever," many would die, and there was no real hope (with the knowledge then available) of controlling the random selection of victims.

Planners in Britain had a further cause for optimism in the progress of science and technology. Faith in medical science was misplaced in the short run, as mortality rates showed, but European medicine was moving in new directions. Even though the germ theory of disease and the cellular structure of the body were still unknown, the rationalism of the Enlightenment came belatedly into medicine toward the end of the eighteenth century. The general systems of one-cause pathology decayed slowly. There was a new trend toward more accurate clinical observation and more extensive autopsy. These changes in turn were associated with the broader social and economic development of Western Europe. The Industrial Revolution brought rapid urbanization and with it the development of hospitals, where many of the uprooted came for their final medical

8. PP, 1830, xxi (57), p. 49.
9. Mungo Park, *The Journal of a Mission to the Interior of Africa in 1805*, 2nd ed. (London, 1815), II, 190.

treatment and ultimate dissection. The new era of hospital practice made possible mass clinical observation far beyond the range of doctors who merely worked at the bedside of individual patients.[10]

During the Napoleonic Wars, doctors accustomed to hospital work went to the tropics with the armies, and the new generation of military doctors took with them the new precision, the new techniques, and a knowledge of new work in the basic sciences. Priestley and Lavoisier had opened an interest in the chemistry of respiration, with obvious implications for the study of the tropical fevers "known" to be caused by the miasma in tropical air. Closer analysis and speculation about the nature and cause of miasma was one opening for further investigation. Mass clinical observation of various remedies was another.

Very little of the new work, however, was done in West Africa. Britain's medical concern went where the troops went, in this period to either India—to the West to protect the valuable remnant of an old empire, or to the East to create a new one. The only new and substantial West African medical reports came from Sierra Leone; and the best of them came during the Sierra Leone Company's early years, when the company still hoped to use their colony as a base for scientific investigation. Their physician in the 1790's was Thomas Winterbottom, whose *Account of the Native Africans in the Neighbourhood of Sierra Leone* became the pioneer work in African medical ethnography. The whole of the second volume was a study of tropical medicine based on his practice in the colony, and it included a detailed account of the medical practices of the Africans themselves. It was patterned on the work of Benjamin Rush with the North American Indians and based on the assumption that European medical men might learn something of value from the Africans. This enquiring spirit, however, was closer to that of the "enlightened travellers" of the eighteenth century than to the more self-confident attitude that followed the Napoleonic Wars.[11]

Other medical investigations were more narrowly concerned with the problem of European survival. One possible line of inquiry fol-

10. E. H. Acherknecht, *A Short History of Medicine* (New York, 1955), p. 134. R. H. Shryock, "Nineteenth Century Medicine: Scientific Aspects," *Journal of World History*, III, 881–908 (1957).

11. T. Winterbottom, *An Account of the Native Africans in the Neighborhood of Sierra Leone,* 2 vols. (London, 1803), II, esp. 1–4.

lowed the tradition of Lind's detailed assessment of West African geography and its possible medical implications, the object being to select the most healthy places for European posts or settlements. By the early nineteenth century, "medical topography" was recognized as a special department of medical science. One of the early works in their field was presented as a thesis to the Faculty of Medicine in Paris by Charles Stormont, a Scot who had been in Sierra Leone.[12] It described the general topography of West Africa, with information on meteorology, epidemiology, and estimates or statistics of the incidence of disease.

By the 1820's, medical topography was a regular feature in the official reports from the Coast, notably that of Commissioners Wellington and Rowan. If the investigators were not themselves medical men, they could still depend (as Wellington and Rowan did) on the evidence of medical practitioners already established in the settlements. But in the 1820's the West Coast of Africa was not the kind of place to attract original investigators. Most of the medical men there were merely the ordinary run of army doctors, and West African medicine tended to follow the lead of tropical medicine elsewhere.

Tropical fevers, still undifferentiated with any precision, remained the key problem of tropical medicine, and the principal medical controversy of the period involved the continuing uncertainty of classification and diagnosis. It began with the epidemic spread of yellow fever from Africa to the West Indies to North America. In 1793, a disease now recognized as yellow fever appeared as an epidemic in Grenada. Dr. Colin Chisholm, a surgeon of His Majesty's Ordnance, quickly identified it as distinct from the ordinary fevers of the country. He then developed the hypothesis that it came to Grenada from West Africa in a ship carrying refugee settlers from Bulama Island. For scientific purposes, he identified it as "malignant pestilential fever," but the popular name "Bulam fever" followed from the supposed source and became one of the common terms for yellow fever during the next half century. The epidemic was so severe and spread so rapidly that every military doctor in the West Indies had the opportunity to see hundreds of cases. The same privilege was soon visited

12. Charles Stormont, *Essai sur la topographie médicale de la côte occidentale d'Afrique et particulièrement sur celle de la colonie de Sierra Leone* (Paris, 1822).

on the medical men of the North American coast, especially in Philadelphia.[13]

The result was a burst of medical interest in fevers, with a stream of articles and books, first from the West Indies, then from America, and finally in Britain as well. There, it developed into a fifty-year controversy, with ramifications far beyond the initial problem of correctly explaining a single epidemic. The original argument turned on the correct classification of "Bulam fever"—whether it was a separate disease or merely a more serious form of the ordinary fevers of the tropics. This was by no means the petty question it may appear. Chisholm claimed that "Bulam fever" was infectious, and its spread could be prevented by proper quarantine. He thus raised questions of public medical policy. William Pym took up the case for quarantine and fought for decades (though mainly without success) for the adoption of more stringent quarantine regulations in the military services.

The assumption of infection raised further medical problems involving the nature of disease itself and the transmission of disease from one individual to another. From this point, the quarrel could be further extended to the attack or defense of the systems of monistic pathology. Throughout, there were important implications for the treatment of "fevers." Chisholm defended his position with a two-volume study of yellow fever in 1801 and a later work in 1822, and others came to his support, at least in part.[14] Critics attacked from many different points of view, and initially they carried the day by sheer weight of numbers and reputation.[15] But even the immediate issue of classification was not settled, and the broader issues rising from the controversy were not to be settled for many decades.

13. Colin Chisholm, *An Essay on the Malignant Pestilential Fever introduced into the West Indian Islands from Boullam, on the Coast of Guinea* . . . (London, 1795).

14. C. Chisholm, *An Essay on Malignant Pestilential Fever* . . . , 2 vols. (London, 1801); C. Chisholm, *Manual of the Climate and Diseases of Tropical Countries* (London, 1822); William Pym, *Observations upon Bulam Fever* . . . (London, 1815); Nodes Dickinson, *Observations on the Inflammatory Endemic, Incidental to Strangers in the West Indies from Temperate Climates, Commonly Called Yellow Fever* . . . (London, 1819), pp. 1–9.

15. T. Trotter, *Medica Nautica*, 3 vols. (London, 1797–1803). I, 325–32; Henry Clutterbuck, *An Inquiry into the Seat and Nature of Fever* (London, 1807); E. N. Bancroft, *An Essay on the Disease called Yellow Fever* (London, 1811); E. N. Bancroft, *A Sequel to an Essay on Yellow Fever* (London, 1817); W. Ferguson, "On the Nature and History of Marsh Poison," *Transactions of the Royal Society of Edinburgh*, IX, 273–98 (1823), esp. pp. 294–95; E. Doughty, *Observations and Inquiries into the Nature of Yellow Fever* . . . (London, 1816), esp. pp. 1–9.

Meanwhile, medical men practicing in West Africa could follow any one of three different schools of thought about classification. They could have "Bulam Fever" as a separate and infectious disease. They could consider it as merely one of the many varieties of "endemic ardent" or "yellow fever" (in both cases meaning malaria) of the tropics. Or else, they could use a geographical classification, which named each variety of "fever" according to the part of the world where it was prevalent. By this system, neat distinctions were possible between Coimbatore Fever, Guzzerata Fever, Seringapatam Fever, and Coromandel Fever, without even leaving India.[16] In practice, West African practitioners were not so concerned about terminology as the medical writers at home. They continued to treat remittents, intermittents, and an occasional case of "yellow fever," which might or might not be the disease now called by that name.

Gradually, however, yellow fever was recognized as a separate entity, if only when it took an epidemic form, and there was some clearing of the air as medical men attempted to be more precise. The effort to achieve a new level of precision was especially marked in the new analysis of the cause of fevers. The yellow fever controversy raised new hypotheses, and Chisholm himself made a distinction between two sources of infections: Bulam fever was caused by infectious *effluvia* thrown off by persons already infected, while the *miasmata* of swamps was the cause of all other tropical fevers.

The connection between the type of miasma and the type of disease could be carried further still. Dickinson, for example, took the position that *both* human effluvia and marsh miasmata were the causes of ordinary tropical fevers (in short, malaria), while yellow fever was caused solely by *change* of climate aggravated by drunkenness and overeating.[17] Johnson also accepted human effluvia as a cause of fevers and argued further that the type of effluvia inhaled by the victim controlled the symptoms of the fever that would follow. Thus, the effluvia of a typhus victim would produce typhus, while the effluvia of a malaria victim would produce malaria.[18] In trying to establish a mode of transmission from one fever victim to the next, these men were more nearly correct than the majority of their colleagues, though

16. James Johnson, *The Influence of Tropical Climates on European Constitutions,* 2 vols. (Philadelphia, 1821), I, 67. First published London, 1813.

17. Dickinson, *Observations,* pp. 7–8.

18. Doughty, *Observations,* pp. vi–vii; Johnson, *Tropical Climates,* I, 32–38. See also Bancroft, *Essay on Yellow Fever,* pp. 156–97.

they took as their starting point the older belief that fevers must be transmitted by some quality of the air.

Most authorities never departed from the theory of gaseous transmission, nor from the association of tropical fevers with the miasmata of marshes or swamps. Popular opinion still held with the traditional connection between fevers and dampness, and especially between fever and tropical rain or dew, and it was supported by ancient folk fears and aversions. After all, reptiles and insects flourished during the rains. The rains produced mold and mildew, and a "foetid and disgusting odour" escaped from the ground during the rainy season. Thomas Winterbottom tried to defend the rains as harmless in themselves, but by the 1820's the residents in Sierra Leone blamed the rains and not the marshes for their fevers.[19]

Advanced medical opinion in Britain kept the fear of marshes and tried to work toward a more precise chemical definition of the harmful gas. The phlogiston theory was now dead, while a new theory suggested that a combination of nitrogen and oxygen might be at fault. Others suspected "azotic gases." Chisholm thought it was more likely to be "hydrogenous gas, or a combination of hydrogenous gas and carbonic acid." Thus, one tendency was to define and isolate the offending gas, but other authorities still held with a broader spectrum of gasses, merely relabeling it "vegeto-animal effluvium" for the sake of greater scientific precision.[20]

The most careful study of the empirical evidence came from William Ferguson, who reached a verdict widely accepted as authoritative. According to him, marsh poison was neither vegetable nor "aqueous putrefaction." Nor was it necessarily always to be found associated with marshes. It must therefore be connected in some way with the drying process. There was evidence for this view in the presence of fevers along the margins of swamps, or along drying water courses. Large bodies of water were not only safe; they seemed to have the capacity to absorb miasma passing over them. Ferguson's studies also showed some of the other characteristics of the dangerous gas. It

<hr>

19. Winterbottom, *Native Africans*, I, 37–39. See also Stormont, *Topographie médicale*, pp. 38–47.

20. See C. Chisholm, *Malignant Fever* (1801), I, 270–81; Johnson, *Tropical Climates*, I, 39; John MacCulloch, *Malaria: An Essay on the Production and Propagation of this Poison* . . . (Philadelphia, 1829), pp. 21–77. First published London, 1827.

was heavier than air and tended to creep along the ground. It gathered strength during the night and was dissipated somewhat by the strength of the sun. The only real preventive was the cultivation of the land, which allows the pestilential gases to escape from the earth and thus exhausts its "morbific principle by a constant succession of crops."[21]

Ferguson's study was, in many ways, an accurate piece of pure empiricism. It took account of the behavior of many varieties of mosquitos, without being aware that mosquitos were being described. In other hands, similar views could be developed more fully. John MacCulloch carried this trend to its logical conclusion. He imported the term "malaria" from Italian—not as a name for the disease, but for the poison that causes many diseases in both tropical and temparate regions. For him, it was the danger above all others: "This is the Destroying Angel, the real pestilence which walks at noon day; and to which all the other causes of mortality are but as feeble auxiliaries in the work of destruction. This is Malaria, the neglected subject to which I am desirous of calling attention, that, by this, its powers may be diminished. . . ."[22]

Before he finished, MacCulloch had arrived at something approaching a whole system of pathology based on his malarial gas. He was not universally followed, but he helped lead other investigators into a fruitless *cul de sac*.

By the 1820's, there was a broad measure of agreement among medical men on the Coast. They were now convinced that fevers were caused by a noxious gas, originating from the decay of animal or vegetable matter and not simply from the proximity of marshes.[23] Like Ferguson's work, the new view represented a kind of progress. It accounted for the empirical data with greater care and precision than ever before, going as far as men could go without shifting completely from a gas theory to a mosquito theory. (There were, indeed, occasional hints to suggest a mosquito theory, but they were only hints. Winterbottom, for example, coupled the fact that African villages in the bush were both mosquito-infested and unhealthy. There were other suggestions that the ova of insects found in low

21. Ferguson, "Marsh Poison," pp. 273–94.
22. MacCulloch, *Malaria*, p. 8.
23. See answers to the Commissioners' Questionnaire, PP, 1830, xxi (57), pp. 63 ff.

or swampy ground might be a cause of fevers.[24] Such hints were not
yet enough to distract men from the apparently overwhelming evidence in favor of a miasma theory.)

Most of the suggested public health measures followed the miasma
theory, combined with some of the apparent lessons of broadening
experience. The Sierra Leone Company, for example, thought they
had discovered a panacea in the nature of food and shelter provided
for Europeans in the colony. They were struck by the fact that the
death rate of their "Upper Servants" had dropped by 1802 to only
about twenty to forty per thousand per annum. At the same time,
that of the "lower orders" remained shockingly high. The upper
servants were better fed and better housed, while the lower orders
were less well cared for. They were also less often imbued with the
religious zeal of the Evangelical officials in the colony. Hence they
were more given to drunkenness and fornication, and these sins received increasing emphasis as "predisposing causes" of fever, in step
with the growth of Evangelical piety in Britain.[25] The Company's reaction was to dispense with the services of subordinate officials, who
could be neither properly controlled nor cared for. The early possibility that Europeans might be settled in the colony was quietly

24. Winterbottom. *Native Africans*. I, 79–80; Edward Griffith and others, "Supplemental History of Man," in G. Cuvier, *The Animal Kingdom*, 16 vols. (London,
1827–1835), I, 137.

25. PP, 1803–1804, v (24), 23–24. The Parliamentary Committee on Sierra Leone
accepted the Company's explanation. (Report of the Committee, PP, 1803–1804, v
(24), p. 6.) In fact. the Company's claim of 20 to 40 per thousand per annum as a
death rate for their "Upper Servants" would have been very low and seems to indicate that they were nearly all "acclimatized" by this time. though the numbers involved were too small to have much statistical validity. Other evidence, however,
indicates a more general pattern of lower death rates in West Africa for the higher
officials than for those in subordinate posts or for soldiers. A statistical survey of all
forces stationed in West Africa between 1819 and 1836, for example. showed a death
rate of only 209 per thousand mean strength among the officers, as against 483 per
thousand for other ranks. (PP, 1840, xxx [C. 228], p. 24.) The most likely explanation of this pattern is the fact that "upper servants" and officers tended to acquire
an immunity, after which they could return for several tours of duty on the Coast,
whereas the artisan class or the common soldiers served their time and went home.
Thus William Dawes and Thomas Ludlam both served three terms as Governor of
Sierra Leone under the Company, and three other Governors served twice. Later on,
others, notably Sir Charles MacCarthy, served long terms under the Crown. These men
probably acquired at least a limited immunity against *falciparum* malaria, while many
others died within the first year. Among the very small group of European officials,
there were enough of these immune long-term residents and returnees to affect the
statistical mortality of the group as a whole. The very high death rate among the
European soldiers may also owe something to psychological depression in the face of
imminent death, to drink, and to the severity of military punishments.

dropped, and the only European settlers encouraged after the early 1790's were capitalists of means, who might establish plantations.[26] By contrast, the Bulama Island Association placed its faith in technology and spent a good deal of time and energy thinking up ways to prevent high mortality on a possible second venture. Wadström studied the problem of a pure water supply.[27] Philip Beaver thought the principal errors of his first attempt had been lack of shelter on arrival at the beginning of the rains. The obvious remedy was better timing and the preparation of prefabricated houses that could be erected immediately on landing.[28]

The suggestion was taken up by Anders Johansen, a Swede who worked as a publicist for the Bulama Association. He invented a tropical house for pioneering conditions and an improved type to be built once the settlement was established. The latter was a new design for tropical architecture, which took full account of medical theory. It was to be raised about ten feet off the ground on stilts, to avoid the noxious vapors arising from the ground. The exterior walls were protected from direct sunlight by a broad verandah on all sides, with further protection in the form of venetian blinds or awnings around the verandah. The house was further insulated by a double roof, with free circulation of air between the inner and outer shell. The interior was also air conditioned. A water-driven air pump maintained a constant circulation of air, which could be cooled by water, warmed by a fire, and kept insect free by smoke treatment, before it was led into the house through a system of ducts. Although the house was never built, it was a most ingenious attempt to bring technology to bear on the problems of tropical life. In both conception and detail it foreshadowed a great deal of modern tropical architecture.[29]

Later suggestions for public action to improve tropical health followed the rising concern about sanitation in Britain itself. Dr. Chisholm and his successors in the yellow fever controversy went beyond their key recommendation of quarantine. Chisholm proposed a whole sanitary code for West Indian towns, including compulsory building in brick and stone rather than wood, widening the streets, control of

26. Sierra Leone Company, *Report* (1791), 11; Sierra Leone Company, *Account of the Colony*, pp. 49–53; Statement of the Directors, PP, 1803–1804, v (24), pp. 23–24.
27. Wadström, *Colonization*, I, 28–31.
28. P. Beaver to Bulama Island Association, 24 June 1794, CO 267/10.
29. Andrew Johansen, *Description of Bulama Island* (London, 1794), p. 20; Wadström, *Colonization*, I, 49 and II, diagram, plate I.

privies and stables, butchershops and slaughterhouses. Dr. Sweeney, the Surgeon of the Forces at Cape Coast, recommended similar measures for West Africa and added some new ones. He wanted, among other things, to move the African town to a new site at some distance from the European fort— in short, the "sanitary segregation" that was to become a popular panacea in the early twentieth century. His other suggestions were to drain the surrounding country, improve the water supply to the forts, and clear the brush for some distance around the area where Europeans lived. Clearing the brush was, indeed, the most popular anti-fever measure of all.[30]

Little enough was done along any of the lines suggested, and the results were far from promising. Some authorities came to the conclusion that West Africa was hopeless and nothing could be done. Dr. William Barry, the principal medical officer in West Africa at the time of the 1826 investigation, held that no sanitary regulations or any other improvements could make an appreciable difference to the health of the troops, his principal concern.[31] The facts were on his side, but many authorities continued to hope, and they put their faith, where public measures either failed or were not attempted, in personal precautions to avoid the "predisposing causes" of fevers.

There was plenty of room here for personal action to forestall the influence of malarial poison. The very concept of "predisposing" causes left an opening for older ideas to live on in the face of the new developments in medical science. Humoral pathology in slightly changed forms reappeared in the work of James Johnson, perhaps the standard author on tropical medicine in this period. He held that perspiration was especially dangerous because of a sympathetic relation between certain organs of the body, or the "consent of parts." Thus, if the skin perspires, there will be a sympathetic reaction from the liver, which then increases the quantity of bilious secretion. In hot climates, this "cutaneo-hepatic sympathy" will bring on a chain of responses: heat leads to perspiration, leading to a degree of liver malfunction, weakening the body, and thus preparing the way for the

30. Charles Dunne to African Committee, 16 November 1811, T 70/35; G. A. Robertson, *Notes on Africa . . . with Hints for the Melioration of the Whole African Population* (London, 1819), p. 24; Sir N. Campbell, Memorandum on the Gold Coast, November 1826, SLA, Gold Coast Misc., 1826–1827; Chisholm, *Malignant Fever* (1795), pp. 204–10; M. Sweeney to James Rowan, 20 September 1826, PP, 1830, xxi (57), p. 88. See also Stormont, *Topographie médicale,* p. 68 for an anti-clearing opinion.

31. PP, 1826–1827, vii (312), p. 108.

Figure 1. Johansen's design for an air conditioned
tropical house, as modified by C. B. Wadström.

Explanation

a. The ground on which the House is to be erected & which ought to be
covered with a Coat of cement or mortar, to prevent the ascent of Vapours from
the Earth.

b. A small trench which may be made all round the House through which
water should be constantly running if the Situation admit of it, to prevent
Ants & other Insects from entering the House.

c. Pillars on which the dwelling House should be raised to a proper elevation above the ground in order to give a free circulation of Air underneath, to
carry off the Vapours. These pillars may be covered with bricks & plastered
if found necessary.

(continued on following page)

d. A Fire Urn or grate from which the Smoke rises through the opening in the top of the Roof.

e. The Roof also double, like the floor, in order to give a free circulation to the Air & render the roof, & consequently the room, cool.

f. The stairs to be wound up in order to render the house a place of defence, in case of necessity, particularly at night time.

g. Curtains to let down on the side the Sun enters, but moveable Venetian blinds are preferable.

h. A Gallery covered by the projecting roof of the House all round in order to keep off the Sunshine.

To Mr. Johansen's Invention I have added an apparatus which I have seen frequently used in Germany for blowing their furnaces in Situations where they have water-falls. But where that advantage is wanting, a sufficient quantity of water for cooling a House may be easily raised by a pump.

i. Is a Cistern from which the water falls through the pipe *k* full of holes by which the Air enters & is forced downwards by the violent discent [*sic*] of the water into the close barrel *l*. The water dashing on the basons *m* is broken into froth & falls into the lower part of the barrel *n*, whence it runs off by the hole *o* and may then supply the above mentioned trench *b*. The Air being disengaged from the broken Water & confined on all sides is driven into the pipe *p*, by which Mr. Johansen's pipe *q* under the earth is furnished with a constant stream of Air, which ascending through this pipe spreads itself into the air reservoir under the floor of the house & continues the ascent through the side pipes. The cool and purified Air thus delivered by these pipes, being specifically heavier than the Air in the room, descends toward the floor & takes the place of the rarefied Air which constantly ascends till it escapes by the opening in the top of the Roof.

onset of fever. But excessive perspiration was not alone among the predisposing causes. Johnson listed "plethora—inanition from excessive evacuations—depressing passions—excess, whether in eating, drinking, or gratification of the sensual passions—mental or corporeal exertions—extremes of atmospheric heat and cold, especially alternations of these or of heat and moisture—sollunal influences," and a few more.[32]

The recommended personal regimen therefore remained as diverse and as broad as it had been in the eighteenth century. The key was still "moderation, regularity, and temperance," and above all not living as the "natives" did. In detail, this normally meant the avoidance of alcoholic drink, sexual intercourse, and eating meat. These were, of course, nothing but the proscriptions of traditional Christian asceticism, and they underscore the continued half-conscious belief in a connection between morality and disease. The principal change was a gradual shift of emphasis. Joy and sorrow—and indeed all mental activity—were more frowned upon than they had been a few decades earlier. Light exercise tended to fall into disfavor, while bathing was now more often permissible. At the same time, the recommended clothing increased in quantity and weight. Cotton was less popular, while linen and especially flannel next to the skin was increasingly recommended. The popularity of flannel came partly from its ability to absorb dangerous perspiration, and partly from the belief that change of temperature rather than uncomfortable heat was the most serious danger.[33]

Other advice was more specific. The gauze net or *canopeum* now made its apperance, though not merely as a protection against mosquitos. The cloth was supposed to filter the dangerous effluvia, and it was recommended as a head net for naval crews sent ashore on the West African coast. Other prophylactic measures were connected with the old belief in artificial "acclimatization," to protect against the inevitable "seasoning sickness." Chisholm, for example, was convinced that tropical air contains more oxygen than temperate air—an old belief set in terms of the new chemistry—but the preventive measures were traditional. The newcomer, according to Chisholm, should have himself bled and purged when the ship crossed the Tropic of

32. Johnson, *Tropical Climates*, I, 32–33. See also I, 8–27.
33. For some representative advice, see Henry Meredith, *An Account of the Gold Coast of Africa . . .* (London, 1812), pp. 42–50; Johnson, *Tropical Climates*, II, 228–93; MacCulloch, *Malaria*, pp. 132–64.

Cancer, and again on arrival at his tropical destination. This prophylactic treatment could be topped off by a course of calomel,
tartarized antimony, and doses of sea water.[34]

The more valuable prophylactic use of chinchona bark retained
some popularity during the 1790's and then began to decline, though
it continued in the official practice of the Navy. The printed Instructions for Surgeons for 1814 and 1825 ordered ship's surgeons to give
chinchona to all men going ashore in the tropics, at the rate of "a
drachm of bark in half a gill of sound wine" both morning and
evening. They were, furthermore, to report the results to the Commissioners for Transports and Sick and Wounded Seamen.[35] Depend-
ing on the quality of the bark used, this treatment would have been
beneficial, but the instructions were not often followed in practice.
The men disliked the taste, and surgeons followed the medical
fashions which, after the 1790's, had gradually moved into an anti-
chinchona phase.[36]

The unpopularity of chinchona came from several sources. The best
of the barks, and after the 1790's this meant *Chinchona succirubra*
or "Red Bark" from Ecuador, might contain up to 4 per cent by
weight of the anti-malarial alkaloids. But other barks that looked
very much the same also found their way into the British market in
the early nineteenth century, and they sometimes contained no alkaloids at all. Even an occasional shipment of *C. succirubra* which had
been poorly preserved might be free of anti-malarial qualities.[37] There
was thus room for pharmaceutical error, and there was room for
error in diagnosis. Dr. Wade in Bengal had tried bark extensively on
his patients, and he published the finding that it was not only useless
for the treatment of fevers but could in some cases be an active
poison. Chisholm in the West Indies and others in North America
during the yellow fever epidemics of 1793–94 also reported that the
drug was useless—as it surely was for the treatment of yellow fever.[38]

Chinchona thus became involved in the yellow fever controversy.
Chisholm, who distinguished yellow fever from other fevers, recom-

34. MacCulloch, *Malaria*, p. 138; Chisholm, *Malignant Fever* (1801), II, 56–57;
Trotter, *Medica Nautica*, I, 339–40.
35. *Instructions for Surgeons of the Royal Navy* ([London], 1814), pp. 13–14.
36. A. Bryson, "Prophylactic Influence of Quinine," *Medical Times and Gazette,*
VII (n.s.), 6–7 (7 January 1854).
37. J. E. Howard, *Illustrations of the Nueva Quinologia of Pavon* (London,
1862), esp. p. 15 on *Chinchona succirubra.*
38. Chisholm, *Malignant Fever* (1801), I, 364–68.

mended mercury treatments with calomel as far preferable to chinchona. Those who made no such distinction took up mercury for all
tropical fevers, and calomel gradually came into more common use
—and in larger doses.[39] The authority of James Johnson was soon
added to the anti-chinchona school, with a special emphasis on bleeding as the best alternative. As he put it, "In these scrutinising days
of investigation and experiment, the lancet has dispelled the mists
of prejudice, the phantoms of debility and putrescency, with the de-
lusions of the Brunonian school; and bleeding is justly regarded as
the paramount remedy. . . ."[40]

As it happened, the two treatments combined in a new phase of
popularity for heroic doses of calomel, heroic bleeding, and a combination of other minor remedies which might include blisters, and
perhaps chinchona bark at the later stages of the disease as a "tonic."
Some carried the new fashion to extremes. Doughty recommended
taking as much as two pounds (or about thirty-two ounces) of blood
the minute a patient appeared to suffer from fever, following this
with mercury treatments. Others took from twenty to fifty ounces of
blood at the first sign of disease, and still more later on. Blisters were
applied to the head, the nape of the neck, and the stomach, theoretically in order to relieve the pressure of blood on the internal organs.
Blue ointment, a mercurial preparation, was occasionally rubbed into
the skin of the arms and legs and applied to the blistered sores in
order to increase the intake of mercury. In the last stages of illness,
blisters were sometimes applied to the extremities in order to arouse
the patient to life. Most painful of all was the night-cap blister, which
covered the whole head.[41]

There is every reason to believe that these new forms of treatment
were positively harmful, aside from the unnecessary pain caused by
the blisters. Sixteen to twenty ounces of blood is the amount normally
taken from the donor for a blood transfusion. It would certainly
cause no harm to a healthy individual. To take 100 ounces, as was
often done, meant taking half of the blood in the body, and it would
certainly have caused some harm, even to a healthy individual. As
little as twenty to fifty ounces, taken from a patient with malaria,

39. Chisholm, *Malignant Fever* (1801), I, 418–519; Clutterbuck, *Inquiry,* 404–5,
40. Johnson, *Tropical Climates,* I, 53.
41. Doughty, *Observations,* pp. 11–12; Dickinson, *Observations,* pp. 121–68;
A. Bryson, *Report on the Climate and Principal Diseases of the African Station* (London, 1847), pp. 243–44 and 246–47.

could be very serious. Anemia normally accompanies malaria, and any victim needs all the blood he has.

The mercury treatments would have had a similar result. Malaria is seriously dehydrating. Calomel is a strong purgative, causing still more dehydration. But the dosage of the early nineteenth century was not merely enough to purge the intestinal tract. The intention was to produce a profuse salivation, since it was observed that a patient who salivated after mercury treatment usually lived. In this case, the doctors mistook the sign of recovery for the cause of recovery. They tended to load the patient with more and more calomel until he either died or recovered. At times the dosage went as high as fifty to sixty grains a day for four or five days, in some instances exceeding a total of 500 grains.[42]

These two treatments in combination, or either one of them in its more extreme form, would certainly have been enough to kill a malaria victim already on the borderline between life and death. It can be assumed, therefore, that they had some influence, and probably a significant influence, on the high death rates of the 1820's. The inference is further strengthened by the fact that the mercury-bleeding combination reached a peak of acceptance in the 1820's, precisely the decade when the qualitative impression of West Africa as the "white man's grave" reached its peak. In spite of the progress of European medicine generally, the trend in tropical medicine, as it was practiced on the West Coast of Africa, was clearly one of declining efficiency.

But even in its worst decade there were some signs of change. Chinchona began to come slowly back into favor, especially in the later 1820's, building up its reputation from its continued use as tonic in the latter stages of a fever. As early as 1822, Chisholm himself was advising chinchona bark as a prophylactic, but only against further attacks of fever once recovery had begun.[43] More important still, in 1820 Pelletier and Caventou in France isolated two alkaloids of the chinchona bark, and the sulfate of one of these, quinine, gradually came into pharmaceutical use. During the 1820's the price was still prohibitive for ordinary use as a superior substitute for raw bark, but the Clapperton-Oudney-Denham expedition of 1821–25 and Clapperton's later expedition with Lander were both supplied with quinine, though in quantities too small to be used

42. Bryson, *Principal Diseases*, pp. 240–44.
43. Chisholm, *Manual*, p. 52.

prophylactically. By 1826 a few of the doctors in West Africa were experimenting with the new drug and reporting excellent results, even though they were still using it in conjunction with bleeding, blisters, calomel, and even ordinary chinchona bark.[44] The way was at last prepared, though the reformed treatment of fever would not be the standard procedure for another quarter century.

Compared with their overwhelming interest in tropical fevers, medical men had relatively little time for writing or research about other tropical diseases. Dysentery was simply the "fluxes" and was treated in the same way it was treated in temperate climates. Medical men on the Coast were not concerned in most cases with the treatment of Africans. They therefore paid little attention to Guinea worm, leprosy, elephantiasis, yaws, and the other diseases that seemed more serious for the African population than for the intrusive Europeans. Investigation of these diseases was more often left to the plantation surgeons of the West Indies.

Only Thomas Winterbottom reported extensively on the treatment of Africans in West Africa. He was particularly interested in yaws, which he correctly believed to be infectious and transmitted by contact. He was also correct in stating that Guinea worm is not caused (as many then believed) by impure water, but by "animalcules" which enter the body through the skin. In other respects as well, his work on minor tropical diseases was far ahead of his time. He pointed out, for example, that there was no such thing as sun stroke in Sierra Leone, either among Africans or Europeans. Europeans in the tropics, however, continued to have "sun stroke" for the next century and a half, and as recently as 1958 the British Medical Council was still trying to abolish the term from the classification of heat illness.[45]

44. E. H. Acherknecht, *Malaria in the Upper Mississippi Valley, 1760–1900* (Baltimore, 1945), pp. 101–4; A. A. Boahen, "British Penetration of North-West Africa and the Western Sudan, 1788–1861" (Unpublished Ph.D. thesis, London, 1959), p. 252; R. L. Lander, *Records of Captain Clapperton's Last Expedition to Africa . . . With Subsequent Adventures of the Author*, 2 vols. (London, 1830), II, 333–37; Dr. Sweeney to James Rowan, 20 September 1826, PP, 1830, xxi (57), pp. 87–88; Dr. Alexander Stewart to Commissioners, 4 November 1826, PP, 1830, xxi (57), p. 58.

45. Winterbottom, *Native Africans*, II, esp. 38–40; *The Times*, 5 September 1958. Most of the reported cases of "sun stroke" were in fact cerebral malaria. See S. F. Dudley, "Yellow Fever as seen by the Medical Officers of the Royal Navy in the Nineteenth Century," *Proceedings of the Royal Society of Medicine*, XXVI, 443–56 (1932), p. 443.

Whether or not medical practice was successful in solving the problem of survival, the evidence of medical men impinged on policy decisions at many points around the periphery of medical thought. One point of constant interaction between tropical medicine and tropical policy was the old rivalry between West Africa and the West Indies. Whatever the facts of European mortality in West Africa—and they were bad enough—the West India interest was anxious to show the West African "climate" in the worst possible light. They felt threatened by the possibility of West African production of tropical staples. The humanitarians, their chief political opponents in Britain, were identified with the settlement at Sierra Leone, and therefore that colony became a prime target.

From the 1790's onward, almost any medical writing about West Africa had some political overtones. Chisholm was not merely a scientist. He used his work on "Bulam fever" to damn the African coast as its source, and along with it the humanitarians and all of their works. Both the lay defenders of the "Saints" and some medical journals took up the other side of the case. Dr. Elihu Hubbard Smith of New York attacked Chisholm in a scientific journal, claiming that he had invented "Bulam fever" in order to cast aspersions on West African colonization. Thus the yellow fever controversy was a trans-Atlantic political issue from the beginning.[46]

Much of the later publicity given to European mortality in Sierra Leone was politically inspired, though the facts themselves were mainly true. The many articles and pamphlets of James MacQueen, the newspaper *John Bull*,[47] and other anti-humanitarian organs carried a running campaign during the 1820's, which linked the bad "climate" of Sierra Leone and the defense of West Indian slavery. *The Times* joined in and roundly condemned Bathurst for yielding to "the mixture of quackery and hypocrisy which has instigated a certain class of people in this country to press upon the Government the retention of a costly grave for British subjects, by nicknaming it a school for the civilization of negroes." Their solution was to give up all West African settlements and concentrate on more hopeful areas.[48]

In the face of this kind of attack, even before the Wellington and

46. See Chisholm, *Malignant Fever* (1801), I, xv–xvi and 98–102.
47. See, for example, leaders of 15 August 1824 and 30 August 1829.
48. *The Times,* 17 and 21 November 1827.

Rowan report, the humanitarians and the pro-West African faction
were thrown on the defensive. It was impossible to deny the facts of
European mortality, and it was difficult to advocate further African
activity in the face of these facts. But there was one possible way out.
It was an ancient and universally accepted belief that Negroes were
immune to the "climate," even though white men died. Medical
opinion of the 1820's still sustained this conclusion in spite of Wellington and Rowan's suggestion to the contrary.[49] The obvious solution had been advocated long ago by Lind—that is, to staff the West
African posts with Westernized Africans. As early as 1823 the possibility of using Africans as missionaries was seriously considered by
the Church Missionary Society. After 1825, the idea of using African
personnel in government posts was widely discussed.[50]

The line of government strategic decisions from 1826 to 1830 was
mainly a surrender in the face of the African "climate." Sierra
Leone's reputation was given a final turn downward in 1829 by the
appearance of a disastrous yellow fever epidemic, which came just
in time to influence the Parliamentary Committee of 1830. There
would be no extension of the British sphere of interest in West
Africa. It would, indeed, contract within the limits of irreducible
commitments to the anti-slavery blockade and to those people already settled in Sierra Leone through British agency. But as it withdrew, the government accepted the outlines of a policy of Africanization. Sir George Murray announced that in future all official posts
would (as far as possible) be filled by people of color, either native
Africans or men born in the West Indies, and this policy was to be
followed until all positions were filled by men of African descent.[51]
The decision grew mainly from the medical failure, but it also drew
its detail from several decades of stategic thought and exploration;
and it rested on some further basic assumptions about culture, race,
and the process of culture change.

49. Chisholm, *Malignant Fever* (1801), I, 141–42; Winterbottom, *Native Africans,*
I, 65 and II, 13, 22–23; Johnson, *Tropical Climates,* I, 2–4; Doughty, *Observations,*
p. 50; Dickinson, *Observations,* pp. 12–13. Ferguson, "Marsh Poison," pp. 297–98.
50. E. Stock, *A History of the Church Missionary Society,* 4 vols. (London, 1899–
1917), I, 244.
51. Report of the Select Committee on Sierra Leone and Fernando Po, PP, 1830,
x (661), p. 3; Sir George Murray, Commons, 15 June 1830, 2 H 25, cc. 402–5.

8

TOWNS

AND ELEPHANTS

... Geographers in Afric-Maps
With Savage-Pictures fill their Gaps,
And o'er inhabitable Downs
Place Elephants for want of Towns.
—Swift, *On Poetry*

It is almost an accepted conven-
tion that no book shall deal with African exploration without some
reference to Swift's famous lines on cartography. Geographers of the
early nineteenth century began the wholesale replacement of elephants
with towns, at least in West Africa. The increase in geographical
knowledge between 1790 and 1830 was greater than that of any
comparable period. Explorers followed virtually the whole course of
the Niger. They crossed West Africa from the Guinea Coast to the
Maghrib. The major cities were either visited or known by hearsay
and their positions were plotted with tolerable accuracy. Chains of
mountains, the important drainage, the principal political units—all
these were located and described in outline. New maps had every
right to the towns, but geographers might well have left a liberal
sprinkling of elephants, symbolically representing certain remaining
areas of ignorance and misunderstanding, especially in the field of
ethnography. In cartography and political geography, the work of
scholars in Britain was closely integrated with that of travellers on
the spot. Many of the explorers were tough, practical men without a

broad general education; but they were well briefed in the existing
state of geographical knowledge, and they knew precisely what data
was needed to fill out the picture. The educated public also followed
the course of geographical scholarship. The unknown heart of the
African continent captured the imagination, and works of geographical synthesis were widely read along with the accounts of the explorers. In scholarly circles, new information was rapidly rechecked
and fitted into the existing pattern of knowledge.

This geographical tradition was organized and reinforced after
1788 by the work of the African Association and the scholarship of
James Rennell, who followed his initial reports for the Association
with *Elucidations of African Geography* in 1793. Using this work as
a base, Rennell continued with a series of commentaries on the new
explorations. By the end of the century his scholarly prestige stood
so high that Mungo Park deferred to Rennell's view on the Niger
problem, even though it differed from his own.[1]

Paul Jacob Bruns in Germany meanwhile published an even more
detailed and systematic treatment of the whole continent in six volumes, of which one and one-half were devoted to West Africa.[2]
Bruns's synthesis in time replaced Rennell's as the most authoritative
work on African geography; but it reached British readers at second
hand, and Rennell remained the geographer with the greatest popular
reputation.

The scholarly syntheses were, in any case, received as mere hypotheses to be checked and amplified on the basis of new information, and
new data was by no means limited to the work of the more spectacular exploring expeditions. It was now more frequently sought from
people already in Africa. Rennell's map, for example, was checked
with the cooperation of the Secretary of State for Colonies, who
passed a dozen copies to the African Committee for distribution to
officials of the African posts. They were asked both for their criti-
cisms of the map and for answers to a geographical questionnaire.[3]

1. J. Rennell, "Geographical Illustrations of Mr. Park's Journey," in M. Park, *Travels in the Interior Districts of Africa*, 2nd ed., 2 vols. (London, 1799), II, iii-xcii; "Account of the Life of Mungo Park," in M. Park, *The Journal of a Mission to the Interior of Africa in 1805*, 2nd ed. (London, 1815), pp. 46-51.

2. P. J. Bruns, *Neue systematische Erdbeschreibung von Africa*, 6 vols. (Nuremberg, 1793-1799).

3. Minutes of the African Committee, 12 November 1802, in J. J. Crooks (ed.), *Records Relating to the Gold Coast Settlements from 1750 to 1874* (Dublin, 1923), p. 99.

Information about coastal waters increased constantly, in spite of a decline of trade after 1807. The technology of seafaring was itself improving, and the Navy had its own need of charts for the anti-slavery patrols. A new *African Pilot* with a set of 24 sheets of charts and a book of sailing directions appeared in 1807 to replace the standard *English Pilot* which had served throughout the eighteenth century. In 1819 it was supplemented by Lt. Edward Bold's *Merchants' and Mariners' African Guide,* which dealt with both navigation and commerce. The commercial side was carried further still by Captain Adams's *Remarks on the Country Extending from Cape Palmas to the River Congo,* containing a manual of mercantile practice with full information on systems of currency, prices, and the goods in greatest demand on each section of the coast.[4]

During the 1820's the Admiralty began to sponsor coastal surveys to correct the charts of certain regions, such as the Windward Coast and the navigable course of the Gambia. The French, however, were first in the field with an official pilot guide, covering the whole coast from Cape Bojador to the vicinity of the modern city of Conakry. It was immediately translated into English; but British publications of this kind were left to private enterprise until 1856, when the Hydrographic Office published the first volume of the official *African Pilot,* from the Straits of Gibraltar to the Cameroons.[5]

Hearsay information about the interior was also gathered and collated with increasing care. Rennell received and used reports from British Consuls in the Maghrib. Travellers in Morocco, like J. G. Jackson, were increasingly careful to record what they might hear of the far side of the desert.[6] From time to time, a North African traveller to the Sudan might even appear in England. One such, known to the English as "El Hage Abd Shabeeny" of Tetuan, had spent twelve

4. *Laurie and Whittle's New Sailing Directions for the Coasts of Africa, from Cape Spartel to the Cape of Good-Hope* . . . (London, 1807), published to accompany the charts of the *African Pilot;* E. Bold, *The Merchant's and Mariners' African Guide* (London, 1819); John Adams, *Remarks on the Country Extending from Cape Palmas to the River Congo* (London, 1823), pp. 223–65.

5. Great Britain, Hydrographic Office, *The African Pilot, or Sailing Directions for the Western Coast of Africa. Part I Cape Spartel to the River Cameroons* (London, 1856); W. F. Owen, *Narrative of Voyages to Explore the Shores of Africa, Arabia, and Madagascar* . . . , 2 vols.(London, 1833): T. Boteler, *The West Coast of Africa, from the Isles de Los to Sierra Leone* (London, n. d. [c. 1831]); A. Roussin, *Memoir on the Navigation of the Western Coast of Africa from Cape Bojador to Mount Souzos* (London, 1827), translated from French by Lt. James Badgley, R. N.

6. James Grey Jackson, *Account of the Empire of Morocco* (London, 1809), pp. 237–66.

years in Timbuctu and Hausa before his visit to Britain. His account
was published in England in 1820 and later used extensively by
Jackson.[7]

Still other notices came from northeastern Africa. J. L. Burckhardt,
who was sent by the African Association in 1808 to penetrate the
Western Sudan by way of Egypt, wandered in the Levant for almost
a decade. He travelled south to Nubia and along the Red Sea but was
unable to move west of the Nile valley. He was, however, able to
collect hearsay information, bringing news, for example, of the rise
of the Sokoto Fulani.[8]

Captain G. F. Lyon had even better opportunity to gather information during his long residence in Fezzan. At his base in Murzuk he
interrogated men from the caravans trading to Bornu and Hausa and
slaves passing northward toward Libya and Egypt. The itineraries he
collected gave stages and travel times to the opposite side of the
desert and on to Nupe, Dagomba, Gonja, and Ashanti. They also
showed the route westward to Timbuctu, Jenne, and back across the
desert to Tafilelt.

All of this North African information, whether itineraries or geo-
graphical speculations, had the defects of earlier Maghribi accounts.
The detail and accuracy dropped off sharply south of Adamawa,
Zaria, or Nupe—that is, in the "middle belt" of modern Nigeria.
Reporters from a distance, like Lyon, were thus unable to follow the
course of the Niger after it flowed south of Nupe. The dominant
North African hypothesis about the Niger was still set in the classical
Islamic mold, and men like Lyon and Jackson followed it, concluding
that the great river must ultimately flow into the Nile.[9]

Among scholars in Europe, the most careful collation of North
African information was the work of Baron Walckenaer, who collected and published itineraries leading into the desert and beyond,
trying to fix the position of towns and oases by cross-reference.[10]
T. E. Bowdich planned to translate this work into English but the
intention was cut off by his death. His interest, however, is evidence
of the link between Maghribi and Guinean sources of information,

7. It first appeared in *The Literary Gazette,* No. 171 (1820).

8. J. L. Burckhardt, *Travels in Nubia* (London, 1819).

9. G. F. Lyon, *A Narrative of Travels in Northern Africa in the Years 1818,
19, and 20* (London, 1821), pp. 121–63.

10. C. A. Walckenaer, *Recherches géographique sur l'interieur de l'Afrique sep-
tentorionale . . .* (Paris, 1821).

since Bowdich himself was the most important collector and collator
of information gathered on the southern approaches to the Sudan. A
long chapter in his *Mission to Ashantee* took up where Rennell left
off and attempted a new statement of the outlines of Sudanese geography.[11]

Others collected geographical data—on the Coast, in Kumasi, or
even further afield in America. Dupuis, Bowdich's successor in
Ashanti, attempted to correct what he considered to be Bowdich's
errors. G. A. Robertson published information from Lagos, Bonny,
and Lahou (on the Ivory Coast), showing, among other things, the
trade route from the Gold Coast to the Niger.[12] In Brazil, a careful
interrogation of Hausa slaves led to a correct solution of the Niger
problem—the conclusion that it did indeed flow into the Gulf of
Guinea.[13] Even *The Times* fed the public interest by publishing an
account of the route from Lagos to Hausa, gathered from Hausa
merchants in the port.[14]

The flow of new hearsay data was a striking change from the
previous century. Information of this kind must have been available
in earlier decades, but Europeans now began to collect and publish
whatever they could find out. The hiatus in successful exploration between Park and Clapperton was, therefore, no hiatus in the growth of
geographical knowledge. By the 1820's the way was open to a solution of the Niger problem, first by scholarship then confirmed by
exploration.

After Mungo Park had shown that a large river (identified as the
Niger of the ancients) flowed from west to east, five general theories
emerged to explain its course beyond Sansanding, where Park's reporting ended. Rennell thought it ran into Lake Chad or some equivalent inland lake and disappeared there through evaporation. Park
himself thought it probably emerged as the Congo or Zaire of lower
Guinea, though he never bothered to argue the point in public.[15]
The theory of an outlet into the Nile had been familiar for centuries.

11. T. E. Bowdich, *Mission from Cape Coast Castle to Ashantee* . . . (London,
1819), pp. 161–227.

12. J. Dupuis, *Journal of Residence in Ashantee* (London, 1824); G. A. Robertson, *Notes on Africa* . . . *With Hints for the Melioration of the Whole African
Population* (London, 1819), especially pp. 179–80, 185–88, and 206–7.

13. Menèzes de Drumond, "Lettres sur l'Afrique ancienne et moderne," *Journal
des voyages*, XXXII, 190–224 (December, 1826).

14. *The Times*, 18 May 1815.

15. Park, *Journal of a Mission*, II, 46–51.

In 1829, Lt.-Gen. Sir Rufane Donkin published an even more outlandish Mediterranean hypothesis. He suggested that the Niger
flowed into Lake Chad, then out of Lake Chad toward the north,
disappearing under the desert in an underground stream that finally
emerged in the Gulf of Sidra.[16]

The correct identification of the Oil Rivers as the mouths of the
Niger was first made by the German geographer, Christian Gottlieb
Reichard in 1802. In the following year, he worked out the theory in
more detail and published again, this time with his own map of
northern Africa. His argument rested on the rate of flow of the
known portions of the Niger. Both Park and al-Idrīsi long before had
described a river much too large to be evaporated from the surface of
a lake the size of any known to exist in Africa. Furthermore, the flow
of water from the system of rivers extending from the Formosa on
the west to the Rio del Rey on the east was enough to account for the
Niger's flow—and was far too great for a smaller watershed, limited
to the immediate hinterland.[17]

In other respects Reichard followed Rennell, and one particular
was to have important geographical consequences. Reichard's Niger,
like Rennell's, flowed from the foothills of the Futa Jallon Mountains
northward to the latitude of Timbuctu and then directly eastward
through the heart of Hausa to the vicinity of Lake Chad (or about
15° East). There it picked up tributaries flowing from points still
further east. Other tributaries were assumed to flow down from the
north, through an apparently well watered region lying between Lake
Chad and Tibesti, where in fact there is nothing but desert. By accepting Rennell's concept of a Niger basin stretching out to the east
and north of Lake Chad, Reichard vastly magnified the Niger Valley.
By the time the river reached its destination in the Bights it drained
an imaginary river basin twice the size of the actual Niger basin, and
one that included most of northern central Africa.

Reichard's theory found its way into English geographical thought

16. R. Donkin, *A Dissertation on the Course and Probable Termination of the
Niger* (London, 1829).

17. C. G. Reichard, "Ueber die Vermuthung des Dr. Seetzen zu Jever, dass sich
der Niger in Afrika viellicht mit dem Zaire vereinigen könne," *Monatliche Corre-
spondenz zur Beförderung der Erd-und-Himmels Kunde,* V, 402–15 (Gotha, May 1802);
Reichard, "Ueber den angekündigten, nun bald erscheinenden, Atlas des ganzen
Erdkreises," *Allegemeine Geographische Ephemeriden,* XII, 129–70 and map opposite
p. 265 (August 1803), esp. pp. 157–67.

through the work of the French geographer, Malte-Brun, and it appears to have been first published in England in 1816.[18] From that time onward a number of English theorists took up some variant of the Oil Rivers thesis. G. A. Robertson, for example, believed that three parallel branches flowed out of a large lake near Gao directly toward the Bights. Thus for him the Niger basin lay entirely to the west of the Niger delta.[19]

The most important and best publicized of the British theories, however, was that of James MacQueen. It was so well publicized, indeed, that MacQueen has often been given credit for Reichard's discovery. MacQueen was more a publicist than a scholar, and his geographical work was accompanied by a detailed plan for British West African strategy. From a geographical point of view, his construction of the West African map was very much that of Reichard, even though he claimed not to have seen Reichard's work until after his own was published. His vision of an eastern as well as a western Niger basin was even more extensive than Reichard's had been. For MacQueen, Niger drainage began at about 28° East, or almost the longitude of Alexandria. His eastern Sahara was even narrower than Reichard's, confined to the north of the Tropic of Cancer and thus only half its actual width. If this projection had been true, the well watered region to the north and east of Lake Chad would have had an area equivalent to all of the actual agricultural land in West Africa south of the desert. No wonder, then, that MacQueen worked so hard to direct British strategic entry toward the Bights rather than Sierra Leone.[20]

MacQueen also made a serious error about the political geography of the interior. Perhaps because he knew that many of the peoples of the Western Sudan were Muslim, he assumed that they must be under "Arab domination" and ruled by white North Africans. The belief fitted well with his racial views. Since he held that Negroes were congenitally inferior, he believed they could never have created or maintained elaborate political structures like the Empire of Bornu or the Hausa city-states.[21] In fact, there had been cultural diffusion

18. C. Malte-Brun, *Précis de la géographie universelle* . . . 8 vols. (Paris, 1810–1829), IV, 635; "Appendix No. IV," in M. Park, *Journal of a Mission*, II, 364–66.
19. Robertson, *Notes on Africa*, frontispiece map.
20. J. MacQueen, *Geographical and Commercial View of Northern Central Africa, Containing a Particular Account of the Course and Termination of the Great River Niger in the Atlantic Ocean* (Edinburgh, 1821).
21. MacQueen, *Northern Central Africa*, pp. 185–87.

across the Sahara for centuries, but conquest from the north had been
a rare occurrence. The nineteenth-century states in the Western Sudan
were ruled by sub-Saharan Africans and based on an indigenous political and cultural tradition, in spite of their considerable cultural
debt to Islam. "Arab domination" in countless variants, however,
became a commonplace of ill-informed thought about Africa for a
century to come.

In its broader pattern, MacQueen's synthesis dominated British
geographical thought for a generation, even though he himself revised it drastically in 1840, and explorers modified many points of
detail. But acceptance was not immediate. Throughout the 1820's the
Niger question was still open, and hotly debated in the reviews. The reports of Denham and Clapperton were greeted by the
Quarterly in 1826 as further proof that the Niger really flowed eastward to the Nile. *Blackwood's* answered with an article (probably
written by MacQueen himself) in further defense of the Oil Rivers
hypothesis. As an indication of public interest, the *Edinburgh* gave its
reviewer twice the usual space to deal with Denham's and Clapperton's book, and it followed up with another long reconstruction of
African geography based on the Clapperton-Lander expedition.[22] The
Niger question was finally closed only when the Oil Rivers theory
was confirmed by the emergence of Richard and John Lander in
1830. With that, the principal mystery was solved, and public interest
in West African geography began to decline. The classic age of West
African exploration was finished.

The reporting of the explorers during this classic age had a special
place in forming the British image of Africa. It was the first solid information about the recent Western Sudan. It came from Europeans,
who wrote vividly in a way that appealed to their contemporaries. It
caught the wide public interest generated by the Niger problem and
the romance of the unknown. But the data of the explorers was very
uneven in quality. It was very good within the narrow range of geographical problems that were their special concern. Otherwise it was
often less complete and less accurate than the accounts of the eighteenth-century "enlightened travellers." The earlier generation of
European visitors to West Africa had come out with a broad educational background and a universal curiosity, even though their spe-

22. *Blackwood's Edinburgh Magazine,* XIX, 687–709 (June 1826); *Edinburgh
Review,* XLIV, 173–209 (June 1826) and XLIX, 127–49 (March 1829).

Figure 2. A slave-trade fort on the coast of Ghana.
Fort St. George, Elmina, formerly the principal Dutch post
on the Gold Coast. (Photograph by the author.)

Figure 3. The Accra waterfront. The former English Fort James
(*upper right*) and the Dutch Fort Crèvcoeur (*center,* now Ussher Fort)
stood side by side in the era of the slave trade. (Photograph by the author.)

Figure 4. West Africa according to Reichard. (Photograph of original.)

Figure 5. West Africa according to MacQueen. (Photograph of original.)

Figure 6. "The Oil Rivers." A creek in the Niger Delta in 1832.
(From Allen, *Picturesque Views on the River Niger.*)

Figure 7. A scene on the Niger. This illustration
from Captain Allen's *Picturesque Views* combines an appeal
to the English taste of the period with a certain didacticism.
A romantic aspect comes out in the exaggeration of the hills
on the far side of the river, helping to spur the lure of the Niger
as a scene for British enterprise. The decapitation scene
in the foreground appeals to the "Gothick" aspect of the romantic movement
while it also underlines the alleged "savagery" of the African people.

Figure 8. The Attah of Igala holding court.
(From Allen, *Picturesque Views.*)

Figure 9. The rooftops of Timbuctu, Sankoré Mosque in the distance.
(From Barth, *Travels in North and Central Africa.*)

Figure 10. The entrance of a caravan into Timbuctu.
(From Barth, *Travels in North and Central Africa.*)

Figure 11. A man and woman of Gaman. (From Dupuis.)
The decapitated head is still another way of showing
the alleged character of the people in illustrative form.

Figure 12. Street scenes in Kumasi. (From Bowdich.)

Figure 13. Dixcove Fort, an English trading fort on the Gold Coast.

Figure 14. Muslims from Dagomba and Salaga
in the costumes of their countries. (From Dupuis.)

cific mission might be the collection of botanical specimens in one spot. The new generation were men of a different stamp. They were selected for their ability to make a difficult journey and still survive. Many of them were military officers. Others had made their reputation by hard travel in the past.

Mungo Park as an individual and the emissaries of the African Association as a group represent a transitional phase between the enlightened travellers and the nineteenth-century explorers. They were often selected for their background and interest in Africa. The best, like Park himself, were very good indeed. Park was surprisingly successful in stepping over the culture barrier that entangled so many of his predecessors. His basic attitude was one of neutrality toward the African way of life. He simply told what he had seen, without arrogance, without special pleading, and (since he was not a scholar) without interpretation. His work has rightly become one of the classics of European travel literature, but the amount of space he could devote to ethnographic description was relatively small in comparison with the enlightened travellers who saw one society at leisure.

Park's successors tended to be less well educated for the task at hand, though a lack of formal education was not necessarily a bar to good reporting or careful research. Clapperton was mainly self-educated, yet he located Kano within 50 miles of its actual position, calculating the longitude by dead-reckoning. More important (and unfortunately more rare among his colleagues) he portrayed the culture of the Western Sudan with sympathy and an unusual degree of modesty.

When ignorance was combined with cultural arrogance, the result was quite different. Richard Lander also lacked a formal education, but he saw Africa through a haze of cross-cultural misunderstanding. Where his report touched on African culture, it was usually to poke fun and provide a little comic relief for his readers. The queer superstitions and peculiar doings of the Africans were made to look as ridiculous as possible in contrast to the "achievements" of Western civilization. This was probably Lander's own attitude, but it was also a way to tickle the prejudices of his audience and play on their sense of superiority. As a result his errors were more serious and more frequent than those of other travellers. In his view, for example, all African states were complete despotisms, and the enforcement of Muslim law in Hausa was nothing but the whim of the judge. He stated bluntly that none of the *mallams,* the educated class in Hausa, could actually read Arabic. Clapperton, in contrast, was candid enough to admit that he was not sufficiently educated in Christian theology to discuss the subject on the same level as Sultan Bello. It is hard to avoid the conclusion that Lander was not merely ignorant but intentionally disparaging in order to increase the popular appeal of his books.[23] He was by no means the last traveller to Africa to write in this vein.

All of the travellers over the long routes in the interior faced a special problem in their many-sided role as the only source of information about Africa. They had an adventure story to tell, and they knew they would be read mainly for the sake of their adventures. They also travelled fast, often under conditions of difficulty and danger. They spent long periods down with malaria, which is psychologically depressing in the best of circumstances. They were therefore in no position to check facts or work to a critical standard, even if they wanted to do so. It was the easiest course to stop short with a personal narrative combined with geographical detail. Very often little of Africa emerged, beyond a rather flat backdrop to set the scene.

What was not actually culture-bound tended to be naive and superficial. Denham included a good deal of information about Bornu, but his description of the Bornu "character" shows how little he got below the surface to Sudanese life: "The Bornu people, or Kanowry, as they are called, have large unmeaning faces, with flat Negro noses, and mouths of great dimensions, with good teeth and high foreheads. They are peaceable, quiet, and civil; they salute each other with courteousness and warmth; and there is a remarkable good-natured heaviness about them which is interesting. They are no warriors, but revengeful; and the best of them given to commit petty larcenies, on every opportunity that offers."[24]

The passage reads like the opinion of a badly educated tourist after his first brief trip abroad. Yet it was taken seriously: it was almost the only information available.

The reporting from the Coast was different, in quality, quantity,

23. R. L. Lander, *Records of Captain Clapperton's Last Expedition to Africa . . . with Subsequent Adventures of the Author,* 2 vols. (London, 1830), esp. I, 270–85.

24. D. Denham and H. Clapperton, *Narrative of Travels and Discoveries in Northern and Central Africa in the Years 1822, 1823, and 1824,* 2 vols. (London, 1826), I, 316.

and methods of gathering information. There was a persistent tradition of enlightened travel, and the Sierra Leone Company in their earlier and more hopeful years recruited scientists as members of their African staff. They were able to draw especially on the African interest of the Swedenborgians. Augustus Nordenskiold, one of the more eccentric of Wadström's group, went out to Sierra Leone as the official mineralogist. He considered himself something of an alchemist, and he had dreams of discovering the pure people in the heart of Africa. He died, however, in 1792, shortly after his arrival. Adam Afzelius, on the other hand, became the Company's botanist and did valuable work. In spite of the loss of his initial collections in the French raid of 1794, he stayed on and lived to return to Sweden with his specimens.[25]

Still other visitors to Guinea had strong scholarly interests. Bowdich, Golbéry, Mollien, and Dupuis all belong to the tradition of the Enlightenment. Thomas Winterbottom was the culminating field investigator of that school, by far the most competent and careful field ethnographer to visit West Africa before the second half of the nineteenth century. His *Account of the Native Africans in the Neighbourhood of Sierra Leone* was partly the result of his own field work and partly a work of ethnographic synthesis. Aside from his contribution to medical ethnography, which was unique for Africa at this period, his general ethnography was the first publication of its kind based on fieldwork by an English scholar. It was so far in advance of the general development of ethnographic fieldwork that Winterbottom has nearly become a forgotten figure in the history of anthropology.

Even though many of his substantive findings have long since been superseded by newer work, he made the first serious efforts to apply critical standards to field investigations; and his warning to other ethnographers is as valid today as it was a century and a half ago:

The difficulty of procuring satisfactory intelligence from the natives of Africa, respecting themselves or their country, is known only to those who have made the experiment; they frequently lead Europeans into error by answering questions in the affirmative, merely to avoid trouble and escape importunity.

25. R. L. Tafel, *Documents Concerning the Life and Character of Emanuel Swedenborg,* 2 vols. (London, 1875–1877), I, 640–42. The Afzelius papers, including his journals from Sierra Leone, are preserved in the University Library, Uppsala.

The questions themselves sometimes awaken jealousy of those to whom they are addressed; feeling that the curiosity of Europeans has some sinister end in view. It requires also much time, and a fund of patience, to propose the necessary queries; to vary them in such a manner as to enable the natives to comprehend their precise import; and to compare testimonies of different individuals in order to avoid the risk of misconception. Even interpreters are not to be implicitly relied on, as they are apt to give to answers that colour which they perceive will be most agreeable to their employer.[26]

He put this critical spirit to work in his own investigations. Among other things, he tried to overturn the widespread myth about the prevalence of cannibalism in West Africa. After checking the earlier European reports, he came to the conclusion that, aside from occasional ritual cannibalism, there was not a single authentic account by a reliable witness. The prevalence of the myth arose instead from the fact that most Africans "appear struck with horror when questioned individually on the subject; though at the same time they make no scruple of accusing other nations at a distance, and whom they barely know by name, of cannibalism."[27]

Other visitors to the coast, who were by no means scholars, occasionally tried to investigate and report in the light of existing culture theory. Philip Beaver, whose physical problems were at least as great as those of the explorers in the interior, still took time to investigate the culture of the Africans near Bulama Island. He even tried to assign them a place on the traditional scheme according to their "stage of civilization." Since they practiced hunting, fishing, pastoralism, and agriculture all at the same time, the task was beyond him. He thought that African culture was "debased," but he also saw a common humanity behind the differences in custom. As he put it in one instance: "Powdering the hair is only painting it white, and I see no rational difference between that, and the Bijugas filling theirs with red ocre, except, that red ocre best becomes a black countenance."[28]

G. A. Robertson continued the relatively unbiased tradition of the eighteenth-century merchants. His manual of mercantile affairs was designed for practical men of business, rather than scholars, but it included a good deal of ethnographic information, especially on the commercial customs and the nature and distribution of political

26. T. Winterbottom, *An Account of the Native Africans in the Neighbourhood of Sierra Leone,* 2 vols. (London, 1803), I. v.

27. Winterbottom, *Native Africans,* I, 166–67.

28. Philip Beaver, *African Memoranda* (London, 1805), pp. 318–36, quotation on p. 326.

power in each African state. He was no reformer. Perhaps for this reason, he was less culture-bound than many of the humanitarians, who were committed to the goal of civilizing and Christianizing Africa.[29]

Thomas Edward Bowdich was both an official and something of a scholar, though with less critical sense than Winterbottom. His report on Ashanti included a record of the traditional history back to the beginning of the eighteenth century, and it extended to aspects of African culture that were often neglected. In addition to the more usual description of customs and "superstitions," he noted down bits of Ashanti music and gave a chapter to Ashanti law and constitution. As a result, readers at home had a much better picture of Ashanti as a functioning society than they had of the Fante states after almost three centuries of contact.[30]

But the tradition of enlightened travel to West Africa was slowly dying in the early decades of the nineteenth century. Neither the government nor the Sierra Leone Company sponsored professional scientists after Winterbottom and Afzelius, except on the exploring expeditions. The African Institution, however, tried to keep up the tradition of research by the questionnaire method. In 1810, they published one of the most elaborate questionnaires so far, with 114 questions to serve as a guide to the investigations of any traveller who happened to be in Africa. The questions were somewhat slanted toward geographical and statistical information, but about half were broadly concerned with the history, laws, politics, and culture of the people. In this sense, it was the forerunner of a whole succession of later ethnographic questionnaires.[31]

The Institution itself published two brief articles based on the questionnaire. One was the work of Henry Meredith, governor at Winnebah on the Gold Coast, who dealt with Angona, the small Akan state in his immediate hinterland. The second, by Thomas Ludlam, discussed the Kru people of Liberia, who were already in the habit of coming to Sierra Leone as transient laborers.[32] Later writers

29. Robertson, *Notes on Africa, passim.* A part of Robertson's work was reprinted in Germany for its ethnographic contribution as "Die Republik der Fantees an der Westküste von Afrika," *Ethnographisches Archiv,* X, 142–92 (Jena, 1820). For traders' ethnography see also J. Adams, *Remarks,* pp. 8–43.

30. Bowdich, *Mission to Ashantee, passim.*

31. "Queries Relative to Africa," African Institution, *Reports of the Committee of the African Institution,* 18 vols. (London, 1807–1824), Fourth Report, pp. 75–82.

32. African Institution, *Reports,* Fourth Report, pp. 82–93; Sixth Report, pp. 87–102.

also occasionally used the questionnaire more loosely as a guide to general orientation.[33]

Other questionnaires, for administrative rather than scholarly purposes, came into use at about the same time. Both sets of Commissioners, Ludlam and Dawes in 1810 and Wellington and Rowan in 1827, circulated questionnaires to the commanders of the forts and other European residents. The questions of 1810 were mainly concerned with political and economic prospects, or the state of the slave trade. The Commissioners were not interested in African society as a functioning whole, but only in selected aspects that might affect the future British position. Both the questions and the answers were much less sophisticated than those of the amateur scholars. The flavor of ethnocentric suggestion is clear from the question on the African character:

> 9. What is the general character of the people; more particularly, can Europeans confide in them with safety? Are they remarkable for fidelity to one another in times of danger? Do they repose confidence in Europeans, or in one another, where their pecuniary interests are concerned? Are they revengeful; or are quarrels, especially between families, easily made up? If shipwrecked or distressed Europeans fall into their hands, how do they treat them? Are they fond of war? Are they much bigotted to ancient customs? Do they readily change part of those customs (their mode of building or dress for instance) in imitation of Europeans? What customs do they most rigidly adhere to? What means have been tried (by persuasion, instruction, example, &c.) to wean them from their most prejudicial customs?[34]

Answers from the eight commanders of Gold Coast forts were more culture-bound than the usual attitudes expressed by eighteenth-century slave traders. George Richardson of Anomabu struck a note that was representative of the group. "The natives in general are addicted to many vices, but particularly stealing, lying, deceit, imposition, &c. &c. Europeans cannot confide in them with safety, . . . they are much bigotted to ancient customs; some of them do attempt improvements in their houses in the European manner, but their dress is always the same. Europeans have tried, in vain, to convince them of the folly of their more absurd customs; but they do not wish to enter much on the subject."[35]

33. As may have been the case with Peter McLachlan's *Travels into the Baga and Soosoo Countries* (Freetown, 1821), a brief ethnographic report prepared by the Assistant Staff Surgeon of Sierra Leone, first incorporated in his official half-yearly report, and then separately published.

34. PP, 1816, vii (506), p. 156.

35. Answer dated 16 August 1810, PP, 1816, vii (506), p. 161.

The answers give some insight into the "official mind" on the Gold Coast, showing among other things how rare the attitude of a Winterbottom or a Bowdich was among the administrative class. A similar arrogance was echoed by the press at home. High adventure was one thing, and Mungo Park was avidly read. Ethnography was another, and Winterbottom's book was generally neglected. The *Edinburgh Review* completely missed Winterbottom's point. The reviewer devoted his space to an essay against the slave trade, brushing off the Africans themselves as a people "divided by different shades of barbarism, and disputed limited of territory, plunged in the darkest ignorance and superstition."[36] The *Anti-Jacobin* openly attacked Winterbottom, especially for his failure to recognize the "fact" of African inferiority.[37]

Bowdich fared little better, though his mission to Kumasi was a "discovery," and his work was more widely read than Winterbottom's had been. *Blackwood's* thought it might improve the racial reputation of Africans by showing that they were "capable of improvement."[38] The reviewer in the *Quarterly,* however, used it as an occasion for poking fun at African customs and took Bowdich to task for attempting to write seriously about African language or music. As for history, "The 'history' of the Ashantees, to which Mr. Bowdich has dedicated a whole chapter, is, like that of all other savages who can neither read nor write, the history of a day, and little worthy of notice."[39]

Even though writing about African ethnography was unpopular in some quarters, it was still widely published and read, smuggled in, as it were, under the guise of travel literature. The edition and publication of collected travellers' tales was continuous, while ephemeral literary fads rose and fell. Some collections placed a new emphasis on personal narrative and reduced the space given to "manners and customs," but the tradition of Astley's *Voyages* and the *Universal History* also persisted. It was especially important in the editions of John Leyden and Hugh Murray. Leyden began the series with his *Historical and Philosophical Sketch of the Discoveries and Settlements of the Europeans in Northern and Western Africa at the Close of the Eighteenth Century,* first published in Edinburgh in 1799. Its

36. *Edinburgh Review,* III, 355 (January 1804).
37. *Anti-Jacobin Review,* XVIII, 47 (May 1804).
38. *Blackwood's,* V, 175–83 and 302–10 (May–June 1819).
39. *Quarterly Review,* XXII, 286 (January 1820).

title notwithstanding, the work was mainly concerned with the society and culture of the Africans themselves. The achievements of the
explorers fell into second place. Taking his point of departure from
moral philosophy, Leyden believed that, "By contemplating their
manners and customs, we may discover the simple and unmixed operation of those principles which, in civilized society, are always combined with extraneous circumstances."[40]

He thus reaffirmed the eighteenth-century search for man-in-general, and his work passed through several editions in both English
and French to become a summary and text for a new generation of
colonial theorists and planners. Hugh Murray, the Scottish geographer, joined in the preparation of later revisions, and Murray too had
an interest in ethnological theory. The size, scope, and title of the
publication changed gradually through the early nineteenth century.
The history of colonization dropped out, and the discoveries of the
most recent explorers were added. In all, the enterprise lasted more
than half a century, with a final edition in 1853, after Murray's
death.[41]

The most ambitious and complete publication of African information, however, came from France. Between 1826 and 1831, Baron
Walckenaer edited a series of twenty-one volumes, designed as the
first stage of a world-wide collection of voyages. In fact, he never
got beyond Africa. Five and one-half volumes devoted to West Africa brought back into print very nearly the whole canon of earlier
African travels, plus the recent explorations in the Western Sudan.
The format was similar to Astley's *Voyages,* with authorities edited
and interlaced to form a running account of each geographical region. It made easier reading, but it often obscured the original
source.[42] Some other French publications were equally elaborate.
Grasset de Saint-Saveur's *Encyclopédie des voyages,* for example, depicted West African costume in twenty-eight hand-colored plates.[43]

Periodical publication of travellers' accounts was also a Continental

40. Leyden, *Historical and Philosophical Sketch,* p. ix.
41. J. Leyden and H. Murray, *Historical Account of Discoveries and Voyages in
Africa,* 2 vols. (Edinburgh, 1817); R. Jameson, J. Wilson, and H. Murray, *Narrative
of Discovery and Adventure in Africa from the Earliest Ages to the Present Time*
(Edinburgh and London, 1830); Hugh Murray, *The African Continent* (Edinburgh,
1853).
42. C. A. Walckenaer (ed.), *Histoire générale des voyages,* 21 vols. (Paris,
1826–1831).
43. J. Grasset de Saint-Saveur, *Encyclopédie des Voyages,* 5 vols. (Paris, 1795), IV.

phenomenon. Malte-Brun's *Annales des Voyages* ran through 24 volumes between 1809 and 1814. It was succeeded by the *Nouvelles Annales des Voyages et de la Géographie et de l'Histoire* and by the *Journal des Voyages, Découvertes et Navigations Modernes*, which published 44 volumes between 1813 and 1826. The German equivalent was the *Journal für die neuesten Land- und Seereisen*, published in Berlin. None of these was chiefly concerned with Africa, but the French journals kept track of French accounts from Senegal. All of them lifted and republished translations of the major British explorations and occasionally printed a review of recent British activities.[44]

As English interests pushed out to many parts of the overseas world, the major English travel collections came to be less concerned with Africa. Less than 3 per cent of Kerr's voyages was devoted to African material, and Pinkerton's gave Africa no more space than North America, and less than Asia.[45] This tendency was redressed to some extent by the publication of smaller compendia, specifically designed to catch the public interest in African exploration. Some of these synthesized and popularized the new information at a high level of competence. Catherine Hutton's *Tour of Africa* is an example of the better work of this kind. She selected from the work of the travellers so as to produce an account of a single tour of Africa told in the first person. In spite of this eccentric presentation, she told her story without the usual single-minded concentration on the slave trade, and with less cultural bias than most.

In a more limited sphere, Frederick Shoberl's account of Mauritania and Senegambia for children was equally well done. He simplified and explained, as is characteristic of this type of literature but the result was a well balanced description of Wolof culture and political structure, with some information on surrounding peoples.[46]

Most popularization came nowhere near the quality of these two,

44. See, for example, N. V., "Coup-d'oeil sur la guerre des Ashantis et sur l'état des possessions anglaises de la Côte-d'or," *Journal des Voyages*, XXV, 169–89 (February, 1825).

45. Robert Kerr (ed.), *A General History and Collection of Voyages and Travels* . . . , 18 vols. (Edinburgh, 1811–1824); John Pinkerton, *A General Collection of the Best and Most Interesting Voyages and Travels in All Parts of the World*, 17 vols. (London, 1808–1814).

46. Catherine Hutton, *The Tour of Africa . . . with the Manners and Customs of the Inhabitants*, 3 vols. (London, 1819–1821); F. Shoberl, *The World in Miniature. Africa. A Description of the Manners and Customs of the Moors of the Zahara, and of the Negro Nations between the Rivers Senegal and Gambia*, 4 vols. (London, n. d. [c. 1821]).

and many editors used the medium of travel literature for their own
didactic purposes. An imitation of Catherine Hutton's format, for
example, taught cultural chauvinism by concentrating on the evil of
"heathen" customs.[47] Charles Hulbert's two scissors-and-paste com-
pilations of Africana were designed to attract British emigrants to
South Africa.[48]

Travel books compiled for the young were especially inclined to
moral preaching. At best, they merely boiled down selected passages
from the explorers,[49] but many editors combined exhortation with an
easy disregard for the facts. One, for example, presented authentic
travel narratives interlarded with fanciful accounts, endowing the
Western Sudan with "mountains covered with impenetrable forests,
and barren solitudes parched by the raging heat of the torrid climate."[50] Another used the travellers for a juvenile anti-slavery tract,
concentrating on the horrors of the slave trade and the virtue of the
English for abolishing their share of it. As for the Africans, they were
dismissed with such statements as: "Bornou is a very considerable
tract of country, north west of Darfur; and may be described as resembling the other tribes, in ignorance, ferocity, and power." Or, in
regard to Timbuctu: "The people being negro, and so much separated from other nations, are very ignorant and of course superstitious."[51]

The ignorance was certainly mutual, since this was published before Clapperton had reached Bornu or Caillié, Timbuctu. While the
intention was to encourage morality and support of Christian missions, the obvious by-product was racial and cultural arrogance.

Little of the writing about Africa was, in any case, politically neu-
tral—nor could it be in an era when first the slave trade and then
West Indian slavery were debated in Parliament. Both the humanitarians and their opponents needed data to support their efforts in
Britain. Wilberforce frequently appealed to the Sierra Leone officials
of the 1790's for evidence to support the case he was about to make
in the House. In 1804, he wrote to Lord Muncaster with a list of
eight propositions about Africa and the Africans, asking Muncaster

47. *Travels in Africa* (Dublin, C. Bentham, 1821).

48. C. Hulbert, *The African Traveller* . . . (Shrewsbury, 1817) and *Museum
Africanum* (Shrewsbury, 1822).

49. Mrs. Barbara Hofland [née Houle], *Africa Described* (London, 1828).

50. William Bingley, *Travels in Africa, from Modern Writers* (London, 1819),
p. 202.

51. Isaac Taylor, *Scenes in Africa* (London, 1820), pp. 31 and 33.

to check through his library of African travellers and furnish proof
that these points were correct.[52] Defenders of slavery and the trade
did the same kind of thing, and old "evidence" like the horrors of
Dahomey depicted by Dalzel in the 1790's cropped up for thirty years
and more, with a drumming repetition that must have carried conviction to the casual reader.

There was not yet an established professional or scholarly group
whose business it was to receive, check, and assimilate new cultural
data from overseas for the sake of knowledge itself. To some extent
this function was performed by the publishers of travel collections
and their editors, but it was rarely done in a way that measured up to
the best standards of scholarship as then understood. So far, only
geographers posed an effective series of concrete questions suggesting
the data they needed.

Anthropology had only reached its barest beginning as a body of
systematic knowledge. The discipline, as it is now understood, was
still divided between biology on one hand and moral philosophy on
the other. While moral philosophers were anxious to use ethnographic data, they did not see it as a part of their work to collect
these data or to assimilate them in a systematic way.

Leadership in organized ethnography came from other sources.
One of these was an extension from the biological study of man, and
the key figure was James Cowles Prichard. Originally trained as a
physician, his first interest was physical anthropology, which formed
the bulk of the first edition of his *Researches into the Physical History of Man* (1813). As times passed, however, the new editions
took on a new emphasis. By 1826, the two-volume second edition
already contained an ethnographic survey of Africa based on the
reports of the travellers.[53] The final five-volume version (and with it
Prichard's greatest reputation) came only later, but the base was laid
in the 1820's. Guidance for travellers began even earlier with such
efforts as the African Institution's ethnographic questionnaire of
1810. By the 1820's the word "ethnography" was coming into use.[54]

52. Wilberforce to Z. Macaulay, 23 August 1793 and Wilberforce to Muncaster,
18 December 1804, in Wilberforce, R. I. and S. (eds.), *Correspondence of William
Wilberforce*, 5 vols. (London, 1838), II, 409–13 and III, 203.

53. J. C. Prichard, *Researches into the Physical History of Man*, 2nd ed., 2 vols.
(London, 1826), I, 250–81.

54. As in the title of the *Ethnographisches Archiv* published in Jena, but the precise
meaning was still uncertain. Adriano Balbi's *Atlas ethnographique du globe* (Paris,
1826) was in fact a set of tables of language classification, rather than a broader study
of human culture.

The new science was then new enough, yet familiar enough, to be worthy of a playful lampoon in the *New Monthly Magazine*.[55] The way was prepared for the more extensive developments to follow.

Meanwhile, travellers reported selectively—even though their criteria for selection were rarely conscious or based on a desire for systematic knowledge. The pattern was, indeed, little changed from that of the later eighteenth century. The interest in commerce remained, but with a new bias, as the need for new openings to replace the slave trade became evident. From 1805, government-sponsored expeditions carried orders to report on trade and markets. Partly for the same reason, political structures and military capabilities of inland states attracted a new interest. Outward signs of political authority, however, were still reported more accurately than the constitutional base on which they rested. In religion, "superstitious practices" still held little interest, unless they took the form of spectacular festivals or rites particularly abhorrent to Europeans.

Even in the area of their special concern, travellers often made curious mistakes. African agriculture was still widely misunderstood, though it necessarily formed the base for economic development. The principal error was the continuing assumption of tropical exuberance. If African soils were endlessly rich, the usual West African practice of shifting cultivation could only be understood as an irrational and ignorant use of the land—but West African soils were not rich. Travellers also missed the relationship between shifting cultivation and the systems of land tenure—and the influence of both on African concepts of real and personal property. Leyden, for example, reported at one stage that all African agriculture was communal, that all contributed their labor and received a share of the crop. This, in his view, discouraged individual enterprise and hence economic development. He was, of course, wrong on both counts, and the error was partly corrected in later editions. Still, the belief persisted that each African town or village was surrounded by large tracts of unused land, which would be granted freely to anyone who cared to undertake the labor of cultivating it.[56] This land was often considered ripe for the skill and direction of the European entrepreneur.

New interests also appeared. One was a concern for African

---

55. W. E., "Anthropology," *New Monthly Magazine,* XXII, 505–09 (1828).
56. Leyden, *Historical and Philosophical Sketch,* pp. 99–101; Leyden and Murray, *Discoveries and Voyages in Africa,* II, 491.

women and the place of women in African society. It echoed John
Millar's emphasis on the position of women as the touchstone for
judging social development (and the final edition of Millar's *Distinction of Ranks* did not appear until 1806). Winterbottom, for example, accepted Millar's distinction in preference to Montesquieu's view
that money was the true mark of civilization.[57] Polygyny was also a
repulsive institution to most European travellers, who saw it as male
oppression of the weaker sex. In part, this new sympathy reflected the
rising status of women in Europe—not yet, to be sure, to positions of
equality with men, but deserving of chivalrous protection. Mungo
Park's report of kindness shown him by some African women caught
the public imagination more than anything else in his narrative. The
incident was set to music and became a popular song, inspired in part
by its political usefulness as an attack on the slave trade. In this case,
the association of womanhood, motherhood, and a common humanity
appears to have been a convenient way to by-pass the unsympathetic
image of African men. Then, too, the new concern for African
women was fully supported by the romantic movement: one aspect of
Lovejoy's "diversificationism" was the admiration of exotic beauty.
Golbéry caught this spirit in his praise of the *Sénégalaises:* "Those
who imagine that black, or shades of black, are sufficient to designate
in painting a young and handsome negress, have no correct idea of
her charms; the roses likewise combine with the carnations, and as
we say in Europe, when speaking of a beautiful complexion of an
African beauty, that it is an union of ebony and roses."[58]

African arts and crafts were also favored by romanticism. As classical standards declined, exotic designs were more acceptable. Even
Richard Lander, who otherwise had little admiration for things African, admired African skill in painting, sculpture, leather and iron
works, dyes, and textiles.[59]

African languages received new attention as well, though for more
practical reasons. At the turn of the eighteenth century, the science of
linguistics had reached a stage of development roughly equivalent to
that of biology a century earlier. European philologists were taking
inventory of the languages of the world. Enormous surveys of several

57. Winterbottom, *Native Africans,* I, 144 and 188.
58. S. M. X. Golberry [S. M. X. de Golbéry], *Travels in Africa Performed during
the Years 1785, 1786, and 1787,* 2 vols. (London, 1803), II, 310. See also F. B. Spilsbury, *A Voyage to the Western Coast of Africa* (London, 1807), pp. 22–23.
59. Lander, *Clapperton's Last Expedition,* I, 305–7.

hundred languages were published by P. S. Pallas in 1786–87 and Lorenzo Hervas y Panduro in 1800–05. Pallas took notice of some thirty African languages, and Hervas was the first to identify Amharic as a Semitic language.[60]

By the 1790's, West African languages had entered the picture. Even before Europeans had direct access to the West African interior, comparative vocabularies were collected from Africans in other parts of the world, as Oldendorp had done earlier in the Danish West Indies. Ulrich Jasper Seetzen took down vocabularies supplied by Negro Africans in Cairo, and his information was ultimately published by J. S. Vater of Königsberg.[61] Later on, in 1816–17, J. L. Burkhardt again used Cairo as a listening post for linguistic data from West Africa, tapping the information of pilgrims passing through on the way to Mecca.[62] Other travellers in the Maghrib, and especially Lyon, recorded brief vocabularies of sub-Saharan languages, as they met informants from south of the desert; and the explorers continued the work of vocabulary collection as they began to move into the interior.

Meanwhile, the practical need for a knowledge of African languages was increasing along the West African coast, as travellers began to penetrate beyond the range of accepted European *linguae francae*. Adanson had learned Wolof for his ethnographic studies in Senegal. Mungo Park used Mandingo as the most convenient *lingua franca* for the Senegambian interior. For similar practical reasons the French Senegal Company compiled a dictionary, perhaps in the seventeenth century, giving about 2000 words in French and their equivalents in eleven languages of the Senegambia.[63]

The most serious linguistic studies, indeed, came from the Guinea Coast. Sierra Leone was a natural base. The pioneer linguist there was Henry Brunton of the Edinburgh Missionary Society, who worked on the Rio Pongas in the later 1790's and reduced the Susu language to writing in Roman characters. Among other works, he published a Susu grammar and vocabulary, an abridgement of the

60. Holgar Pedersen, *Linguistic Science in the Nineteenth Century* (Cambridge, Mass., 1931), pp. 9–10. R. N. Cust, *A Sketch of the Modern Languages of Africa*, 2 vols. (London, 1883), I, 25–26.

61. J. C. Prichard, "Abstract of a Comparative Review of Philological and Physical Researches as applied to the History of the Human Species," *Reports of the British Association for the Advancement of Science*, II, 529–44 (1832), p. 531.

62. Burckhardt, *Travels in Nubia*, pp. 477–83.

63. *Mémoires de la Société Ethnologique*, II (2), 205–67 (1845).

Bible, and some devotional works of his own composition. These included three dialogues on the advantages of literacy, the absurdity of the Susu religion, and the superiority of Christianity over Islam.[64]

Other visitors took a hand in linguistic research, at least in an amateur way. Winterbottom worked with Bullom, Temne, and Susu, publishing a brief grammatical study, the usual vocabularies, and a suggested system of orthography for African languages.[65] At this stage, however, most orthography was so careless and unstandardized, and most travellers were so lacking in broad linguistic background, that the pioneer work had little or no permanent value to scholarship.

Even so, a few of the early travellers approached the theoretical problems of linguistic science, if only in a very unsophisticated manner. Bowdich in Ashanti tried to assess the relationships between Akan languages, concluding that Ashanti was the "Attic" of the group, others, such as Fante, being derived from it. He was on weaker ground in his discussion of the origin of language, claiming both that language was revealed to man by God and that languages develop in an evolutionary manner from "primitive simplicity."[66] At the very least, people interested in such questions were now actually carrying on research in Africa.

The most systematic investigations of this period were those of Mrs. Hannah Kilham, who spent most of the period 1820–1832 on linguistic research for the sake of more effective missionary work. She made three separate trips to Sierra Leone or the Gambia, sponsored by some English Quakers; and she produced an exercise book for teaching Wolof to English-speakers, some translations into Wolof, and a substantial comparative vocabulary of English words with their equivalents in some thirty African languages. She was also interested in technical problems and prepared a brief guide for discovering the grammar of an unknown language and reducing it to writing with a phonetic orthography.[67]

As the new linguistic data flowed in from Africa, it was studied by

64. Winterbottom, *Native Africans*, I, 218 *n.*
65. Winterbottom, *Native Africans*, I, 337–62.
66. Bowdich, *Mission to Ashantee*, pp. 344–50 and 503–12.
67. Peter Bedford and others, "Address to Friends," 22 May 1820, Thomas Hodgkin Papers; Hannah Kilham, *African Lessons. Wolof and English* (London, 1823) and *Specimens of African Language Spoken in the Colony of Sierra Leone* (London, 1828). See also C. P. Groves, *The Planting of Christianity in Africa*, 4 vols. (London, 1948–1958), I, 286–88.

European linguists. In the first decades of the nineteenth century
Johann Christoph Adelung was compiling the last of the great inven-
tories of world languages. The final version, completed after Adelung's death by Johan Severin Vater, contained the first detailed and
systematic discussion of African languages.[68] As such, it served as the
point of departure both for Prichard's treatment of West African
languages in his *Researches into the Physical History of Man* and
for Balbi's *Atlas ethnographique du globe.*

The classification of African languages was barely beginning,
though the group now known as the Bantu languages was understood
to be a single family. The Portuguese had recognized the similarity
between Kikongo on the west coast and the "kaffir" languages of
southeast Africa as early as the seventeenth century. This affinity and
its extensions throughout southern Africa was rediscovered and publicized in Britain in the later eighteenth century by William Marsden,
the Orientalist.[69] In West Africa, the only commonly recognized
affinities were in the Mande and Akan families, and in the more obvious unity of the various Fulbe dialects spread across West Africa
from the Atlantic to the Cameroons. Otherwise, the languages were
only arranged in rather uncertain regional groupings.

In spite of these beginnings of serious scholarly study, the British
stereotype of "the African character" drew far more from the reports
of the travellers, than it did from the synthesis of the scholars. But
scholars and travellers alike were virtually unanimous about one
point—there was such a thing as an "African character," different in
significant ways from the character of man in Europe. There was, of
course, disagreement about the exact ingredients of this character
but the range of opinion was somewhat narrower than it had been
in the later eighteenth century. There were now more (and more
varied) sources of information, and a common image of "the African" was well publicized. Individual writers could hardly do more
than adjust the focus or alter the detail.

It was generally believed that African emotions tended toward
extremes: "The understanding is much less cultivated among the
Negroes than among Europeans; but their passions, whether benevo-

68. J. C. Adelung and J. S. Vater, *Mithridates oder allgemeine Sprachenkunde*
4 vols. (Berlin, 1806–1817), III, 1–305.
69. H. H. Johnston, *A Comparative Study of the Bantu and Semi-Bantu Languages*
2 vols. (Oxford, 1919–1922), I, 1–5; C. M. Doke, "Bantu Language Pioneers of the
Nineteenth Century," *African Studies*, XVIII, 1–27 (1959).

lent or malevolent, are proportionately more violent. . . . Though addicted to hatred and revenge, they are equally susceptible to love, affection, and gratitude."[70]

This belief, with various modifications, was extremely common. It was based more on the general theories of the eighteenth-century environmentalists than on observation. A hot temper and violent passions were the prime characteristics of southerners. The travellers, of course, knew this before they left England, and their reports were influenced accordingly.

Further discussions of the "African character" tended to list virtues and vices as a kind of balance of good and evil, following a tradition borrowed from moral philosophy. Different lists were surprisingly uniform. The chief African vices were held to be indolence, ferocity, cowardice, and superstition. The virtues were mild manners, a peaceful disposition, politeness, charity, respect for the aged, and sometimes gratitude and nobility of character.[71] Different opinions merely shifted the balance of these traits, adding here and subtracting there. A poet still writing in the mood of noble savagery with anti-slavery overtones, for example, might idealize the virtue side of the ledger. James Montgomery's "The West Indies" hinted at a highly Christian paradise in Africa:

> There, as with nature's warmest filial fire,
> He soothes his blind, and feeds his helpless sire;
> His children sporting round his hut behold
> How they shall cherish him when he is old,
> Train'd by example from their tenderest youth
> To deeds of charity, and words of truth.[72]

Or the balance might be struck on the negative side, with reservations, as with Durand: "The character of the blacks is nearly the same everywhere: they are indolent, except when animated by the desire for vengeance; implacable, perfidious, and dissimulating when they have received an injury, in order that they may find an opportunity of avenging it with impunity: on the other hand, they are

---

70. Leyden, *Historical and Philosophical Sketch,* p. 98.

71. A convenient summary, based on a wide variety of sources, is found in Abbé Henri Baptiste Grégoire, *De la littérature des nègres, ou recherches sur leur facultés intellectuelles, leur qualités morales, et leur littérature* (Paris, 1808), translated by D. B. Warden as *An Enquiry Concerning the Intellectual and Moral Faculties, and Literature of Negroes* . . . (Brooklyn, N.Y., 1810), pp. 89–106.

72. J. Montgomery, *Poetical Works,* 4 vols. (London, 1828), I, 36. "The West Indies" was first published in 1807.

gentle and hospitable to every one, but inclined to larceny, and re-markable for an extreme inconstancy of taste and conduct."[73]

In extreme cases, the positive qualities might drop out altogether. Nollan, the commander of Secondi fort reported in 1810: "Like the inhabitants of all barbarous countries, the natives here are addicted to many vices, and their characters as liars, thieves, and cheats are noto-riously known. If they possess any virtues, I must confess they have entirely escaped my observation. . . ."[74]

The derivation of the lists is curious, both on the side of virtue and the side of vice. The vices of cowardice and sloth were standard "southern" vices, recognized as such in a centuries-old European tra-dition having nothing to do with empirical data from tropical Africa. The vice of "superstition" represented little more than a reaction to religious difference between Europe and Africa. Cowardice, on the other hand, was not so frequently reported as idleness, and many writers maintained a contradictory listing of both ferocity and cow-ardice. The explanation appears to be that all "savages" were nat-urally ferocious, and southern savages were expected to be cowards as well.

Laziness was the vice most frequently reported, and the emphasis was repeated from several sides. It was believed to be characteristic of Negro slaves in the West Indies. It was reinforced by mistaken ob-servation in West Africa, where the myth of tropical exuberance encouraged the Europeans to think that Africans had no need to work. In addition, agricultural work in West Africa was often sea-sonal, on account of alternation of dry and wet periods. The usual dry-season under-employment became a wet-season labor shortage. The dry-season pattern might look like simple laziness. Lethargy pro-duced by certain intestinal parasites and other African diseases may also have reinforced the impression.

On the side of virtue, reflections of environmentalism combined with other data drawn from actual observation. A formal politeness

73. J. B. L. Durand, *A Voyage to Senegal* (London, 1806), p. 99.

74. PP, 1816, vii (506), p. 176. For other summary views of the "Negro character" see M. Park, *Travels in the Interior Districts of Africa*, 2nd ed. (London, 1799), pp. 261–64; Golbéry, *Travels in Africa*, I, 70 and II, 310; J. Corry, *Observations upon the Windward Coast of Africa . . . made in the Years 1805–1806* (London, 1807), esp. p. 60; PP, 1816, vii (506), pp. 156–97; J. MacLoed, *A Voyage to Africa, with Some Account of the Manners and Customs of the Dahomean People* (London, 1820), p. 129; John Adams, *Sketches Taken During Ten Voyages to Africa, Between the Years 1786 and 1800 . . .* (London, 1822), p. 72; Balbi, *Atlas ethnographique*, table 19.

is still common in many West African cultures. It must have been all the more striking to travellers who expected to find savages. Respect for the aged is equally characteristic—partly for theological reasons, connected with the veneration of ancestral spirits. The code of African hospitality is often rigorous, and so important to travellers that it could hardly escape notice.

The most significant aspect of the virtue column, however, was the attribution of Christian virtues to the Africans. Faith, hope, and charity had appeared occasionally in the literary image of the noble savage, whether African or not. They appeared again in the Christianized noble African of the anti-slavery writers. The result was not so favorable to Africans as it might appear to be. Europeans always paid lip service to the Sermon on the Mount, but they also admired aggressive self-assertion. The sin of pride was the cardinal sin for theologians, but rarely in the moral attitude of the ordinary person. This moral ambivalence in European thought, however, was not mere hypocrisy. Europeans still retained a genuine respect for child-like simplicity and submissiveness—lost long ago by themselves, according to their own mythology, in the Garden of Eden.

During the European Middle Ages, men hoped and expected that somewhere beyond the seas there might still be a terrestrial paradise. The belief had, indeed, contributed to the early travellers' accounts, which had been, in turn, one foundation for the motif of the noble savage.

In another direction, the medieval tradition influenced the missionary image of the potential convert. As early as the sixteenth century, Spanish missionaries in Mexico had laid special emphasis on the meekness and humility of the Indians, qualities which allegedly made them especially susceptible to Christian influence.[75] The description they gave of the Indians was strikingly similar to the virtue side of the nineteenth-century balance sheet of African character, and the picture of the Africans as natural Christians was to grow in strength as time passed.

In contrast to the standardized picture of "the African character," new data about African cultures led those with a more specialized knowledge to emphasize the diversity of peoples and civilizations. According to Prichard: "we find in general that the whole country is

75. J. L. Phelan, *The Millennial Kingdom of the Franciscans in the New World* (Berkeley, Cal., 1956), pp. 56–57.

divided between a great number of small and distinct tribes, who
have no connexion with each other than can be discovered by resemblance of language or by any other trait. On passing over a river,
or a ridge of mountains, the traveller finds the race of men completely changed, as far as the race can be distinguished by customs
and peculiar language."[76]

Others agreed, and the most common practice was to draw a sharp
distinction between the "superior" peoples of the interior and the
"degraded" nations of the coast. The old belief in the good interior
was reinforced by Mungo Park's early reports of dense population,
brisk commerce, and relatively stable political order beyond the head-
waters of the Gambia.

Particular peoples also came in for special praise or blame. The
French writers tended to think highly of the Wolof in the hinterland
of Gorée.[77] The Mandinka,[78] Hausa,[79] and Ashanti[80] were also sin-
gled out as islands of barbarism in a sea of savagery. The British preference for Ashanti over their Fante allies was a curious choice, since
Ashanti was a constant threat, if it was not actively hostile. The cultures of Ashanti and the Fante states were remarkably similar. Yet
Ashanti was the only non-Muslim state to be consistently praised,
and the Fante were usually roundly condemned. In this case, it appears that the myth of the interior plus Bowdich's glowing account
combined with the existing dislike of partly-Westernized Africans. In
Sierra Leone, and for similar reasons, the British approved of the
Maroons and disapproved of the Nova Scotians. As the liberated
Africans began to come ashore from the slavers, the British also
thought better of the Yoruba than of the Ibo or Bakongo.[81] Though
they neglected formal ethnography, they had firm opinions about the
qualities of distinct African cultures.

76. Prichard, *Researches* (1826), I, 250.
77. Durand, *Voyage to Senegal,* pp. 98–99; Golbéry, *Travels in Africa,* I, 70–74.
78. Golbéry, *Travels in Africa,* I, 73; Report of the Commissioners on African Settlements, PP, 1812, x (101), p. 5.
79. Jackson, *Morocco,* p. 247; Leyden and Murray, *Discoveries and Voyages in
Africa,* II, 486–87.
80. Torrane to African Committee, 20 July 1807, T 70/35, f. 66; Dupuis, *Residence
in Ashantee,* lxiv; *Edinburgh Review,* XLI, 341–43 (January 1825); [J. MacQueen]
"British Settlements in Western Africa," *Blackwood's Edinburgh Magazine,* XXVI,
342 (September 1829).
81. See, for example, R. C. Dallas, *The History of the Maroons from their Origin
to the Establishment of their Chief Tribe in Sierra Leone,* 2 vols. (London, 1803), I,
87–88; Spilsbury, *Western Coast of Africa,* p. 38; H. I. Ricketts, *Narrative of the
Ashantee War with a view of the Present State of Sierra Leone* (London, 1831),
pp. 191–93 and 209.

9

BARBARISM:

ITS PHYSICAL CAUSES

Faced, as they were, with the neces-
sary adjustment to the era of "legitimate trade," the British began
to look more closely at African society. Any rationally conceived policy required some understanding of what Africa would become if left
to herself, and what she might become under British influence. This
understanding, in turn, called on the theoretical knowledge of
scholars and scientists—on their beliefs about the nature of race, environment, and culture.

British discussions of Africa in the early nineteenth century necessarily took their departure from the eighteenth-century image of
Africa. They began with the accepted "fact" that Negro Africans
were, at best, barbarians who had never known civilization. They
were also Negro in race. Were these two factors related? If so, what
was the precise nature of the relationship? Would the racial heritage
of the Negroes prevent the rise of civilization in Africa, or would
their racial characteristics themselves change with the "improvement"
of the African way of life? In the priority of logic, the first answer
was necessarily that of the physical anthropologists. If they made

a convincing argument that African man was biologically incapable of change, there was no need to consult moral philosophers or other social theorists.

The starting point for biological science in the early nineteenth century was the knowledge and theory built up in the great age of biological classification. Physical anthropology was still largely undifferentiated from the amorphous body of biology in general. Biological knowledge was itself constantly changing, but it was still firmly pre-Darwinian. New evidence was brought forward, and new theories were propounded. The new theories were often no more accurate, by modern standards, than the ones they replaced, but they were more important: in an age where the prestige of science was steadily increasing, the dicta of the scientists began to carry a new kind of weight. The biological view of race could no longer be ignored as Granville Sharp had ignored it in the 1770's, and it could no longer be put off by a mere citation of scripture as the humanitarians had tended to do since the 1780's.

At the same time, much of the new prestige of the biologists came from their work in fields with little immediate application to questions of race. Paralleling the development of clinical medicine, the first decades of the nineteenth century saw the true foundation of comparative anatomy and paleontology. This work was centered in France and especially associated with the name of the Swiss scientist, Baron George Cuvier (1769–1832). Like the earlier problem of classification, it was concerned with the whole animal kingdom, and the varieties of man were not given serious or concentrated attention. Data on the physical structure of the African race were still drawn from Soemmering, and the even more suspect evidence of Edward Long was sometimes cited by reputable biologists.

The only important attempt to correct some of these errors by actually investigating African anatomy was that of Thomas Winterbottom in Sierra Leone during the 1790's. Winterbottom had an opportunity to examine large numbers of Africans, which was not possible in Europe. He was also concerned for religious reasons to undermine the polygenist position summed up by Charles White at the end of the century. With more data, it was easy enough to show that Soemmering had generalized about African skull capacity by measuring only a few skulls. In fact, skull capacity varied greatly from one individual to another irrespective of race. Winterbottom showed that Soemmering had simply mistaken the anatomical features of a few individuals for the characteristics of the Negro race as a whole.[1]

The old libels of popular belief were still more serious than Soemmering's scientific errors, and Winterbottom set out systematically to refute these on the basis of his African experience. One of the basic supports of polygenesis, for example, had been the assumed difference between African and European nervous systems—the belief that African women could give birth without pain, that the Negro nervous system was generally less sensitive in matters of touch and taste, though not in eyesight. The Negro brain, bile, and blood had also been held to be of a different color from those of other races. It was a common belief that Negro sexual organs were larger, that Negro women menstruated in greater quantity and with less disturbance than Europeans, that Negro women had long and pendulous breasts as an inherited physical trait. All these points were corrected easily enough on the basis of a few years of medical practice among Negroes.[2]

Another support for polygenesis was the claim that Africans mature faster than Europeans and have a shorter life span, thus approaching the pattern of animals. The idea originated from the uncritical and mistaken observation by West Indian planters and travellers to Africa. Winterbottom made a careful investigation of the age of sexual maturity among the "Nova Scotians" at Sierra Leone and found it was not significantly different from that of Europeans. The question of longevity, however, was more difficult for lack of statistical data. Winterbottom was a careful scientist. He left the question open, rather than come out with a snap judgement which might have strengthened his case.[3] In this work, as in other aspects of his many-sided investigations, Winterbottom had no immediate successors, but it stood for half a century as a mine of evidence. The defenders of African equality and African membership in a common mankind could and did draw on it freely.

The theory of polygenesis was declining in British anthropological circles after the turn of the century, and for several reasons. The unfettered rationalism of Long, Kames, and White now met with an increasing current of theological opposition. The Evangelical movement, the religious revival, the disappointment with the French Revo-

1. T. Winterbottom, *An Account of the Native Africans in the Neighbourhood of Sierra Leone*, 2 vols. (London, 1803), II, 255–56.
2. Winterbottom, *Native Africans*, I, 190–91; II, 214–15 and 270–71.
3. Winterbottom, *Native Africans*, II, 263.

lution after its early promise—all of these turned some men back
to the Bible, and the Bible seemed perfectly clear. God had "made of
one blood all nations of men for to dwell on the face of the earth,
and hath determined the times appointed, and bounds of their habitation" (Acts 17:26). Influential biologists were also more inclined
than before to support monogenesis. Blumenbach in his later work
used Winterbottom's evidence and arrived at a new and authoritative statement, which was accepted with variations by the other eminent biologists of the period—by Cuvier in France and by Lawrence
and Prichard in England.[4] While several of the lesser authorities remained convinced polygenists and kept the belief alive, the center
of that school was now in France, represented principally by Bory
de Saint-Vincent and Geoffroy de Saint-Hilaire.[5]

This temporary resurgence of monogenesis countered the poly-
genetic insistence on Negro inferiority, but it did not necessarily imply
a belief in human equality regardless of race. Even monogenists used
the hierarchical forms of race classification, though the idea of the
"Great Chain of Being" was gradually losing ground. Blumenbach
restated his older five-fold classification in 1795. Even though he was
now a conscious publicist in defense of Negro abilities, he continued
to believe that the non-European races were "degenerations" from
the white race.[6] Other views, and especially those on the Continent,
were still less favorable. In 1809 Lamarck classified all mankind as
Bimania, sub-divided into six races arranged in order from Caucasian
at the top to Negro at the bottom. Cuvier followed a similar order in
1817, but returned to a three-fold division into Caucasian, Mongolian, and Negro. This system had the advantage of simplicity, and
it reflected the Biblical division according to the descendents of Ham,
Shem, and Japhet. With Cuvier's immense prestige behind it, the
three-fold classification gradually displaced Blumenbach's system and
became the most common schema from that time onward.[7]

    4. J. F. Blumenbach, "Contributions to Natural History," in T. Bendyshe, Ed.,
Anthropological Treatises of Johann Friedrich Blumenbach (London, 1865). First
published in 1806; G. Cuvier, *The Animal Kingdom,* 16 vols. (London, 1827–1835),
I, 80; Sir William Lawrence, *Lectures on Physiology, Zoology, and the Natural History
of Man* (London, 1819), p. 493; J. C. Prichard, *Researches into the Physical History
of Man,* 2nd ed., 2 vols. (London, 1826), II, 586–87.
    5. A. C. Haddon, *History of Anthropology,* 2nd. ed. (London, 1934), p. 40;
J. Barzun, *Race: a Study in Modern Superstition* (New York, 1937), pp. 64-65.
    6. J. F. Blumenbach, "On the Natural Varieties of Mankind," in T. Bendyshe, Ed.,
Anthropological Treatises of Johann Friedrich Blumenbach, pp. 264 ff.
    7. E. W. Count (Ed.), *This is Race* (New York, 1950), pp. 40 and 706.

Cuvier's view epitomized the beliefs of Continental scientists, with results that were unfortunate for the racial reputation of the Africans. His system was not only openly hierarchical, it also made the implicit assumption that race and culture are intimately connected. His summary description is worth quoting in full, if only for its tone of racial and cultural chauvinism.

The Caucasian, to which we ourselves belong, is chiefly distinguished by the beautiful form of the head, which approximates to a perfect oval. It is also remarkable for variations in the shade of the complexion, and colour of the hair. From this variety have sprung the most civilized nations, and such as have most generally exercised dominion over the rest of mankind.

The Mongolian variety is recognized by prominent cheek-bones, flat visage, narrow and oblique eyes, hair straight and black, scanty beard, and olive complexion. This race has formed mighty empires in China and Japan, and occasionally extended its conquests on this side of the Great Desert, but its civilization has long appeared stationary.

The negro race is confined to the south of Mount Atlas. Its characters are, black complexion, woolly hair, compressed cranium, and flattish nose. In the prominence of the lower part of the face, and the thickness of the lips, it manifestly approaches to the monkey tribe. The hordes of which this variety is composed have always remained in a state of complete barbarism.[8]

English writers on physical anthropology were more moderate in their anti-Negro strictures and increasingly suspicious of such clear divisions into neat categories. Both Sir William Lawrence and James Cowles Prichard, the most influential British authorities of their time, abandoned the "Great Chain of Being." Both were impressed with the range of individual difference within any of the major racial groupings. Lawrence followed Blumenbach's five-fold system, but only for the sake of convenience, holding that lines of classification were merely conventional and arbitrary. At the same time, he believed firmly in white superiority—not as the highest term in a series but as the single superior race standing above all of the "dark races" grouped together at a lower level. The conception followed Blumenbach, but, where Blumenbach saw only a small degree of separation between the races, Lawrence emphasized the gulf he believed to exist between the superior Europeans and their degenerate off-shoots.[9]

Like the earlier biological writers, Lawrence had to find grounds for his belief in qualities that were not scientifically measurable. He

8. Cuvier, *Animal Kingdom,* I, 97.
9. Lawrence, *Lectures,* pp. 327–29 and 549–72.

found one criterion in esthetics—that is, in self-admiration of his own physical type. He also called in ethnographic evidence in order to "prove" an inborn racial difference of intellect, and (a new emphasis as the nineteenth century progressed) in natural moral character as well.

The distinction of colour between the white and black races is not more striking than the pre-eminence of the former in moral feelings and in mental endowments. The latter, it is true, exhibit generally a great acuteness of the external senses, which in some instances is heightened by exercise to a degree nearly incredible. Yet they indulge, almost universally, in disgusting debauchery and sensuality, and display gross selfishness, indifference to the pains and pleasures of others, insensibility to beauty of form, order, and harmony, and an almost entire want of what we comprehend altogether under the expression of elevated sentiments, manly virtues, and moral feelings.[10]

On the face of it, this opinion is hardly more favorable than that of Cuvier, but it was qualified in a number of ways. In discussing Africans in particular, Lawrence accepted the usual stereotype of the African character, and with it the accepted list of African virtues. From these, it could be deduced that Negroes were not so inferior in morality as he believed them to be in mental ability. Furthermore, he thought of racial endowments as a kind of average for the whole group: individual Africans might well excel beyond the usual standard of the white race. In addition, Lawrence's racial views, like those of Charles White before him, were no bar to humanitarian sentiments, and he included an attack on slavery and the slave trade in his scientific lectures.[11]

James Cowles Prichard was even more closely associated with the humanitarian movement, and his major contribution to British thought about Africa was to continue Blumenbach's work as a defender of Negro ability. He despised the African way of life but insisted there was no physical limitation to the *potential* achievement of any people, no matter what their racial type. He also followed Blumenbach in minimizing the differences between the major racial groups—so much so that he preferred not to use an overall classification. While there were roughly recognizable differences between Africans, Asians, and Europeans, there were innumerable transitions as well. "The swarthy nations of Africa do not appear to form that dis-

---

10. Lawrence, *Lectures*, p. 476.
11. Lawrence, *Lectures*, pp. 364, 478–79, 491, and 493–94.

tinct kind of people, separated from all other races of men by a broad line, and uniform among themselves, which we ideally represent under the term *Negro*. There is perhaps not one single nation in which all the characters ascribed to the negro are found in the highest degree, and in general they are distributed to different nations in all manner of ways, and combined in each instance with more or fewer of the characters belonging to the European and the Asiatic."[12]

It was partly on account of this belief that Prichard moved gradually away from purely physical anthropology. In his later years he came to believe that language was the only valid criterion for classifying the peoples of the world. As early as the 1826 edition of the *Physical History of Mankind,* he laid out a mixed linguistic-physical classification of African races. He found three great divisions: the northern Africans who resemble Europeans in physical appearance; the "red or copper-colored" peoples stretching in a belt across Africa from Ethiopia to Cape Verde and including the Fulbe of West Africa; and finally the "woolly-haired" peoples. This group was in turn subdivided into the Negroes of the Guinea coast and western savannas, the Bantu-speaking peoples of central and southern Africa, and the Hottentots of the far southwest.[13]

One observation that bothered many of the early nineteenth-century classifiers of race was the fact that physical characteristics—skin color, form of hair, skull shape, and facial features—seemed to vary independently of one another. In addition to Prichard's solution of loose physical classification modified by language, it was possible to search for a single, rationally valid criterion, which could then serve as the sole basis of classification. If this were successful, it might also be possible to rank the races of man in an order of merit on physical grounds alone.

Scientists approached the problem by looking for some definite link between physical traits and mental ability. The effort began in the eighteenth century. Soemmering believed the form of the skull showed the psychological make-up of its former owner, and he tried to prove that Negro skulls were intermediate between those of Europeans and those of monkeys. Camper's facial angle was a further step. From the 1790's onward the supposed link between psychology and physiology was a special concern of the French school of *Idéalogues,*

12. Prichard, *Researches* (1826), I, 356.
13. Prichard, *Researches* (1826), I, 241–42.

among whom Cabanis, Vicq d'Azyr, and Destutt de Tracy were perhaps the most important.[14]

The most influential step in this direction in the first decade of the nineteenth century came from the new science of phrenology. The principles were first laid down by Franz Joseph Gall (1757–1828) of Vienna and further developed with the collaboration of Johann Gaspar Spurzheim (1774–1832) of Trier. The essence of the phrenological system was the belief that the human mind could be divided into thirty-seven different "faculties," each of which was to be found in a different part of the cortex. For any individual, the strength or weakness of each of these faculties could be discovered by carefully measuring the shape of the skull. Thus character could be analyzed merely by external examination of the head.[15]

Phrenology was, of course, mistaken on almost every point. Even the correct guess that different "faculties" were located in discrete portions of the brain was covered over by the incorrect assumption that these qualities would, in turn, influence the external shape of the head. Nevertheless, its original claims were limited: it was not conceived as a key to physical anthropology, only to the psychological make-up of individual men. But it soon began to spread beyond these early claims. If it seemed to work for individuals, why not for nations and races as well? The desire to overgeneralize about races, social classes, and nations was, in any case, a common intellectual failing of the early nineteenth century. Gall himself warned against any such misuse of his invention, but it was all too convenient. New devotees, particularly outside of the Germanys, were anxious to broaden the system to its fullest social implications. It was taken up in England by George Combe, who had himself been converted by Spurzheim in 1816. Through Combe's efforts, the system acquired a popular following first in the British Isles and later in North America; in time Combe himself was to use the system for the analysis of race.[16]

Meanwhile, some influences from phrenology made their way into the thought of established biologists. Lawrence used phrenological evidence as early as 1819 to prove that race and culture were inter-

14. Barzun, *Race,* pp. 58–60.
15. For a convenient summary of the system see J. C. Flügel, *A Hundred Years of Psychology, 1833–1933,* 2nd ed. (London, 1951), pp. 36–44.
16. George Combe, *A System of Phrenology* (New York, 1845), p. 423. The first edition was published in 1819 under the title *Essays on Phrenology*. Later editions were much enlarged. The fourth London edition of 1836 served as the basis for the American edition of 1845.

connected as part of the permanent order of things. He stopped short of using it as the basis for race classification, but the implications were clear—if head shape was the key to character and mental ability, then headshape was an outward physical sign of the greatest importance. The head was the outer covering of the brain. Hence it should be the prime criterion for race classification. But there were serious problems. The phrenological system consisted of thirty-seven independent variables, and these were not quantitatively measurable. Furthermore, skin color was too obvious a trait to be ignored.

By the 1820's the importance of headshape was emphasized by a new kind of problem. W. F. Edwards, an English scientist living in Paris, was inspired by the writings of Amadée and Augustin Thierry, who had seen racial rather than individual character as the key to historical change. He set out to bring anthropology to the aid of history and arrive at a large-scale, scientifically established, racial history of Europe. With his work confined to Europe, skin color was no longer in question. Racial sub-types had to be distinguished in some other way. Edwards made his bow to phrenology and chose "the form and proportion of the head and face" as the crucial trait for distinguishing one race from another.[17] His theories had nothing directly to do with Africa, but their indirect influence was to be of the greatest importance. If racial interpretations of European history could be made to look "scientific," racial explanations of African culture seemed all the more plausible.

The full impact of these developments was to come only in the 1830's and 1840's. English thought during the first three decades of the century was more generally favorable to Africans than it had been in the recent past or would be in the decades that followed. With polygenesis out of fashion, Lawrence preaching humanitarianism, and Prichard consciously working to use science for humanitarian ends, the contrast with Continental opinion was apparent. In 1827, the English editors of Cuvier's *Animal Kingdom* found it necessary to explain and modify his strictures on African capabilities.[18] The views

17. W. F. Edwards, "Des caractères physiologiques des races humaines, considérés dans leurs rapports avec l'histoire . . . ," *Mémoires de la Société Ethnologique*, I (1), 1–108 (1841). First published as a separate book in 1829. See also Edwards, "Esquisse de l'état actuel de l'Anthropologie ou de l'historie naturelle de l'homme," *Mémoires de la Société Ethnologique,* I (1), 123-25 for the author's retrospective appreciation of his own earlier achievement.

18. Edward Griffith and others, "Supplemental History of Man," in G. Cuvier, *The Animal Kingdom,* 16 vols. (London, 1827–1835), esp. I. 172–74.

they expressed were essentially those of Lawrence. While accepting race difference as a fact, they added: "Man as we see him around us, morally speaking, is a creature of art and education. . . . Knowledge, then, is not indigenous to his mind: it is an exotic, acquired by art, and approaches more or less to perfection, in proportion to the care and industry employed in its cultivation."[19]

Thus, while many—perhaps most—English authorities believed in the inferiority of other races, they also left room for the operation of "moral causes," which might drastically modify or even eliminate the "barbarity" of African culture. Even within the narrow range of race theory, there remained an opening for the "lower races." With polygenesis disposed of, it was necessary to assume that these "inferior races" had become inferior at some finite point in time—and not long ago, since the creation itself was thought to be only a few millennia away. If their "inferiority" had been acquired so quickly, it might disappear with equal speed.

Meanwhile, some of the more naive eighteenth-century suppositions about the origins of race were gradually swept away. The older view that dark skin color might represent the inheritance of an acquired suntan over several generations had some obvious faults. Travellers pointed out that the darkest people in Africa were the Wolof living near Cape Verde, not the people living nearest the equator.[20] Nor were the white creoles of the West Indies turning darker in successive generations of tropical life.[21] Newer explanations arose, such as the belief that African skin color came from the habitual breathing of "phlogistonated" air,[22] but this too fell before the test of empiricism. By the early nineteenth century, the most prominent of the British anthropologists had come to believe that acquired characteristics could not be inherited. New varieties must therefore occur in a manner that appeared to be accidental and could not be explained.[23]

19. Griffiths and others, "Supplemental History," I, 113.

20. S. M. X. Golberry [S. M. X. de Golbéry], *Travels in Africa Performed during the Years 1785, 1786, 1787*, 2 vols. (London, 1803), I, 75; J. Corry, *Observations upon the Windward Coast of Africa . . . made in the years 1805–1806* (London, 1807), p. 96.

21. Prichard, *Researches* (1826), II, 532–36.

22. Richard Shannon, *Practical Observations on the Operation and Effects of Certain Medicines in the Prevention and Cure of Diseases to which Europeans are Subject in Hot Climates and in these Kingdoms* (London, 1794), p. 395.

23. Prichard, *Researches* (1826), II, 548–49; Lawrence, *Lectures*, 508–10; William

William Wells, an American physician settled in London, seized on the element of uncertainty, and on the recent developments in tropical medicine, to produce a theory of racial origins through natural selection. (It was, incidentally, more nearly precursory of Darwin's later discovery than any other theory of the early nineteenth century.) Wells began with the proposition that Europeans and Africans differed most markedly in their resistance to disease, not in external traits like skin color. He cited the recent data from Africa, showing that Europeans could not create a self-reproductive society in tropical Africa. Nor, he claimed, could Africans permanently reproduce their own kind in the north. Furthermore, among men as among animals, individual variations are constantly produced by nature. Of these accidental varieties born in Africa, some would be, "better fitted than others to bear the diseases of the country. This race would consequently multiply, while the others would decrease, not only from their inability to sustain the attacks of disease, but from their incapacity of contending with their more vigorous neighbours. The colour of this vigorous race I take for granted, from what has been already said, would be dark."[24]

By the same process, a superior race would emerge in the north, and here the color would be light—not because skin color gave immunity to disease, but because this particular skin color accidentally accompanied climatic adaptation.

It goes without saying that the evidence on which this theory was based was erroneous. African immunity to the "tropical climate" was not racial but environmental in origin, and Africans could survive perfectly well in the north. Nevertheless, the only important point separating Wells's theory from Darwin's was the fact that Wells dealt only with human races, while Darwin dealt with all animals. Wells's statement also lacked the full justification that Darwin was to supply, and it was put forward so diffidently that it seems to have

---

C. Wells, *An Account of a Female of the White Race of Mankind, Part of Whose Skin Resembles that of a Negro; with some Observations on the Causes of the Differences in Color and Form Between the White and Negro Races of Men Appended to Two Essays: One Upon Single Vision with Two Eyes and the Other on Dew . . .* (London, 1818), pp. 435–46.

24. Wells, *Account*, pp. 435–36. A degree of relative immunity is found with the "sickle-cell" trait and perhaps with certain other hemoglobin characteristics. While these are clearly genetic, they are not "racial" in the sense that they invariably accompany certain physical types.

had little direct influence on the formation of Darwin's ideas. It was only called to his attention after the publication of *The Origin of Species*.[25]

The indirect influence of Wells's idea was much greater. The essence of the theory was restated by Prichard in 1826, and from that point it went on to become one of the common hypotheses about the origins of race differences.[26] It explained in ostensibly scientific and evolutionary terms why, to all appearances, the Europeans were not able to survive on the Coast. It also suggested that, whatever Europeans might think of their own racial superiority, in the conditions of tropical Africa, the Africans themselves were the more "vigorous" race. When, in the 1830's and '40's, culture contact and race contact were discussed in increasingly evolutionary terms, Wells's hypothesis would be developed and expanded in a variety of ways.

Wells's hypothesis was important in still another direction, and one more closely connected with the Africans. He accepted the common view that the supposed cultural inferiority of the Africans was somehow related to their physical type. But he remained uncertain as to which was cause and which effect. The possibility remained that "Negro features" were the result of a "low state of civilization" and would "improve" as the Africans became more civilized. After all, as he pointed out, ancient Egyptian art showed people who were clearly negroid in appearance. Yet modern Egyptians were not Negroes. Could this change be one that somehow accompanies the rise of civilization? He left the question unanswered.[27] Others, however, did not, and the possibility remained that, even though race and culture were linked, an "improving" culture could "improve" racial characteristics as well.[28] Thus even the most binding assumptions of racial inferiority and an iron-clad link between race and culture failed to prove that inferiority was necessarily permanent. Scope remained

25. R. H. Shryock, "The Strange Case of Wells' Theory of Natural Selection," in M. F. Ashley (Ed.), *Studies and Essays in the History of Science and Learning in Honor of George Sarton* (New York, 1944).

26. Prichard, *Researches* (1826), II, 575–82. Darwin was, of course, familiar with Prichard's work, as he was with Robert Knox's *The Races of Man* (London, 1850), where the theme of natural selection among human races was given even greater emphasis.

27. Wells, *Account,* pp. 438 ff.

28. This view was put forward by J. C. Prichard in many of his writings. For his final argument on the subject see Prichard, *Researches into the Physical History of Man,* 4th ed., 5 vols. (London, 1851), II, 388 and 340–46 or his *Natural History of Man,* 4th ed., 2 vols. (London, 1855), I, 97–101.

for the operation of moral causes—even to the extent of removing "physical inferiority."

These racial theories might seem, at first glance, to have an important bearing on British policy toward Africans in the Old World or the New. The theory of polygenesis had, indeed, been used in the 1790's as a defense of the slave trade, but "scientific" racism played only a minor role in the debates about slavery after the Napoleonic Wars. In part, the decline of racist arguments is explained by the anti-slavery position taken by the humanitarians themselves. They did not claim full equality for all races of men, only the minimum condition of monogenesis. As the argument usually ran, the Negroes' right to freedom derived from the Christian charity that was owing to any of God's creatures, regardless of racial character. It appeared in the motto of the Anti-Slavery Society, inscribed under the picture of a Negro in chains: "Am I not a Man and a brother?" Any monogenist—and at this period any orthodox Christian—necessarily had to answer in the affirmative. With this point safely accepted, humanitarian pamphleteers could concede the inferiority of African culture and character. As one of them put it: "The Negro may indeed have rather more of that volatile sensibility, or irritability, which seems to make all human character as it approaches the sun,—warmer, yet weaker;—their sentiments more ardent, seem to be more transient than ours; and their faculties may be somewhat different, but certainly not beyond the power of habit and education to model and assimilate."[29]

The argument could be given a further turn, and the claims of the Africans made to appear the more pressing *because* of their assumed inferiority. Sir William Lawrence himself put the case for racist paternalism in a way that strongly suggested a "white man's burden."

In the warm and long disputes on this subject [of Negro slavery], both parties have contrived to be in the wrong regarding Negro faculties. The abolitionists have erred in denying a natural inferiority so clearly evinced by the concurring evidence of anatomical structures and experience. But it was only an error of fact, and may be the more readily excused as it was on the side of humanity.

Their opponents have committed the more serious moral mistake of perverting what should constitute a claim to kindness and indulgence into justification or palliation of the revolting and antichristian practice of traffic in human flesh. . . . Superior endowments, higher intellect, greater capacity for knowledge, arts, and science, should be employed to extend the blessings of civiliza-

29. *West African Sketches* . . . (London, 1824), p. 22.

tion, and multiply the enjoyments of social life; not as a means of oppressing the weak and ignorant, of plunging those who are naturally low in the intellectual scale still more deeply into the abyss of barbarism.[30]

In the atmosphere of religious revival, any argument that could be made to appear immoral was hardly useful in political debate. Pro-slavery writers therefore dwelt on the political and economic expediency of continuing slavery. When they took up the question of race they placed the emphasis on emotional xenophobia and cultural chauvinism, rather than pseudo-scientific racial theories. Cobbett had the touch. In a single paragraph he could ring the changes on nationalism, sexual competition, and economic self-interest, jumping from the enlistment of Negro soldiers as a disgrace to the King's uniform, to the "disgusting spectacle" of miscegenation and mixed marriage in England, to the taxpayer's burden in supporting the colony of Sierra Leone—where, unaccountably, the Africans were condemned as "sable intruders."[31]

And there was a fund of racial xenophobia to play on. In a period before Negroes were a common sight in English cities, even the missionaries going out to Africa were caught short by the unfamiliar appearance of the people they had come to "save." As William Singleton, a Quaker missionary agent, reported of his own arrival in Bathurst in 1821: "The first object that engaged my attention as I passed along the beach was the great variety in the countenances and forms of the natives. Some appeared to possess so little of the human face, so little indication of intellect, that, at the first glance, I was rather painfully affected . . ."[32]

Some humanitarian publicists were fully aware of the need to combat prejudice, both scientific and emotional. Building on the body of pro-Negro arguments gathered together by Blumenbach and James Ramsay, a literary tradition grew up in defense of the Negroes. Blumenbach continued his earlier work with a new publication in 1806. In this, he drew on the new biological researches of Winterbot-

30. Lawrence, *Lectures,* p. 364.
31. *Cobbett's Annual Register,* I, 701–2 (June 1802).
32. [William Singleton and others], *Report of the Committee Managing a Fund Raised by Some Friends for the Purpose of Promoting African Instruction; with an Account of a Visit to the Gambia and Sierra Leone* (London, 1822), p. 25. See also John Morgan, *Reminiscences of the Founding of a Christian Mission on the Gambia* (London, 1864), p. 45, for a similar reaction on the author's first arrival in Bathurst in 1827.

tom and leaned even more heavily on literary authority to extend and amplify his list of eminent Negroes. He concluded that, "there is no so-called savage nation known under the sun which has so distinguished itself by such examples of perfectibility and original capacity for scientific culture, and thereby attached itself so closely to the most civilized nations of the earth, *as the Negro.*"[33]

Another important work dating from the period of slave-trade abolition was Abbé Grégoire's *De la literature des nègres*, which drew heavily from Blumenbach and the earlier works and came to stand for the next forty years as the principal thesaurus of pro-Negro debate. The work is therefore especially useful as a touchstone for understanding some of the cultural and racial attitudes of the time, even though the only English translation was published in America.[34] Grégoire was clearly not a scientist. He had only a slight understanding of recent biological developments, but he felt it necessary to begin with a defense of monogenesis, built largely on the work of Winterbottom and Blumenbach. He was obviously much more at home within the range of moral philosophy, and his study of the "African character" was a classic compilation. "The African" that emerged was very much the noble savage with Christian overtones. His only real vice was laziness, and this could be corrected by Christianity and civilization. Grégoire had a mild admiration for what he took to be the African political achievement in erecting limited monarchies and republics, but otherwise he had little respect for African culture.

His final argument was Blumenbach's point about cultural assimilation: if individual Africans could succeed in Western society, then African society as a whole could become "civilized." But Blumenbach and Grégoire both passed over African achievements within African culture, and the weight of Grégoire's evidence merely extended and amplified Blumenbach's list of Negro worthies. It was now lengthened to more than eighty pages of biographical detail, replete with Latin odes of Negro composition.[35]

One Negro writer used the work of the anthropologists for his

33. Blumenbach, "Contributions to Natural History," p. 312.

34. Abbé Henri Baptiste Grégoire, *De la litérature des nègres, ou recherches sur leur facultés intellectuelles, leur qualités morales, et leur litérature* (Paris, 1808), translated by D. B. Warden as *An Enquiry Concerning the Intellectual and Moral Facilities and Literature of Negroes . . .* (Brooklyn, 1810).

35. Grégoire, *Enquiry*, pp. 155–241. See also *Anecdotes of Africans* (London, 1827) for a later derivative English work in the same vein.

own ends. The Baron de Vastey of Haiti argued the case for monogenesis in the orthodox way, but he admitted that there were different racial endowments which worked to the advantage of people
of African descent living in the tropics. He cited Montesquieu's opinion that southerners were cowards and agreed that this was the case
of all Europeans who came to live in hot countries. Men of African
descent, however, were not subject to the same climatic determinism,
and if Europeans wanted to prove their superiority they would have
to do so by showing they could survive in the tropics as successfully
as the blacks.[36]

The main line of English pro-African argument, however, was
epitomized in a sermon by the Reverend Richard Watson, delivered
in 1824, when he was Secretary of the Wesleyan-Methodist Missionary Society. Although Watson had absorbed the Blumenbach-
Grégoire data about the achievement of individual Negroes, his principal defense remained the Biblical authority for monogenesis, which
was still more convincing than science. Watson was also perceptive
in picking out the two principal enemies of racial equality—the
planters and the scientists:

[T]he first is composed of those who have had to contend with the passions and vices of the negro in his purely pagan state, and have applied no
other instrument to elicit the virtues they have demanded than the stimulus
of the whip, and the stern voice of authority. . . . The second class are our
minute philosophers, who take the gauge of intellectual capacity from the
disposition of the bones of the head, and link mortality and the contour of
the countenance; men who measure mind by the rule and compasses; and estimate capacity for knowledge and salvation by a scale of inches and the acuteness
of angles.[37]

Watson spoke for religious orthodoxy, and religious orthodoxy
had a strong appeal. On the other hand, Thomas Fowell Buxton was
probably correct in gauging the opinion of the British ruling class in
1830, when he admitted in the House of Commons that his belief
in racial equality was a minority position. Not many would agree,
he said, "that there is no difference between the Black and the White,

36. Baron J. L. de Vastey, *Reflexions sur une lettre de Mazères, ex-colon français,
adressée à M. J. C. L. Sismonde de Sismondi, sur les noires et blancs, le civilisation de
l'Afrique, le Royaume d'Hayti, etc.* (Paris, 1816).
37. Richard Watson, "The Religious Instruction of Slaves in the West India Colonies
Advocated and Defended," *Works of the Rev. Richard Watson* (London, 1834), II, 94.
The sermon was first preached in April 1824.

except that which is produced by superior opportunities of receiving information."[38]

The crucial question was the kind and quality of this racism. In 1830 the belief was still rare than the African race was inevitably condemned to a permanent state of "barbarism." Both science and religion, each in its own way, held the door open to improvement through "moral influences."

38. Thomas Fowell Buxton, Commons, 15 June 1830, 2 H 25, c. 399.

BARBARISM:

ITS MORAL CAUSES

While most Britons assumed that
African culture and African race were somehow interdependent, the
accepted social theories still gave priority to man's moral, rather than
his physical nature. In spite of the growing prestige of the new
biology, most educated men were still trained in the classical tradition
of humane letters. They were neither accustomed to the scientific
outlook nor imbued with the fullest faith in the conclusions science
might reach. They believed, to be sure, what science had to say in new
areas of knowledge, but belief stopped short when it came into conflict with older preconceptions. Not only the authority of the Bible,
but the more general attitude of seeking truth by reference to literary
authority retained much of its old strength, even after a century of
rationalism.

The tradition of humane letters was principally an ethnocentric
tradition. It was concerned with European society, and with its roots
in Mediterranean civilization. Western civilization was thought of as
the only true civilization, the only one epitomizing mankind's path
of progress. Non-Western societies were, at best, exotic variants from

the main stream of history. They were, in present-day jargon, "control groups" against which Europeans could measure their own achievements.

The nature of human progress was, indeed, the principal concern of social theory in the early nineteenth century. The idea of progress had infiltrated many aspects of Western thought since the middle of the seventeenth century. Eighteenth-century rationalists had helped it along in the variant readings of Condorcet in France or the Scottish moral philosophers, and most versions were still optimistic: it was still far too early for the later nineteenth-century belief that the "less fit" must go to the wall to make room for the "fittest." With the French Revolution, the optimistic strain was sometimes continued, as it was with utopians like William Godwin, but disillusionment also set in. As the early promise of the French Revolution degenerated into the long wars for European hegemony, this attitude was sometimes expressed as a revived Christian pessimism, sometimes in secular forms. In 1789 Thomas Malthus published his *Essay on Population* as explicit ammunition against the more naive hopes, but the idea of progress itself was barely shaken. In decades following the Napoleonic Wars, it went on to new heights, carried there by a generation of publicists who saw around them the material fruits of the Industrial Revolution and the "moral" fruits of the Evangelical revival. English society seemed not only richer but better—more devout, wiser, more just than any the world had seen before.

With progress so notable, writers in many fields became more conscious of change as a factor to be explained. Dynamic forms of analysis gradually replaced the static analysis so common a century earlier, and the new tendency of thought was clear in moral philosophy, as it was in the physical sciences. The static world of mercantilist economics was disappearing in favor of a new school with Adam Smith at its head, and the bare beginnings of development economics were already visible. John Millar, Adam Ferguson, and the rest had laid the groundwork for a dynamic theory of history and society, and they were widely read.

Their work impinged on the British image of Africa at several points, but principally in discussing the "early stages of society," assumed to be that of existing African societies. Most of the Scottish school had something to say about early society, but few made special studies of the subject. Hugh Murray, however, tried to lay down a general and systematic theory of early social development based on ethnographic data. His *Enquiries Historical and Moral Respecting the Character of Nations and the Progress of Society* was largely derived from the older members of the Scottish school, but it remains an important and neglected work in the history of anthropological thought.

His point of departure was the idea of progress: "the aspect of human society is continually changing: it is continually becoming more numerous, more splendid, more civilized. Particular nations may have remained a long time stationary; nay, same have even experienced a temporary retrogradation; still, however, the general progress made by the species is certainly as above described."[1]

He believed that, by understanding the laws of progress, men could influence the course of history, since historical change took place according to the action of observable laws or principles. These laws, however, were not all-determining. Individual action and legislative interference were still possible, within limits. The study of "moral history" was necessary precisely in order to enable the legislator to "strike the medium between a superstitious attachment to what is ancient, and a tendency to rash innovations."[2]

This much was a common attitude of the Enlightenment, but Murray went beyond most of the eighteenth-century philosophers in considering the possible relations between race, climate, and culture. He began with the significant and rare assumption that race and culture are separate facts of the human condition; and furthermore, "that between any two great portions of the human species, (whatever be the age or country to which they belong,) there exists no radical distinction; that the total amount of moral and intellectual endowments originally conferred by nature is altogether or very nearly, the same; and that the wide differences which we observe, arise from the influence of external circumstances."[3]

He regarded racial characteristics as mere adaptations to environment. Though they might survive for some time after an individual

1. Hugh Murray, *Enquiries Historical and Moral Respecting the Character of Nations and the Progress of Society* (Edinburgh, 1808), p. 2.
2. Murray, *Enquiries*, pp. 1–4.
3. Murray, *Enquiries*, pp. 12–13.

had left his ancestral home, they were, for all that, only differences of external form having nothing whatever to do with the "dispositions of the mind."[4]

The direct influence of climate was also dismissed, in explicit disagreement with Kames, Hume, Volney, and Montesquieu, and with the support of new ethnographic data from Africa. He showed that Montesquieu's evidence for the prevalence of despotism in southern countries rested entirely on the despotisms of South Asia. West Africa, well to the south of India, had a whole range of different political systems—"republican" in the case of the Akan states, in other regions a form of chieftancy controlled by intricate checks and balances, in still others an irregular kind of feudalism. The West Africans, furthermore, far from being timid and sluggish, were fierce and tenacious of their independence. Any direct operation of the climate on the individual, then, had to be disallowed, but Murray still left room for the "moral" influence of climate, meaning in this case the role of climate in setting underlying conditions of human ecology.[5]

Murray's own theory of human progress was an intricate system, based in essence on a form of challenge and response. He held that history ultimately moves according to the operation of four progressive principles and two repressive principles. Each of the progressive principles operates in society so that its first influence, when present in a small degree, is negative, but its continued operation brings a reversal, and ultimately progress itself. In the same way, the repressive principles were held to work first toward progress and then against it.

The four progressive principles were a diverse lot. The first was called "numbers collected into one place," by which he meant the formation of social groups. Small groups and small societies were held to be less prone to vice than large ones, but also unable to achieve progress because they could not pool their resources and knowledge. As larger groups were formed, the first result was an increase in vice, but as time passed the value of intercommunication would outweigh the detrimental effects of vice. One conclusion for Africa was that large and complex societies can attain progress (at a

4. Murray, *Enquiries,* pp. 148–49.
5. Murray, *Enquiries,* pp. 140–47.

price), while small and segmented societies cannot; and Africa had many small societies.

The second principle was free communication, within societies and between societies. Murray used the example of culture contact. An individual first encountering other ways of life would initially lose his faith in any real or permanent standard of behavior, but in the longer run he would learn from the experience. The result would be cross-cultural borrowing, hence progress. As examples he cited the European demoralization of the Tahitians, or the corruption of the Spanish *conquistadores* in their contact with Mexican and Peruvian civilizations. In contact between "advanced" and "backward" cultures, both would be corrupted in the first instance, though both might gain in the long run.

The third progressive principle was simply wealth. For individuals and societies alike, the first increase in wealth brings indulgence and sensuality, but as time passes the newness wears off. Refinement and civilization follow.

Finally, there was the category of "Great Public Events," by which Murray meant such instances of social disorganization as war or revolution. These might appear to be completely destructive of progress, since they break down the normal social restraints. But a disorganized society also allows unusual social mobility and makes possible the rise of new and able men to positions of importance.[6]

The two repressive principles were more reminiscent of earlier social theories. The first principle was the necessity for labor. A little labor is progressive, since it makes for a sedate and sober character; but too much work leaves no leisure to cultivate the arts or the intellect. Applied to society as a whole, the optimum conditions for progress were to be found where the environment is neither too hard nor too easy. A moderate environmental challenge might even serve to keep the operation of this principle in its progressive phase. The obvious retort was the Malthusian argument that population pressure would, in the long run prevent progress—in Murray's terminology, by driving this principle into its repressive phase. But Murray answered that population pressure was not necessarily inimical to progress. In easy environments, it might even provide a necessary challenge to be met by the right amount of labor.

The second repressive principle was "coercion," meaning any and

6. Murray. *Enquiries*, pp. 21–63.

all forms of social subordination. A little coercion was necessary
for people to organize a society, but increased coercion would dimin-
ish the liberty of the individual and thus stifle invention, initiative,
and further progress.[7]

For Murray, the repressive and progressive principles were intimately related. The untrammelled action of a progressive principle
would call forth one of the repressive principles as a balance. Following this theory, he outlined the schematic history of mankind.
The basic pattern was the familiar four stages, called by Murray
primitive society, savagery, barbarism, and civilization. The first steps
toward civilization required a warm climate, where agriculture was
easy—in short, the exuberant growth of the tropics. The progressive
principles of wealth and "numbers collected in one place" could soon
make themselves felt. But progress was self-limiting in this setting:
it was soon brought to an end by the repressive principle of coercion.
Coercion would be especially severe, since the other repressive principle, the necessity for labor, could not operate fully in such a soft environment. Progress would therefore cease, as, according to Murray,
it had already ceased in the original cradle of civilization—the belt
of despotisms stretching from Egypt through South Asia to China.
Further progress could only take place where the need for labor made
possible a relaxation of coercion. "Thus, there has been, for the arts
and sciences, a continual progress northward from happier climates
to those less favoured by nature."[8]

One aspect of Murray's thesis—the concept of a moving focus of
"civilization"—was both ancient and persistent. Virgil had traced
the westward course of empire from Troy to Rome. Medieval German theorists justified its further transfer from Rome to Germany.
Geoffrey of Monmouth in twelfth-century England carried it on to his
own country, and Berkeley projected the couse of empire forward
to America.[9]

The idea of moving empire contained two threads, one of westward movement and one of movement to the north. Where Berkeley
chose to emphasize the westerly drift, Murray took the northward
movement and set it in the terms of eighteenth-century rationalism.
The focus of civilization was no longer conceived to move by the

7. Murray, *Enquiries*, pp. 64–95.
8. Murray, *Enquiries*, pp. 147–48.
9. See Loren Baritz, "The Idea of the West," *American Historical Review*, LXVI,
618–40 (April, 1961) for a history of this idea.

will of God, but for purely natural causes resting essentially on the relationship between environment, technology, and political institutions.

Although not solely concerned with West Africa, Murray's theory could serve to explain the "backwardness" of African culture, drawing in many partial explanations made in the past. The connection between labor and civilization, so often assumed, was explained as part of a broader and more elaborate theory. The failings of "despotism" found in some African societies, and the fragmentation of political institutions found in others, were equally taken into account as part of a grand sweep of history. Even the mutual corruption of Africans and Europeans in the course of the slave trade could be seen as a natural result of culture contact in its early stages.

Murray's views were not widely influential, but they represent one version of a series of ideas very widely held by British intellectuals of the period, and in particular by those trained in the Scottish tradition. They were especially compatible to the early Utilitarians, and we find James Mill, in 1817, tracing the stages of human society in India through much the same course of development as that outlined by Murray. With Mill, as with Murray, the key to movement upward through the stages of progress was population growth pressing on subsistence and thus forcing people to organize into a civil society— and into a society which in India stopped with the achievement of despotism. Mill too used African data, especially that provided by travellers like Mungo Park: he believed that Africa illustrated the earlier stages through which India had passed. He borrowed a great deal of his general social theory from John Millar, laying special emphasis on the social position of women as a gauge of the level of development.

While Murray lacked a broad following, Mill did not. Where Murray, for his time and place, was relatively friendly to African culture, Mill was extremely unfriendly to the culture of India. His discussion of Indian society was also drawn for a purpose—specifically to tear down the appreciative view of Indian civilization put forward by Sir William Jones. His attitude, and that of the Utilitarians he influenced, had a new note of cultural arrogance in regard to any and all non-Western peoples. In this respect Murray was closer to the eighteenth-century tradition on which both drew so heavily.

Mill was closer to the dominant attitude of the decades to come, which he himself was helping to create.[10]

Travellers to Africa and publicists writing about Africa sometimes relied on Murray's general theory, or on Mill's. More frequently, they drew on the Scottish intellectual tradition on which both were based. But a common background and the occasional use of the same theoretical principles could lead to a variety of different conclusions. Among the travellers, for example, Golbéry and Winterbottom visited adjacent parts of West African and published in the same year, but their analyses were poles apart. For Golbéry the Africans were vastly inferior to Europeans, but they were the happiest of men:

> Gifted with a carelessness which is totally unique, with an extreme agility, indolence, sloth, and great sobriety; the negro exists on his native soil, in the sweetest apathy, unconscious of want, or pain of privation, tormented neither with the cares of ambition, nor with the devouring ardour of desire.
> To him the necessary and indispensable articles of life are reduced to a very small number; and those endless wants, which torment Europeans are not known amongst the negroes of Africa.[11]

If not quite the noble savage, here at least was the happy savage. Golbéry supposed that Africans had come to achieve this state of bliss through a combination of race, climate, and religion. Race provided the natural bias toward "sloth," which kept the Africans from seeking the unattainable. Climate provided against the need for clothing or shelter, and tropical exuberance supplied plentiful food. African religion gave the necessary fatalism, protection both against fear of the future and the "fatal venom" of *ennui*. Together these conditions made for a society with an extremely high birth rate, where happy and healthy savages could father children until the age of sixty-five or seventy. Hence Africa was densely populated, and the slave trade was to some extent justified as a way of carrying off the excess people.[12]

Winterbottom, on the other hand, contradicted Golbéry's analysis on almost every point. He denied all direct influence of race or climate on human ability and thought of African culture as merely an

10. James Mill, *The History of British India,* 3 vols. (London, 1817). The discussion of culture theory and Indian-culture history occupies I, 91–480. See especially I, 102–7, 180–81, 293–94 and 429 ff.

11. S. M. X. Golberry [S. M. X. de Golbéry], *Travels in Africa Performed in the Years 1785, 1786, and 1787,* 2 vols. (London, 1803), II, 240.

12. Golbéry, *Travels,* II, 231–52.

earlier stage of civilization. Nor was civilization the exclusive property of any single people: "The annals of history prove to us, that
genius and empire have been constantly changing their seats, and that
no people or country have been favoured hitherto with the exclusive
enjoyment of them."[13]

Whatever this might promise for the future of Africa, the African
present was a far cry from Golbéry's Elysium. It was, for Winterbottom, a land of misery based on ignorance, poverty, polygyny, and
slavery. Polygyny stood out as a special evil, epitomizing the low
condition of women and hence the low state of society. It also caused
a low birth rate, slow population growth, and, by implication, slow
progress toward civilization.[14]

The influence of eighteenth-century social thought is as evident
here as it is in the work of Hugh Murray. Still other aspects of that
thought were selected and re-expressed by humanitarian publicists.
Wilberforce, in many ways the intellectual as well as the political
leader of the group, accepted the customary low esteem in which
African culture was then held, but he saw hope for the future in the
rule of law and the process of cultural diffusion:

> How is it that civilization and the arts grow up in any country? The reign
> of law and of civil order must be first established. From law, says a writer
> of acute discernment and great historical research, from law arises security;
> from security curiosity; from curiosity, knowledge. As property is accumulated,
> industry is excited, a taste for new gratification is formed, comforts of all
> kinds multiply, and the arts and sciences naturally spring and flourish in a soil
> and climate thus prepared for their reception. Yet, even under these circum-
> stances, the progress of the arts and sciences would be extremely slow, if a
> nation were not to import the improvements of former times and other coun-
> tries. And we are well warranted, by the experience of all ages, in laying it
> down as an incontrovertible position—that the arts and sciences, knowledge,
> and civilization, have never yet been found to be a native growth of any
> country; but that they have ever been communicated from one nation to
> another, from the more to the less civilized.[15]

13. Thomas Winterbottom, *An Account of the Native Africans in the Neighbour-*
hood of Sierra Leone, 2 vols. (London, 1803), I, 145–51, 176–77, and 215–18.

14. Winterbottom, *Native Africans*, I, 145–51, 176-77, 215–18.

15. W. Wilberforce, *A Letter on the Abolition of the Slave Trade, Addressed to th*
Freeholders and other Inhabitants of Yorkshire (London, 1807), pp. 73–74. The autho
to whom Wilberforce refers might possible be Adam Ferguson. See *An Essay on th*
History of Civil Society (Edinburgh, 1767), Pt. II, Sec. 2. In other respects, howeve
the passage suggests derivation from Adam Smith.

This diffusionist position was, of course, intimately connected with hope for African progress through legitimate trade, so often expressed by Wilberforce and his group in the past. It now found support in general social theory, and came to be buttressed with ethnographic evidence as well. The African Institution, for example, backed its plans for carrying European culture into Africa by pointing to the frequent appearance of a semi-divine culture bearer in the myths of many lands.[16]

In Wilberforce's own explanation of African "barbarism," the belief in cultural diffusion was linked with the equally prevalent idea of a moving focus of civilization. His reconstruction of history found the "original seat of the human race" in Mesopotamia. After the flood, men moved from this original cradle in many directions, but "civilization" moved to the north and west, developing as it went— first to the Egyptians, then Phoenicians, then Greeks, Romans, and ultimately northwest Europe. The root cause of African backwardness came from the fact that the Africans had hived off from the rest of mankind before the rise of Egyptian civilization. They were, therefore, unable to rise with the others. Thus deprived of diffused innovations, they had nevertheless, in Wilberforce's opinion, done very well: "it may be even affirmed, that the Africans, without the advantages to be derived from an intercourse with polished nations, have made greater advancements toward civilization than perhaps any other uncivilized people on earth."[17]

While such dynamic forms of analysis were the new fashion and widely used, they still competed with the older static analysis. Three standard explanations of African "barbarism" recurred constantly. These were race, climate (either through indolence or tropical exuberance, or both), and the evil influence of the slave trade. Most writers either rang the changes on these three, or used them in combination with a favorite bugaboo—the economic evils of insufficient division of labor, or the social evils of polygyny. Even so, the climatic explanation dominated. It found its way into the standard reference works, into Grégoire's defense of the Africans, into MacQueen's

16. African Institution, *Reports of the Committee of the African Institution*, 18 vols. (London, 1807–1824), I, 12–13.

17. Wilberforce, *Letter to Yorkshire*, p. 80. For his historical theory in general see pp. 72–76.

attack on them, into the journals and reviews, and into the supposedly empirical accounts of the travellers.[18]

The direct influence of climate through tropical exuberance was peculiarly ambivalent in its political uses. On one hand it could be used to magnify the sin of the slave traders by showing the African paradise from which the slave was torn:

> ——Is the Negro blest? His generous soil
> With harvest-plenty crowns his simple toil;
> More than his wants his flocks and fields afford: . . .[19]

But much the same picture was used by Golbéry as an apology for the slave trade, and it was used by the British and the West Indian defenders of slavery. After all, if the tropical lands produced food in such abundance, no man would ever work for mere wages.[20]

This use of the myth of tropical exuberance as an ecological cause of barbarism was not weakened in the slightest by the adverse evidence from Sierra Leone, where agriculture had failed so miserably. Other parts of the tropical world still seemed to confirm the older view, and agricultural abundance might yet be found in some part of Africa. At best, a theorist might try to explain why Sierra Leone was a special case, or the exception proving the rule. Charles Stormont, a Scottish physician who spent some time in the colony, came to the conclusion that the African climate enormously increased the fecundity of all nature. But, just as "civilized" man died in that "climate," so also domesticated animals and plants either died before maturity, were imperfect, or failed to bear fruit.[21] Thus the colony could still bring the evils of abundance to the Africans, while withholding its riches from the Europeans.

The slave trade was the most hotly debated of the possible causes

18. [J. Leyden], *A Historical and Philosophical Sketch of the Discoveries and Settlements of the Europeans in Northern and Western Africa at the Close of the Eighteenth Century* (Edinburgh, 1799), pp. 78–79; H. B. Gregoire, *An Enquiry Concerning the Intellectual and Moral Faculties, and Literature of Negroes* . . . (Brooklyn, 1810), pp. 47–48; C. Malte-Brun, *Universal Geography*, 6 vols. (Philadelphia, 1827), II, 519 and III, 20–21; James MacQueen, "Geography of Central Africa," *Blackwood's Magazine*, XIX, 707 (June, 1826); John Adams, *Sketches Taken during Ten Voyages to Africa, Between the Years 1786 and 1800* . . . (London, 1822), pp. 70–71.

19. James Montgomery, "The West Indies," *Poetical Works*, 4 vols. (London, 1828), I, 36. First published 1807.

20. See my *Two Jamaicas* (Cambridge, Mass., 1955), pp. 68–69, and works there cited.

21. Charles Stormont, *Essai sur la topographie médicale de la côte occidentale d'Afrique et particulièrement sur celle de la colonie de Sierra Leone* (Paris, 1822), pp. 24–26.

of African barbarism, and along lines already laid down as far back as the 1780's. Up until 1807, pro-slavery writers reiterated their claim that the trade was a civilizing force: it brought savage Africans into contact with civilized people. At first, the humanitarians had sometimes countered by claiming that Africans were not really savage, but this argument was less heard after the 1790's. The new line was to admit that *coastal* Africa was savage, made so by the evil influence of the slave trade itself. Now both the humanitarians and their opponents could be found roundly condemning African culture, with results that were most unfortunate for the Africans' reputation.

In the realm of theory, the shift in debate posed problems of a different kind. The diffusionists, with Wilberforce at their head, had insisted that trade carried civilization with it. Hence, the seacoasts and river valleys were always the first regions to move upward in the scale. Yet in West Africa, Wilberforce believed the non-maritime interior was the center of civilization and the commercial coast was "degraded." Clearly, in his view, only "legitimate trade" carried civilization, while the slave trade carried savagery.[22] A very few commentators, however, carried on and tried to show that even the slave trade could be a civilizing influence. Captain John Adams went further still as a minority voice and maintained that the slave trade had already begun to act as a culture-bearer—that in time coastal West Africa would emerge as the most westernized part of tropical Africa.[23]

Several commentators on the humanitarian side began to realize as early as 1807 that false hopes might be created by blaming all the "barbarism" of Africa on the slave trade. Governor Thomas Ludlam, for example, wrote to Zachary Macaulay from Sierra Leone, saying, "In the first place, the Abolition of itself will not prevent the Africans from remaining a savage and uncivilized people. To abolish the Slave Trade is not to abolish the violent passions which now find vent in that particular direction. Were it to cease, the misery of Africa would arise from other causes; but it does not follow that Africa would be less miserable: she might even be less miserable, and yet be savage and uncivilized."[24]

22. Wilberforce, *Letter to Yorkshire*, p. 86; William Wilberforce, Commons, 1 March 1799, *Parliamentary Register*, VIII (new series), 139–40.
23. John Adams, *Ten Voyages*, p. 73; *Remarks on the Country Extending from Cape Palmas to the River Congo* (London, 1823), pp. 208–13.
24. Thomas Ludlam to Zachary Macaulay, Sierra Leone, 14 April 1807, printed in Z. Macaulay, *A Letter to His Royal Highness the Duke of Gloucester* . . . (London, 1815), p. 49.

Although it is always hard in retrospect to assess the genuine conviction that might or might not lie behind the aging phrases of polemic, it appears that humanitarians gradually lost their belief in the slave trade as the sole cause of African barbarism. The old phrases were still repeated, and the foreign slave trade remained to be destroyed, but extensive reading of debate and discussion carries the impression that most observers came round gradually after 1807 to the belief that, evil as the slave trade had been, it was only one evil among many.

Attempts to account for the cultural level of the West African interior followed a slightly different course. The old belief in a better interior lost nothing during the first two decades of the nineteenth century, even though explorers were unable for the time being to penetrate to the fabled walls of Timbuctu, Jenne, or Kano. The dominant impression was fortified by Mungo Park, recalled by humanitarians,[25] and supported by commercial enthusiasts, who wanted to push trade routes toward the cities of the Western Sudan.[26]

The natural and immediate explanation on all sides was to consider the civilization of the Western Sudan as a product of cultural diffusion across the Sahara, or possibly westward from the Nilotic Sudan.[27] It was usually assumed, incorrectly as it turned out, that such large and well organized states as the medieval Arab travellers or Mungo Park reported could not have been developed by Negro Africans. They must therefore have been brought to Africa by Islamic influence, but European opinion regarded Islam itself as a mixed blessing. Muslim North Africa was itself thought of as a barbarous country possessing a powerful but totally false religion. Nevertheless, the influence of Islam in sub-Saharan Africa was generally looked on with approval, even in Evangelical circles. The Sierra Leone Company, for example, made a special effort to encourage Muslim visitors to their colony and to establish friendly relations with the Muslim states of the interior. In the light of traditional British opposition to Catholicism, the uncompromising monotheism of Islam had a certain attraction

25. Wilberforce, *Letter to Yorkshire*, p. 86.
26. See, for example, G. Torrane to African Committee, 20 July 1807, T 70/35, f. 66; J. MacQueen, *Geographical and Commercial View of Northern Central Africa* ... (Edinburgh, 1821), p. 185.
27. G. T. Mollien, *Travels in the Interior of Africa* (London, 1820), p. vii; John McCormack, Evidence before Sierra Leone Committee, 1 July 1830, PP 1830, x (661), p. 7; Winterbottom, *Native Africans*, I, 85–86.

for extreme Protestants.[28] Furthermore, Muslim states appeared to have moved at least one step upward from savagery, though it was a step with its own special dangers. As Prichard put it, Islam might well awaken the faculties from the "brutal sloth of savage life," but at the same time render the morals "more depraved rather than improved."[29]

Some writers looked further afield for the ultimate source of Sudanese civilization. Whether diffusionists or not, most European travellers had a classical education. They tended to compare what they saw with what they knew, and they frequently saw African customs as the "degraded" off-shoots of imperial Rome. Mollien, indeed, set out for Africa in the hope of finding "civilized nations, the relics of Egyptian or Carthaginian colonies."[30] The precise origins and routes of cultural diffusion soon came to be an object of scholarly research. In 1821, T. E. Bowdich, the traveller to Ashanti, published the first full-length study of West African culture-history. Picking up an earlier suggestion by Golbéry, he traced the origin of the Ashanti aristocracy back to the highlands of Ethiopia—and their cultural heritage still further back to ancient Egypt. Bowdich's thesis is by no means unknown in present-day historiography, and it was carefully worked out from the archaeological and ethnographic literature then available, as well as his own field work in Ashanti.[31]

During the 1820's the nature of the problem shifted slightly. The new explorations brought new evidence. They also reduced the wilder dreams of a glorious civilization in the interior. Timbuctu, Sokoto, and Kano could hardly rise in reality to the heights of imagined grandeur sometimes portrayed in earlier decades. Some writers looked at the other side of the coin and set out to explain why the interior was so barbarous. An *Edinburgh* reviewer returned to the diffusionist hypothesis and explained that the Western Sudan was stagnant because it had no seacoast, hence no contact with the outside world. He also claimed the topography of the region was such that no large

---

28. C. Fyfe, *A History of Sierra Leone* (London, 1962), p. 67.

29. Wilberforce, *Letter to Yorkshire,* pp. 79–80; MacQueen, "Geography of Central Africa," *Blackwood's Magazine,* XIX, 707; J. C. Prichard, *Researches into the Physical History of Man,* 2nd ed., 2 vols. (London, 1826), I, 278.

30. Mollien, *Travels,* pp. 1–2.

31. T. E. Bowdich, *An Essay on the Superstitions, Customs, and Arts Common to the Ancient Egyptians, Abyssinians, and Ashantees* (Paris, 1821); Golbéry, *Travels,* I, 79.

political units could ever be formed there.[32] He was, of course, wrong on all counts. It was precisely the far interior of the Western Sudan that had had the most intense commercial contact with the outside world through the caravan trade with North Africa. Not only were there no natural barriers to prevent the growth of large states: large states actually existed, as they had for some centuries. Far from being stagnant, several of these states were just then passing through the violent readjustment of religious revolution.

It was, in fact, too early for scholars to attempt a general view of African history with the evidence then at hand. Prichard refused even to try, but others were more courageous in groping for an outline of past events. Hugh Murray sketched a broad pattern that was probably the most common view, even to the point of its vagueness. He thought of Africa as peopled by two waves of migrants out of Asia. The first wave, the Negro Africans, had come at such an early date as to have deviated from the Asian pattern toward "aspect, manners, and institutions" which could be considered indigenous. South of a line extending across Africa from the mouth of the Senegal, along the Niger, and eastward to the Mountains of the Moon, "native Africa" lived its life with relatively little change. North of that line it was subject to recent modification by newer migrations, principally of Arabs and Berbers, and by the influence of these alien cultures.[33] Murray's error was to believe that change in Africa could come only from the outside, and this particular fallacy was to be repeated by several later generations much better informed than Murray's had been.

In any case, the Africanists of the early nineteenth century were not primarily interested in the problems of history and ethnology for their own sake. They wanted to know how Africa had come to be as it was, but mainly for the sake of changing it in the direction of their own desires. Thus knowledge of the moral causes of "African barbarism" was useful knowledge—essential background for the grand problem of deciding how it might be cured.

    32. "Interior of Africa," Edinburgh Review, XLIV, 127–28 (March, 1829).
    33. Prichard, Researches (1826), I, 355; J. Leyden and H. Murray, Historical Account of Discoveries and Voyages in Africa, 2 vols. (Edinburgh, 1817), II, 475–76.

11

TECHNIQUES
FOR
CULTURE CHANGE

Among British enthusiasts for a more active West African policy, the theme of induced culture change was a constant feature. Many civilizations—perhaps most—have overvalued their own way of life and undervalued that of their neighbors. This attitude was one of long standing in the Western tradition, and it increased in force throughout the nineteenth century; but it was accompanied by another, less common belief. Most Europeans thought their own way of life represented values of universal application. Barbarians might therefore acquire "civilization." Even more, for some Europeans, to carry civilization to the barbarians was not only possible, it was desirable. It might even become a moral duty.[1]

The intensity of this belief and the justifications that sustained it differed from time to time, but its roots seem to lie in the theoretical universality of the Christian religion and the injunction to preach the gospel among the heathen. Western missionary efforts had been at a low ebb during the seventeenth and eighteenth centuries, but the

1. See, for example: Alfred, "On the Most Rational Means of Promoting Civilization in Barbarous States," *The Philanthropist*, I, 8–21 (1811).

religious revival in Europe as a whole and the Evangelical revival in Great Britain toward the end of the eighteenth century pointed toward a new and greater burst of missionary enthusiasm. Britain was not alone in catching the spirit of proselytizing Christianity; but Britain was one of the earliest and strongest centers of the missionary revival, and this fact colored much of the British attitude toward West Africa.

The new interest in reforming the barbarians also had foundations in secular thought. During the eighteenth century, Europeans had come increasingly to realize that human misery was not only an evil: to some degree it was a preventable evil. The new humanitarianism drew something from a secularized belief in Christian charity. It also drew from the idea of progress and the new hope for improvement of the human condition. Egalitarian social and political thought, setting forth the rights of man as the rights of all men, encouraged the belief that human progress should be shared by all. This sentiment merged with the new pride in Western civilization and led to the easy assumption that the good life was possible only within the framework of Western culture. Belief in the moral value of spreading Western civilization was not limited to the "Saints" or to those with a narrowly religious concept of civilization. Secular reformers, even enlightened unbelievers, could share some aspects of the missionary zeal to carry the light of "civilization" to the "dark places."

There was also an economic motive. It was widely believed that British economic growth moved forward with the increase in British commerce. If Britain were to trade with West Africa, West Africa would have to produce goods for export. Production for export was not possible without culture change. In 1807, the Committee of the African Institution held that, "Indolence, it must be admitted is a common characteristic of all un-civilized people. . . . But indolence is a disease which it is the business of civilization to cure. The motives and means of industry must be supplied before men can begin to be industrious."[2]

This being the case, the satisfaction of a moral obligation, economic growth for Great Britain, and commercial profits for those engaged in the African trade would all follow from the "civilization" of Africa. There is no use in this context worrying the old question

2. African Institution. *Reports of the Committee of the African Institution*, 18 vols. (London, 1807–1824), I (1807), 27–28.

whether economic profits or moral proscriptions were more important. Certainly both were important, and they were thought to be
nearly identical. Where profit and morality seemed, at the time, to
demand the same action, the two motives can hardly be separated by
retrospective analysis.

This is not to say that all Europeans (or all Britons) believed the
"civilization" of Africa was desirable or even possible. Most people
were either uninterested or apathetic, and a minority were actively
hostile to the idea. It was possible to admit the essential goodness of
the good works planned by the enthusiasts, and yet oppose them in
detail. The greatest fund of hostility was found in a widespread iso-
lationist sentiment, though it took many different and even contradictory forms. Popular xenophobia of the type represented by Cobbett
was one ingredient. Other social reformers went beyond a simple
dislike of strangers and argued that the English poor had first claim
to whatever charity the English nation could supply. From the right
wing of English politics, the West India interest could be counted on
to oppose any activity in Africa other than the suppression of the
foreign slave trade, and West Indian propaganda could draw on
deep-seated Tory sentiments—distrust of religious fanatics, like the
Quakers and Evangelicals with their "Methodistical nostrums," and
an even more profound dislike of paying taxes. "We are expending
our thousands and tens of thousands a year: to do what, Sir? To wash
the Blackamoor white;—monstrous absurdity!"[3]

Some few believed the "civilization" of Africa was not even desirable for the Africans, since Africans were racially incapable of attain-
ing the "heights" of Western civilization. If they also accepted an
image of Africa set in terms such as Golbéry's picture of savage
contentment, then it would indeed be a disservice to increase contact
between Africa and the West. William Mudford, Golbéry's translator, took this line: "Rather let them remain forever in a state of
contented barbarism, than by civilizing their minds, only awaken
them to a bitter consciousness of their fate; or by polishing their
manners render them susceptible of desires which you never mean
them to gratify."[4]

This sentiment was dying out slowly in the first decades of the

3. "Senegal" to the Editor, *John Bull*, 8 June 1823.
4. Translator's note in S. M. X. Golberry [S. M. X. de Golbéry], *Travels in Africa
Performed During the Years 1785, 1786, and 1787*, 2 vols. (London, 1803), II, 262.

nineteenth century (step by step with the decline of the idea of the noble savage) but it was still heard. The more common position was to stop short with a warning of the problems to be surmounted. Lawrence, the biologist, urged missionaries not to expect too much. In his view, the Africans were people of limited capacities: thus only limited "improvement" was possible. Or, in another variant, the problems of climate could be stressed. Edward William White, the Governor of Cape Coast Castle, argued, in terms reminiscent of Hugh Murray's theory of history, that successful acculturation of the Gold Coast Africans could take place only with a degree of coercion to counteract the easy life of the tropics. He therefore pleaded for British annexation and administration to reduce the Africans to civilization and agricultural labor. From the perspective of Downing Street, White's warning meant that real acculturation was so difficult and expensive, it was better to do nothing.[5]

Views like these, simple inertia, government reluctance to spend money on African projects, and the European mortality on the Coast, all tended to keep the political classes in Britain vaguely opposed to any effort to change African culture, even though they might agree in principle that the effort was laudable. A convinced minority of conversionists, however, kept up a steady pressure through the press and Parliament. They could accomplish very little in the way of public action, though their influence helped prevent the complete abandonment of government posts on the Guinea coast.

The way to private action was more open. Western education and Christian missions could operate with little or no government support. The attempt to convert the Africans by teaching and example was continuous from the foundation of Sierra Leone, though the Europeans began with very naive ideas about education and culture change. Only gradually, they formulated more careful and explicit plans for achieving their objectives. The projects of the 1780's had tended to assume that African culture was a texture of wickedness, which the Africans themselves would abandon once a "better way" was shown them. Thus the Sierra Leone Company began with hardly any thought about the possible uses of either education or missionary work. Their original clientele, the Nova Scotians, were both Western

5. Sir William Lawrence, *Lectures on Physiology, Zoology, and the Natural History of Man* (London, 1819), pp. 500–1; Edward William White to African Committee, Cape Coast, 30 April 1814, T 70/36 (also printed version in PP, 1817, vi [431], p. 46).

and Christian, and many of them were literate as well. The Company
therefore began by merely sending a Chaplain for the colony and
some schoolmasters for the children. There seemed little need to
raise the general educational level, and the principal religious problem was the fact that the settlers had "imbibed very inadequate or
enthusiastic notions of Christianity," which is to say, they were Dissenters.[6]

The education policy of Sierra Leone under the Company and
under the Crown continued as it had begun. There was no special
consideration of the proper education for non-Western children, and
any native Africans who were attracted to schools were educated
along with the settlers. It was difficult enough in the first decades
to keep any schools going. Schoolmasters died and were hard to
replace. Still other problems arose during the political struggles of
the later 1790's, and the Company's appropriation for all religious
and educational purposes in 1802 was only £770 for a community
of 1600 people.[7] In spite of these practical limitations, the intention
was to give as much education as possible, following contemporary
English forms. A few of the brighter students were selected in 1794
and again in 1799 and sent to England for advanced training, paid
for by private subscription. Some of these young men advanced rapidly. One of them, a son of the chief of Kafu Bullom, renamed John
Macaulay Wilson, returned to the colony with a medical education
and rose by 1822 to be Assistant Colonial Surgeon.[8]

The mortality problem in the early decades of the new century
underlined the need for still more Western-trained Africans to relieve
Europeans in the subordinate posts of government, in the missions,
and in education itself. The early Governors under the Crown were
especially active. T. Perronet Thompson tried, unsuccessfully, to introduce more advanced education. Governor Charles MacCarthy,
however, was the true founder of what was to be one of the most
extensive systems of public education in the early nineteenth century.
From the beginning of his governorship in 1816, he was impressed

6. Sierra Leone Company, *Account of the Colony of Sierra Leone from Its First Establishment in* [sic] *1793* . . . (London, 1795), p. 80.
7. PP, 1803-4, v (24), p. 38.
8. Sierra Leone Company, *Substance of the Report of the Court of Directors of the Sierra Leone Company to the General Court . . . ,* 7 vols. (London, 1791-1808), V, 49-54, (report for 1801); Evidence of William Greaves, Parliamentary Committee on Sierra Leone (1802), PP, 1803-1804, v (24), p. 37; M. C. P. Easmon, "Sierra Leone Doctors," *Sierra Leone Studies,* II (n. s.), 81-82 (June, 1956).

by the possibilities and the needs presented by the stream of liberated Africans coming ashore from the captured slave ships. He worked closely with the missions, particularly with the Church Missionary Society, and set the precedent of moderately large government subsidies to the mission schools. In doing so, he moved ahead of the English practice of the day, which was to leave education to private enterprise or private philanthropy. In this as in other matters, MacCarthy's long tenure in office, until 1824, enabled him to lay down a form of post-war settlement for the administration of Sierra Leone. In time, the Sierra Leoneans were to look back on his governorship as a kind of golden age.[9]

The new subsidies for schools came at a significant moment for the future of African education. Andrew Bell had recently developed in Madras a system of instruction which economized on staff by using the more advanced students to teach the rest. Bell's system was taken up in England by some of the Evangelicals, and especially by Zachary Macaulay, who helped to found the National Society for the Education of the Poor in the Principles of the Church of England, with Dr. Bell as its director. It was only natural that the "National system" should be adopted in Sierra Leone by the schools of the Church Missionary Society. In the same way, the Methodist missions took up the similar but competing Lancastrian or "British" system.[10] In either case, the missions transferred to Africa a curriculum and method designed specifically to meet the needs of the British working class. Since the goal of both systems was to teach the virtue of hard work and the principles of evangelical Christianity, the choice was natural.

But it implied a decision to present a Western, literary education in Africa, and it was not made without opposition. Many believed that Africans had neither the capacity nor the need for a taste of the Western heritage. Wilberforce himself would have limited the education of native Africans to "our language & religion, habits of industry, the mode of cultivating lands, & mechanical arts," arguing that, "It would be vain to expect to prevail on the people of the sort we have to do with to submit to the drudgery of formal instruction; but in this mode [of learning by imitation] they will insensibly grow familiarized with all we wish them to know."[11]

9. C. Fyfe, *A History of Sierra Leone* (London, 1962), pp. 127–47.
10. C. P. Groves, *The Planting of Christianity in Africa,* 4 vols. (London, 1948–1958), I. 278–79.
11. Wm. Wilberforce to John Clarkson, 27 April 1792, Ad. Mss. 41262A, p. 82.

Other men with experience on the Coast strongly resented partly Westernized Africans. Philip Beaver blamed the political troubles of Sierra Leone on the fact that the colonists were Westernized, Negro Americans. As for any future colony of his own: "I would not take with me a single African who had ever been in London. I would rather carry thither a rattlesnake."[12] In line with this distrust, several commentators wished to limit Western education. One idea was to stop literary education after the most elementary level, continuing only with "useful trades" likely to establish habits of industry. Robert Thorpe, sometime Chief Justice of Sierra Leone, had a grandiose scheme of this kind. He wanted to dot the coast of Africa with British trading posts, each of them with a labor-recruiting center and a school. The quality of the education he had in mind is indicated by his further suggestion that schoolmasters might well be found among artisans condemned to death for their crimes in England.[13]

Still another line of opposition came from certain missionaries, who saw their proper role as that of saving souls, not training black Englishmen. Among these critics was Edward Bickersteth, a Secretary of the Church Missionary Society, who, though a minority voice in his own society, opposed secular education as "fixing the minds of the Natives on worldly advantages," and distracting the attention of the missionaries.[14]

Other problems centered on the *how* rather than the *what* of African education. The rise from "barbarism" to "civilization" was often thought of as a process similar to recovery from a disease. The patient had not only to be cured, but afterwards protected from a relapse which might seize him if he returned to his own people. At the same time, a few observers realized how difficult it was for young students to move sharply across the barriers between their own culture and that of England.

A group of Quakers with an interest in ethnology and linguistics developed a plan for phased acculturation. Rather than begin at once with primary education in English, they preferred to begin with elementary instruction in African languages alone. Once the student had learned about the nature of language and could read and write

12. Philip Beaver, *African Memoranda* (London, 1805), p. 396 n.
13. Robert Thorpe, *A View of the Present Increase of the Slave Trade* (London, 1818), p. 96.
14. The quotation is from Bickersteth's missionary questionnaire in CMSA, CA 1/E5. See also "Private Instructions to E. Bickersteth," n.d., CA 1/E5 and E. Bickersteth to Josiah Pratt, 20 April 1816, CMSA, CA 1/E4.

his own, he could then move on to more advanced education in English. But the full measure of Westernization required a break from Africa itself. Thomas Hodgkin, later to be founder of the Aborigines Protection Society, hoped to set up competitive examinations in each colony, by which students could be selected, brought to England for a complete Western education, and then sent back to Africa to fill the higher posts in colonial government.[15]

A less expensive way of achieving this enforced break between the student and his home environment was to set up boarding schools in Africa. For this reason, two commanders of Gold Coast forts suggested that students should be educated, boarded, and clothed at the public expense.[16] The more sophisticated approach to African education, represented by these ideas, appeared only in the later 1820's, when it could rest on the experience of forty years.

Religious missions also passed from naive beginnings toward a gradual improvement in methods. The Sierra Leone Directors had hoped to convey both Christianity and civilization to Africa, but they began at a time when the English missionary movement was still in its infancy. The older Society for the Propagation of the Gospel was no longer active in West Africa, and the Church Missionary Society was not organized until 1799. In the first decade of the settlement, the Company's chaplain could make little headway even with the Nova Scotians, who preferred their own lay preachers. A few other missionaries came to Sierra Leone during the Company regime, but most of them died within a short time. The only bright spot during the whole period was the work of Henry Brunton in reducing the Susu language to writing, and that was faulty by the standard of later linguistic science.[17]

The early failures are explicable enough. Christian zeal was the only qualification expected of a missionary. In 1796, for example, Dr. Thomas Coke recruited a small group of missionaries from

15. H. Kilham, *African Lessons* (London, 1823), ii; T. Hodgkin, *A Letter from Dr. Hodgkin to Hannah Kilham, On the State of the Colony of Sierra Leone* (Lindfield, 1827), pp. 6–7; Adolphus Back to Thomas Hodgkin, 19 July 1831, ASP, C 112/2; W. Singleton and others, *Report of the Committee Managing a Fund Raised by Some Friends for the Purpose of Promoting African Instruction; with an Account of a Visit to the Gambia and Sierra Leone* (London, 1822).

16. See testimony of W. J. Purchase, Sierra Leone Committee, 24 June 1830, PP, 1830, x (661), p. 31; Smith and Mollan to African Committee, Cape Coast, 23 February 1818, T 70/36.

17. Groves, *Planting of Christianity,* I, 209–17.

among the mechanics and lay preachers of the Methodist connection
and sent them off to Sierra Leone, bound for the theocratically organized Muslim state of Futa Jallon. In his letter of introduction to
its ruler, Dr. Coke promised that his missionaries would be able
to set "an example of all the virtues and all the graces" and were
qualified to instruct the people in "all the important arts of Europe."[18]
It was probably just as well that the missionaries refused to leave
Freetown, where they concerned themselves in sectarian controversy
with the Company's chaplain.

Even such an enlightened and well informed man as Sir Joseph
Banks seriously underrated the strength of Islam in the Western
Sudan, as he also misunderstood the nature of religious conversion.
On the strength of Mungo Park's account, he wrote to Lord Liver-
pool in 1799:

> It uniformly appears [that] the small superiority in useful Acquirements
> which the Moors possess is sufficient to induce the negroes ardently to embrace
> the tenets of the Alcoran, not because these Tenets appear in themselves wise,
> but because those people who teach them, are supposed to have gained from
> them their superiority in the use of the Art they teach, which is the knowledge
> of writing. How much more then would the more intelligible Doctrine of the
> Scriptures if made part of an Education contrived to teach the more useful
> Branches of Mechanics be followed—and how much [more] completely would
> those who are taught be civilized.[19]

More concerted missionary work began in 1804 when the CMS
began sending missionaries to Sierra Leone, followed by the Wesleyan-Methodist Missionary Society in 1811, but the organization was
still haphazard and the death rate was extremely high. It was not
until 1816, when Edward Bickersteth made a tour of inspection and
reorganization, that the CMS mission became an established institution.

Among other things, Bickersteth circulated a questionnaire on
missionary methods and problems. The questions asked reveal some
of the basic policy decisions still to be reached. There were such
matters as the relative emphasis to be given to educational work and
preaching the gospel, the proper language for preaching, whether to

---

18. Dr. Thomas Coke to the King of the Foulahs, quoted in M. J. Holland,
Viscountess Knutsford, *Life and Letters of Zachary Macaulay* (London, 1900),
pp. 116–17.
    19. J. Banks to Lord Liverpool, 8 June 1799, CO 2/1.

work hard with a few individuals or to instruct the masses more superficially, the proper level of missionaries' salaries, and the best way to choose a site for a mission station. The key problem was to organize the mission as a functioning institution, rather than a disorganized group of individuals each separately carrying the Word to the heathen. Mission work, in short, was just beginning to move into a new phase of group effort, based on a body of accumulated experience and a body of theoretical suppositions.[20]

In this situation, missionary methods could hardly escape outside criticism, including the demand that missions should be subject to government inspection and control.[21] Some of the non-missionary critics and observers pointed out serious problems of cross-cultural misunderstanding and tension that might result from missionary work. Philip Beaver lampooned the naive attitude of the early missionaries:

The absurdity of very well meaning persons in thinking that they can overcome vices, customs, or prejudices, immemorially rooted in an unenlightened people, by shocking, instead of gradually enlightening their understandings, has done a great deal of mischief already. To begin by telling a chief, the instant you have got into his country, that of his six wives he must put away five, because it is a great sin, and forbidden by the laws of God, to have more than one will certainly astonish the chief, but will not induce him to part with his wives. . . . When his European instructor goes on from one dogma to another, all alike unintelligible to the present intellectual state of the chief, till he finishes with the doctrine of the Trinity, the belief in which, he tells the chief, is essential to his salvation; the latter, who thought him unreasonable at first, now thinks him outrageously so; and that he is either a mad man, a fool, or an imposter; and to get rid of people professing such doctrines, will be his constant endeavour.[22]

Hugh Murray, on the basis of his broader theory, warned of the special dangers of missionary enterprise, since "intercourse . . . between Europeans and Savages, has a tendency injurious to the character of both." Culture contact was one of his progressive principles,

20. For Bickersteth's report on Sierra Leone see African Institution, *Reports of the Committee, Eleventh Report* (1817), p. 126–52.

21. See G. A. Robertson, *Notes on Africa . . . with Hints for the Melioration of the Whole African Population* (London, 1819), p. 18; A. G. Laing, *Travels in the Timanee, Kooranko, and Soolima Countries in Western Africa* (London, 1825), pp. 391–98.

22. Beaver, *African Memoranda*, pp. 392–93.

and he believed it should be countered by conscious application of a regressive principle, in this case "coercion" in the form of very strict discipline over any missionaries sent into the field. Murray's warning was underscored by one of the early CMS missionaries to Sierra Leone, who pointed out the psychological disturbance likely to result from working in the context of another culture, and the need for Christian perseverance to overcome the hearty dislike of Africans that was bound to result.[23]

According to Murray, damage to the African character should be met with the same prescription—coercion, though not in the sense of physical force. Instead, he believed that missionaries could and should establish themselves as the leaders over their flocks in secular as well as religious matters. Like Banks, he thought such leadership would not be hard to establish, since it would follow naturally from the recognized technological superiority of Europe.

In spite of a minority insistence on the Gospel before all else, technological superiority was the missionaries' trump card. The ends might be spiritual, but, especially among the lay supporters of the missions, the means were material. The dominant attitude of the nineteenth century was a reversal of Samuel Purchas' famous call for English colonization in seventeenth-century Virginia. According to Purchas, "God in his wisdome having enriched the Savage Countries, that those riches might be attractive for Christian suters," the English should go there with the Christian message in order to "sowe spirituals and reape temporals."[24] The new proposal was to sow temporals in the form of economic development and to reap spirituals in the form of conversion for the heathen and a spiritual reward for the Europeans who did God's work.

There would also be an economic reward for the Europeans, and the balance of emphasis varied considerably with different commentators. Some, indeed, would have relegated the spiritual reward to a minor place as the long-run product of missionary work. The missionaries they wanted were technical missionaries, carrying European

23. H. Murray, *Enquiries Historical and Moral Respecting the Character of Nations and the Progress of Society* (Edinburgh, 1808), pp. 422–23; M. Renner to E. Bickersteth, Bashia, 1 May 1816, CMSA, CA 1/E5.

24. Samuel Purchas, *Hakluytus Postumus, or Purchas His Pilgrimes* (Glasgow, 1906), XIX, 232. See R. H. Pearce, *The Savages of America: A Study of the Indian and the Idea of Civilization* (Baltimore, 1953).

material culture to the "savages" rather than Christianity to the "heathen." The preaching of religion was an ultimate aim, but it would come later, after the process of acculturation had already begun.[25]

Those who desired a secular emphasis in the missionary movement were fully in line with the dominant attitudes of their period. In spite of the missionary revival and the hope of changing African culture by direct persuasion, most publicists put their faith in the roundabout influence of "legitimate trade." Just as tropical exuberance was considered to be the sovereign cause of African "barbarism," this was to be the sovereign remedy. But the demand for "legitimate trade" had many shades of meaning. As a least-common-assumption, most commentators understood that trade would create a demand for European goods. This in turn would encourage Africans to perform agricultural work. For many, a flourishing agriculture was civilization enough for Africa.

Occasional explicit and detailed analysis could go further, however, and explain that the wealth of nations depends on division of labor and hence on the exchange of goods. Increasing wealth in Africa would bring leisure, schools, and a developed intellectual culture. Or, in a version published by the *Quarterly Review* in 1823, this theory of economic development could be combined with a sociology of slavery to show that legitimate trade would ultimately put an end to slavery in Africa. In this view, slavery was an institution typical of the middle phases of social development. Primitive hunters had only a rudimentary division of labor. The men hunted and protected the community, while the women did the menial work. There was no need for slavery. But with the invention of agriculture, war prisoners could be put to work. They were therefore enslaved rather than killed. Their labor could also be bought and sold; but, in the absence of an exchange economy, payment was difficult—so difficult that it was most easily arranged by a single payment giving command over an individual's labor for life. Africa was held to have reached this stage of economic development. Further development would bring further specialization, further division of labor, an ex-

25. Murray, *Enquiries*, pp. 421–24; Robertson, *Notes on Africa*, pp. 15–16; *Edinburgh Review*, VIII, 442–50 (July, 1806); T. E. Bowdich, *The British and French Expeditions to Teembo, with Remarks on Civilization in Africa* (Paris, 1821), pp. 7–9; Sir Neil Campbell, "Memorandum on the Gold Coast," November 1826, SLA, Gold Coast Misc., 1826–1827; Alfred, "Means of Promoting Civilization," pp. 16–17.

change economy, and a fluid labor market. At this higher stage slavery
would again be unnecessary.[26]

While all of this might be projected as the automatic working of
economic law, most authorities no longer believed that natural economic law would destroy the overseas slave trade. Both the Sierra
Leone Company in the 1790's and the Company of Merchants after
1807 had found their legitimate trade at a disadvantage in competition with foreign slave traders.[27] It was not gratifying to discover that
commercial and moral advantage did not go together as they were
supposed to do, and various explanations were brought forward.
Some blamed the cupidity of the African slave dealers. Others attacked the criminal behavior of the Americans, Portuguese, French,
or Spanish, who, as citizens of civilized countries, should have been
enlightened enough to give up the trade at the same time Britain did.
Economic explanations were also possible. John Adams, formerly
captain of a slaver, believed that, given the existing level of technology, slaves were in fact a superior product. The cost of their
production was borne by the society in which they grew up. They
were captured in wars that might well have taken place even if there
had been no slave trade. The price in the interior was therefore very
low, and transportation to the coast was cheap. Slaves were locomo-
tive and needed only a little food to keep them going.[28]

Whatever the cause, it was agreed that legitimate trade could enter
Africa only under the cover of military or political intervention. The
question at issue was—what kind of intervention? Even before the
issue could be discussed in the light of peacetime conditions, one
kind of intervention was already present in the form of anti-slavery
patrols by the Royal Navy. Most commentators accepted this much
as an essential beginning. Methods and strategy might be questioned,
but the usefulness of the blockade itself was not seriously doubted
until the 1840's. The issue discussed in the early decades of the
century was thus—what *more* should be done?

If Britain were to make a serious national effort to eliminate African "barbarism," the obvious way to do it was by outright annexation,

26. "The Condition of the Negroes in Our Colonies," *Quarterly Review*, XXIX,
497–99 (July, 1823).

27. African Institution, *Reports of the Committee*, I (1807), 44; African Committee to the Lords of Treasury, 29 April 1812, T 70/32.

28. John Adams, *Sketches Taken During Ten Voyages to Africa, Between the Years
1786 and 1800* ... (London, 1822), p. 73.

as Edward William White and others occasionally suggested. There
was talk of annexing the Fante states on the Gold Coast, or of taking
over the Dutch and Danish forts. The African Committee proposed
a general forward move in 1812 as a wartime measure,[29] but nothing
came of it then; and it was even more difficult to convince the home
government once peace had returned in Europe. The possibility of
annexation was nevertheless open during the first fifteen years of the
century, and projectors were free during this period to make their
plans for enforced acculturation on the assumption of a British administration.

When they did so, it was clear that they often had little faith in
the civilizing nature of legitimate trade operating by itself, even if
the foreign slave trade were suppressed. In the common view, either
the innate racial indolence of the Africans or the bountiful climate
would prevent Africans from responding to purely commercial in-
centives. Managerial cadres of white colonists would therefore be
necessary in order to speed up the process of culture change. A
projector writing for the African Institution argued that European
example, not merely European trade, would be the first necessity:
"Example works more rapidly than precept on all who are quick to
perceive, but slow to reason; and such are children of uncultivated
nations. An African will discern characters as acutely as an Englishman, while much labour is required to make him comprehend a logical proposition."[30]

Furthermore, according to this projector, civilization would not
come simply through the production of goods for the European market. It could come only through the consumption of goods produced
in Europe, and not only luxury goods but the whole range of European material culture. The shift to European habits of consumption
would be crucial: "[If the Africans] . . . can be taught to desire
decent apparel, and comfortable habitations, innumerable blessings
will spring up from these humble shoots. Habits of domestic virtue,
order, and happiness, habits of self-estimation, sense of character
and propriety, a desire for knowledge, prospective industry, and all
the lovely family and social charities which peace and contentment
engender, will gradually be diffused."[31]

29. African Committee to Lords of Treasury, 29 April 1812, T 70/73.
30. African Institution, *Reports of the Committee,* II (1808), 37, This anonymous
project was published by the African Institution, but not necessarily with the full support of the committee.
31. African Institution, *Reports of the Committee,* II (1808), 37.

This was a lot to expect from a change in material culture, and most projectors were less sanguine. They thought European managerial cadres would be necessary—but to give orders, not merely as an example. Virtually all of those who demanded annexation or colonization did so *because* they believed Africans would not respond without some form of coercion. Especially during the 1810's, when the future West African strategy was still in question, several projects appeared, designed to produce enforced acculturation from a limited territorial base.

In Joseph Corry's elaboration of the current scheme for an inland trading-post empire, the nuclear colony on the coast was planned with a managerial force of white settlers to direct a combined system of forced labor and forced education. Slaves would be purchased in the interior. The adults would then go to work on plantations, learning the mechanical and agricultural arts of Europe in the time-honored West Indian way. Children between the ages of five and seven would be trained briefly in "letters, religion, and science" and then pass on to advanced work in "domestic economy, agriculture, and mechanics." At maturity they were to be examined under controlled conditions. Those with high marks would be sent back to their country of origin, there to form small centers for the spread of civilization and Christianity. Those who failed presumably remained slaves and continued their training in the cane fields. Corry had high hopes for this system: "Thus may the long seclusion of the African from the light of truth and revealed religion be annihilated, his inveterate jealousies allayed, his nature regenerated, and his barbarism fall before the emanations of enlightened existence."[32]

Another suggestion came from Henry Meredith, who had served on the Gold Coast. He believed plantations could be established near the European forts, with firm control over the labor force but without slavery, by adopting the Akan institution of the pawn (*Awowa* in Ashanti). In the law of most Akan states, it was possible to borrow money, leaving a member of one's family or household with the creditor as a pledge. During the period of the debt, the pawn's labor took the place of interest. At an earlier period, this institution had operated only within closely related families, but by the early nineteenth century it had already changed, and the position of the pawn was intermediate between that of a domestic slave and that of a free

32. J. Corry, *Observations upon the Windward Coast of Africa . . . made in the Years 1805-1806* (London, 1807), pp. 81-84.

man.[33] According to Meredith's plan, it could be extended still further to become the basis for enforced plantation labor.[34] The difficulty with this scheme or any other scheme for establishing plantations on the Gold Coast was the political disturbance of the Ashanti Wars. The English, Danes, and Dutch all attempted small plantations, but production never reached significant levels and could not do so without effective European occupation.

As time passed it became increasingly clear that the home government was unwilling to annex and administer any part of West Africa. Experimental acculturation by government agency was therefore limited to the existing establishment at Sierra Leone, and human material began to pour in after 1808 as the Navy unloaded liberated Africans from the captured slave ships. The Evangelical promoters of Sierra Leone had had no objection to forced labor under legal control and limited in time. It had, indeed, been a part of Granville Sharp's original utopian project. One of the first devices for the acculturation of the new arrivals was to place them with the European officials or with the settlers as "apprentices." The practice was begun in the last days of the Company, and it was justified as a means of initial training under discipline before the emancipated Africans were allowed to fend for themselves in the fluid society of the colony.

But the use of forced labor as a training device touched off a prolonged storm of protest. It began with the Governorship of T. Perronet Thompson in 1808–10. Thompson himself raised the question in a protest to London. Although he was a Methodist and close to Evangelical circles, the apprenticeship question brought him into direct conflict with the African Institution and ended in his recall. The quarrel was then taken up in Britain and argued with widening ramifications. One issue was that of agriculture vs. trade, and part of Thompson's objection was his belief that the future of the colony lay in its trade with the hinterland.[35] The West India interest was also involved, since they feared that tropical agriculture in Africa, equipped with endless supplies of forced labor, might threaten their monopoly in the British market for tropical staples. The issue was

33. See R. S. Rattray, *Ashanti Law and Constitution* (London, 1929), pp. 47–55 for the Ashanti variant of these practices.

34. Henry Meredith, *An Account of the Gold Coast of Africa . . .* (London, 1812), p. 212.

35. P. Thompson to C. Jenkinson, 6 June 1810, CO 267/28. See L. G. Johnson, *General T. Perronet Thompson, 1783–1869* (London, 1957), pp. 38 ff.

taken up by the defenders of colonial slavery, who used it to show the humanitarians as hypocrites, who practiced slavery in Africa while trying to deny it to the West Indian planters.[36] The controversy ran through the whole decade of the 1810's before it finally died away. It did nothing to stop the practice of apprenticeship in Sierra Leone, but it did serve as a warning that schemes for the "civilization" of Africa through forced labor would be sure to meet a powerful and diverse opposition in Britain.

Both the government authorities in Sierra Leone and those who tried to influence policy from London still hoped to develop the agricultural potentialities of the colony, and in ways that were frequently coupled with the effort to introduce European civilization. The practice of granting land to the settlers was resumed in the early years of Crown administration—this time to the full extent of the initial promises—but quitrents were revived as well. Few of the Nova Scotians or Maroons took up additional land. Instead, Governor Charles W. Maxwell bought some of the land forfeited for nonpayment of quitrents and began cultivating it himself with the labor of liberated African "apprentices." Kenneth and George Macaulay, government servants who were second cousins of the earlier governor, also took up land for plantations. By 1814, Maxwell and the Macaulays held more than half of the cultivated land in the colony.[37]

The tendency toward a plantation form of enterprise, however, was reversed after 1814. Maxwell himself had begun settling some of the liberated Africans in villages of their own. Governor MacCarthy widely extended this practice, reforming the pattern of settlement of the Sierra Leone peninsula. It now came to be dotted with

36. The following tracts are a sample of the controversy: Robert Thorpe, *A Letter to William Wilberforce Containing Remarks on the Reports of the Sierra Leone Company* (London, 1815); Z. Macaulay, *A Letter to His Highness the Duke of Gloucester . . .* (London, 1815); African Institution, *Special Report of the Directors of the African Institution, Made at the Annual General Meeting, on 12th of April, 1815, Respecting the Allegations . . . by R. Thorpe* (London, 1815); Robert Thorpe, *A Reply "Point by Point" to the Special Report of the Directors of the African Institution, and of the Controversy with Dr. Thorpe, with some Reasons against the Registry of Slaves in the British Colonies* (London, 1816); "African Institution and the Slave Trade," *Anti-Jacobin Review*, L, 139–45 (January, 1816); J. Marryat, *Thoughts on the Abolition of the Slave Trade, and Civilization of Africa, with Remarks on the African Institution, and an Examination of the Report of their Committee, recommending a General Registry of Slaves in the British West-India Islands* (London, 1816). The sequence of titles shows the way in which the controversy jumped the Atlantic and ended as a part of the literature pro and contra slavery in the West Indies.
37. Fyfe, *Sierra Leone*, pp. 117–18.

agricultural villages bearing names like Wilberforce, Regent, Gloucester, and Bathurst, each in theory the seat of a Christian parish
with a minister subsidized by the government to superintend and
civilize the new arrivals.[38] Many forms of administration and malad-
ministration were to follow, but the pattern of peasant villages
persisted.

Both the actual settlers on the land and the idea of agricultural
villages found a particular friend and supporter in Britain. William
Allen, a Quaker businessman in London and publisher of *The Philanthropist,* seriously took up their cause in 1810 and followed it for
more than twenty years. Among other activities, he defended the
settlers from the misrepresentations of the Sierra Leone Company
and the African Institution, both of which had often blamed the
Sierra Leoneans for the colony's shortcomings. He also enlisted the
help of Paul Cuffee, a Quaker and a Negro American, to form the
Friendly Society of Sierra Leone. This society was actually a coopera-
tive trading firm, designed to help settlers combine their produce
for sale abroad and to order European goods directly from London.
The English side of the transaction was handled by a non-profit
concern set up for the purpose by Allen and his friends. The Friendly
Society disappeared after Cuffee's death in 1817, but Allen was again
active a decade later trying to establish a model village copied after
the Mennonite communities of southern Russia.[39]

In spite of occasional temporary achievements, the peasant villages
were not the kind of success many had hoped for. Even William
Allen was tempted by the plantation alternative and urged it on
Major-General Turner before the latter became Governor in 1825.[40]
Turner himself was a firm believer in agricultural work as the most
effective agent of civilization: "until it is encouraged and understood
no progress will have been made in Civilization, no foundation laid
for Morals, Religion, or the Decencies of life."[41] Turner's solution
was to use the power of the government to create favorable conditions for European capital investment in plantations. His plan, based
on nonsensical economic reasoning, was to use the government's
control over immigration, and its position as the largest employer of
labor, to depress the rate of wages.

38. Fyfe, *Sierra Leone,* pp. 128–30.
39. Fyfe, *Sierra Leone,* pp. 112–13, 122–23, 132 and 167.
40. Fyfe, *Sierra Leone,* p. 155.
41. Gen. Charles Turner to Bathurst, 22 February 1825, CO 267/65.

Turner died before his plan could be put into operation, but in 1827 Commissioners Wellington and Rowan returned to the necessity for control over labor to speed acculturation. They produced two alternative plans. The preferred recommendation was to send all newly emancipated Africans to a government plantation for several years of forced labor producing crops for export. At the end of the term, they would be given a share of the profits and a small grant of land, subject to quitrent. Presumably they would continue to produce the cash crops they had learned to grow in government service, and the necessity of paying quitrents would be an added incentive. Since the Commissioners realized that this plan was not likely to be accepted in London, they included an alternative: liberated Africans might be given allotments of land immediately, but on condition that they practice European rather than African forms of agriculture. Shifting cultivation in particular was to be discouraged so that peasants would "improve their plots in order to be able to farm them season after season."[42] The Commissioners assumed without question that European methods must be better than African. In the case of shifting cultivation, they could hardly have been more mistaken; and its abolition at that time would have destroyed what little fertility the soils of Sierra Leone may have had.

It was only natural to concentrate on problems of economic development. The projectors of the 1780's had thought little about it, and their unplanned hopes had not been realized. They had, on the other hand, devoted much time and study to political development, but the subject was hardly mentioned by the commentators of the early nineteenth century. The new concern was administration. The question was automatically raised when the Sierra Leone Company decided to pass its burden over to the Crown. Even after the transfer of 1808 and the Crown's resumption of the Gold Coast forts from the Company of Merchants in 1821, colonial government through a chartered company still had its advocates.[43] The establishment of a general West African government based on Sierra Leone was not an adequate solution. Numerous complaints of inefficiency, dishonesty, and muddle continued through the 1820's. Apparently royal government was not even good for trade: in 1829, more than half of the total

42. Report of the Commissioners, PP, 1826–1827, vii (312), pp. 55–56.
43. See, for example, J. MacQueen, *Geographical and Commercial View of Northern Central Africa* . . . , (Edinburgh, 1821), pp. 264–84; J. G. Jackson, *Account of Timbuctu and Houssa* (London, 1820), pp. 251–54.

British trade with West Africa went to the region east of the Volta, where there were no British posts of any kind.[44] Administrative problems filled the bulk of the Commissioners' report in 1827,[45] but the Government's reaction was not to administer better—it preferred to stop administering altogether, if that were possible. The attempted withdrawal of 1826–30 was, therefore, a kind of solution to a much-discussed problem.

Even the withdrawal, however, raised some political questions, at least for Sierra Leone. Throughout the 1820's, the Africanization of the public service (to use the modern phrase) had been suggested as a way of saving European lives. A more thoroughgoing scheme was brought by John McCormack before the Sierra Leone Committee in 1830. McCormack was a merchant, resident in Sierra Leone since 1808. He argued that European officials were not only subject to disease, they were also less competent than the more able Negro settlers. In his opinion, the government of Sierra Leone required no more than four European officials. The other civilian officials, the officers of the militia, and a partly elected Legislative Council could all be supplied by Sierra Leoneans of color.[46]

McCormack's position was supported by the *Westminster Review*, then under the editorship of T. Peronnet Thompson, the former governor. The *Westminster* went further still, and claimed the relative failure of the colony had come about because the "wise views" of Granville Sharp had been set aside in favor of a repressive political regime. The Government had no intention of giving wider representation to Africans, but they accepted in principle the Africanization of the civil service. In both Sierra Leone and the Gold Coast, the militia was to be commanded by African officers. As part of the withdrawal policy, Sir George Murray spoke in Parliament of the Government's ultimate intent to transform Sierra Leone into a "free African colony."[47]

He mentioned no date at which this goal might be realized. Those who discussed African affairs, indeed, had little to say about the dis-

44. PP, 1830, x (661), pp. 110–11.

45. Report of Commissioners Wellington and Rowan, PP, 1826–1827, vii (312), pp. 47 ff.

46. John McCormack, Evidence before Sierra Leone Committee, 1 July 1830, PP, 1830, x (661), pp. 57–72.

47. Hutchinson and Williams to Sir Neil Campbell, Cape Coast, 5 November 1826, SLA, Gold Coast Misc. 1826–1827, f. 32; *Westminster Review*, XV, 506–22 (1831); Sir George Murray, Commons, 15 June 1830, 2 H 25, c. 404.

tant future, and even less about what the Africans might choose to do on their own initiative. The dominant assumption was that Africans could be expected to imitate the West, but little more.

A single projection of the future, made in 1807 by James Montgomery, suggested something quite different. Montgomery ended his long anti-slavery poem, "The West Indies," on a note that rings curiously of modern Pan-Africanism. In the epic poem, African salvation came not through the agency of Western civilization alone, but through that of an African hero, the son of a slave returned from the West Indies. After youthful training combining his father's lore of the West with native sources of savage nobility, he stood forth as a Pan-African messiah:

> He spreads his banner; crowding from afar
> Innumerable armies rush to war;
> Resistless as the pillar'd whirlwinds fly
> O'er Libyan sands, revolving to the sky,
> In fire and wrath through every realm they run,
> Where the noon-shadow shrinks beneath the sun;
> Till at the Conqueror's feet, from sea to sea,
> A hundred nations bow the servile knee,
> And throned in nature's unreveal'd domains,
> The Jenghis Khan of Africa he reigns.
>
> Dim though the night of these tempestuous years
> A Sabbath dawn o'er Africa appears;
> Then shall her neck from Europe's yoke be freed,
> And healing arts to hideous arms succeed;
> At home fraternal bonds her tribes shall bind,
> Commerce abroad espouse them with mankind,
> While truth shall build, and pure Religion bless
> The Church of God amidst the wilderness.[48]

It is fair to say that few in Britain at the end of the slave trade thought in terms even vaguely resembling these.

The formal relations between European and African states were still conducted on the basis of theoretical equality. African heads of state had not yet been downgraded from Kings to Chiefs. The rights of African states in international law were perfectly clear. According to the most respected writers, whatever paramount political authority existed in the non-Western world constituted a sovereign state. Its

48. J. Montgomery, "The West Indies," *Poetical Works,* 4 vols. (London, 1828), I, 63–64. First published 1807.

territory could be legally taken away only by conquest or by treaty of voluntary surrender. Some parts of the overseas world were subject to legal annexation by European powers, but they were very few. According to Blackstone, such *territoria nullius* was limited to unpopulated regions. Vattel, whose opinion was also much respected in England, made additional exceptions. Predatory peoples, hunting and gathering tribes, and nomadic herdsmen were a danger to their neighbors, or else they pursued an "Idle mode of life" occupying "more land than they would have need of under a system of honest labor." Such people might be legally displaced by a more industrious nation in search of land.[49] Even so, virtually all of West Africa would have been exempt. Being sedentary and agricultural, the West African states were legal states. No one suggested at this point that shifting cultivation was a form of nomadism and thus an illicit use of land, though the idea would come with time.

Legal sovereignty, however, was no guarantee of equal treatment. African states were clearly not considered members of the family of nations. They sent no accredited ambassadors to Europe and received none in return. Their dealings with the Europeans were more often conducted through naval officers and colonial governors, and even consuls were rare. Nevertheless, their legal rights were recognized in a series of treaties on which the Europeans based their own rights to their footholds along the Coast.

African states, however, were conceded a stronger position in law than in morality, and the distinction between international law and international morality was of some consequence. In law, for example, right of conquest was considered a valid claim to territory, without regard to the morality of the war that led to it. In West Africa, Britain claimed a moral right to intervene for the suppression of the slave trade, valid against both African and European slave dealers. But there was no legal right to intervene, and legality was guarded by British courts as well as foreign opinion. The Foreign Office therefore sought to broaden the area of legality by international agreement and through bilateral anti-slave-trade treaties.

By extension from the moral right to intervene in the slave trade,

---

49. M. F. Lindley, *The Acquisition and Government of Backward Territories in International Law* (London, 1926), pp. 11–18; William Blackstone, *Commentaries on the Law* (Washington, 1941), p. 53 (Introduction, Sec. 4). First published 1765–1769 Emer de Vattel, *Le droit de gens,* 3 vols. (Washington, 1916), III, 37–38 (Bk. I Ch. 7).

it was possible to claim a moral right to intervene in Africa for the sake of carrying civilization to the barbarians. Arguments to this effect, later summarized in Lord Lugard's phrase, "the dual mandate," were already present: intervention would be for the mutual benefit of Africans and Europeans alike. It might be a question merely of opening new trade routes, as with Mungo Park's second expedition, sent out to see whether "commercial intercourse can be opened . . . for the mutual benefit of the natives and of His Majesty's subjects."[50] Or, the same arguments might justify British domination. James MacQueen used them in this sense. He recognized that Britain had no legal right to any part of Africa beyond what might be purchased and certified by treaty.[51] But morality might provide a claim where law gave none. He argued that Britain had a moral right to intervene because "constant coercion by the arm of civilized man can alone reclaim the savage." Therefore:

> If we really wish to do good in Africa, we must teach her savage sons that white men are their superiors. By this charm alone can we insure their obedience. Without they remain obedient, we never will succeed in rendering them industrious, or in instructing them in any useful branch of knowledge. White men cannot labour in that climate; black men only can labour there. But unless we can command the labour of the latter, so as to direct it to some purpose beneficial alike to themselves and to us, we never can reclaim Africans from their present state of barbarity and ignorance, nor succeed in raising that quarter of the world from its present extremely debased and demoralized state."[52]

While other justifications might not be set precisely in these terms, there existed a broad concensus that Britain had the right, in morality if not in law, to exert informal pressure beyond the walls of the forts or the boundaries of Sierra Leone. The problem was to find the means to exercise this pressure cheaply and efficiently. Military power was available, but its use in West Africa was out of the question except in an emergency. British influence, if it were to carry beyond the reach of ships' guns, would have to be carried in some other way.

The time-honored method on the Coast was economic. All the European trading companies had made payments to African authorities, in customary duties, for ground rent, for favors done, or simply

---

50. Camden to Park, 2 January 1805, quoted in M. Park, *The Journal of a Mission to the Interior of Africa in 1805*, 2nd ed. (London, 1815), p. 53.
51. MacQueen, *Northern Cenertal Africa*, pp. 202–3.
52. MacQueen, *Northern Central Africa*, p. 328.

to secure good will.[53] The Sierra Leone Company had used a similar system of bounties and prizes to direct the settlers, and even missionaries tended to protect their position by regular payments to the ruler when they worked beyond the European colony. Similar subsidies were granted by the royal governors in both Sierra Leone and the Gold Coast, and some kind of monetary payment was the usual inducement offered by the government in return for an anti-slave-trade treaty—both in Europe and in Africa. It was only natural to consider the possibility of extending the subsidies and using them for new purposes,[54] but large concessions would have required large payments. A cheaper and wider form of economic control would be to enforce penalties rather than grant rewards. The possibility of dominating African states by controlling coastal trade was constantly inviting. One obvious place for such a policy was the Gold Coast, where the purchase of the Dutch and Danish forts would have given control over a 300-mile stretch of coast. Similar plans were applied to the region around Sierra Leone, notably by Governor Turner, but the Navy's difficulties in trying to suppress the foreign slave trade showed the practical limitations of the idea.

Client-states in the interior might also be secured by other means. Alexander Laing hoped to use government-sponsored missionary work, applied with real concentration. He argued that, if a single nation in the interior could be converted to Christianity, it would serve as a center for the spread of the Gospel and British manufactures as well. T. E. Bowdich had a more hard-headed scheme for creating a client-state by supplying one country with arms and denying them to its rivals. His choice for this policy was Ashanti, and he claimed Ashanti could be made to cooperate by the threat to by-pass Kumasi with a new trade route up the Volta valley to the market at Salaga. With this threat in the background, the Asantehene could be offered the exclusive right to buy firearms, in return for commer-

53. The African Committee on the Gold Coast spent something more than one hundred pounds a year at the larger forts and as little as thirty or forty at the smaller ones. About half the total went to ground rent, the rest being distributed according to need—for keeping paths open to the interior, to important men in the town outside the fort, or in small sums to the headmen of neighboring fishing villages in return for flying the British flag and maintaining a friendly posture. (S. Cock to Lords of the Treasury, 22 September 1820, printed in J. J. Crooks, *Records Relating to the Gold Coast Settlements from 1750 to 1874* (Dublin, 1923), p. 128.

54. African Institution, *Reports of the Committee*, I (1807), 56–60; Robertson *Notes on Africa*, pp. 21–22; Gen. Charles Turner to Bathurst, 20 December 1825, CC 267/66.

cial concessions in whatever empire he might then conquer. If Ashanti rejected the offer it could still be made to Dagomba or some other state.[55] These schemes were quite unacceptable in the British political setting of the time, but Bowdich was correct in sensing that modern firearms were the key to political power. Outlandish as his suggestion may sound in retrospect, he was merely proposing that Ashanti follow the course Egypt would soon follow in the Nilotic Sudan, or that Zanzibar would follow in East Africa later in the century.

Other projects for spreading British influence called for a measure of more formal political control. The anonymous project published by the African Institution in 1808 included the usual monopoly over coastal trade, the settlement of European managerial cadres at selected centers of plantation agriculture, and, beyond this, an informal protectorate to be established in cooperation with the chiefs. They were to be grouped politically into councils and groups of councils, all ultimately under British protection and control but without the necessity of extensive British administration. British officials would be needed, but only to arbitrate quarrels, keep the peace, and see that justice would be done.[56]

Such ideas might be considered distant relatives of the theory and practice of "indirect rule" as it developed in the twentieth century. If so, the line of descent was long and devious, since the practice of ruling through the indigenous authorities had been used in Spanish America three centuries earlier. In the setting of nineteenth-century Africa, where the combined threats of the Treasury and the "climate" barred the way to most government activity, it was natural to think of economizing on European staff. The existing chiefs were the natural alternative. J. G. Jackson, for example, made much of the possible uses of chiefly self-interest in his project of 1819, calling for a chartered company to exploit the all-desert route from the Atlantic Sahara to Timbuctu.[57]

Jackson's project and the similar suggestion of the African Institution in 1808 were far too extreme to be acceptable in their own time, but they led indirectly to the Niger Expedition of 1841–42 through

---

55. A. G. Laing, *Travels in the Timanee, Kooranko, and Soolima Countries in Western Africa* (London, 1825), pp. 387–98; T. E. Bowdich, *Mission from Cape Coast Castle to Ashantee . . .* (London, 1819), pp. 341–43.
56. African Institution, *Reports of the Committee*, II (1808), appendix, pp. 33–41.
57. Vasco da Gama [Pseud. for J. G. Jackson], *Blackwood's Magazine*, IV, 652–53 (March 1819); Jackson, *Account of Timbuctoo and Houssa*, pp. 247–71.

the mediation of James MacQueen. MacQueen was not an original thinker, but he had read widely in the earlier literature about West Africa. He also had a knack for picking up diverse strands of theory and suggestion and incorporating them in a comprehensive project. The talent was not unlike that displayed by Edward Gibbon Wakefield, the theorist of British settlement in Australasia. The two careers were similar in other ways as well. Both men were able to influence the Establishment, though neither was fully accepted by it, and the practice that followed from their theories was something less than the full-strength dose they prescribed.

We have already seen MacQueen as a strategist and a geographical synthesizer. His suggestions for political and economic penetration of Africa were closely integrated with the Oil Rivers theory of the Niger mouth, and they were equally unoriginal. His theory of culture was racist, but he believed that a limited "improvement" was possible through the agency of "legitimate trade." He followed the line of the African Institution in proposing to deal with the chiefs in the interior by appealing to their economic interests, and he believed that African workers would not work for the mere lure of wages, at least in a land as bountiful as West Africa was assumed to be. All of this was the common coin of the time.

He believed, however, that all problems could be met through a single elaborate scheme, based on a strong post at Fernando Po and another at the confluence of the Niger and the Benue. With these two, Britain would have a competitive advantage on the Niger so strong that her control would amount to monopoly. Hence she could exert the kind of economic pressure chronically suggested, but practically impossible, from coastal bases alone. The key to the project, however, was the position of the chiefs. MacQueen assumed, correctly, that the slave trade continued in part because it served the interest of important groups of Africans with political power. If they would use their power to produce goods for export, rather than exporting manpower, the slave trade would end. They had command over the land. They had slaves who could be coerced to work it. "Only teach them and shew them that we will give them more for their produce than for the hand that rears it, and the work is done. All other methods and means will prove ineffectual."[58]

58. MacQueen, *Northern Central Africa*, p. 189. The plan as a whole is presented on pp. 169–207. The passage quoted makes an interesting comparison with J. G.

Very few Europeans would be needed, since the motive force was African self-interest. What troops were required could come from India. "By these means we should make India the means of preparing for us an Empire of equal importance to replace her strength, when that, in the course of political change, is withdrawn from our allegiance."[59]

Even the assumed racial inferiority of the Africans would rebound to British advantage, since this "weakness" combined with the tropical environment would assure the permanence of the British hold on West Africa. Such people in such a country, MacQueen believed, could never build an industrial machine able to compete with British manufactures. His list of the potential wealth of the Western Sudan reads like a prospectus of the 1780's. An immediate trade worth three millions would fall into British hands, with more to come with development.[60]

For all its plausibility, MacQueen's project was not immediately influential. It came to an audience that had already heard about the promised eldorado in West Africa—had, in fact, been hearing about it for forty years, and there was still nothing to show from the promises. Such cynics as Joseph Hume could point to a level of Anglo-African trade barely recovered to the monetary values of 1787, and these values were now relatively insignificant, compared to British trade as a whole.[61] Aside even from the discouraging mortality figures, MacQueen's project was offensive to important groups which might otherwise have been interested. Many humanitarians were less than pleased with MacQueen's attacks on Sierra Leone, and his substitution of African plantation slavery for the intercontinental slave trade was not quite what they had in mind when they talked about the beneficent consequences to follow from "legitimate trade." The West Indian interest, whom MacQueen sometimes defended, were also violently opposed to the competitive development of tropical agriculture in Africa.

Like the other projects of the early nineteenth century, MacQueen's

Jackson's statement that the African continent could not be explored or its wealth exploited, except "by calling to our aid the cooperation of the native chiefs, by holding out to them the benefits which they will derive from commercial intercourse as a reward for their assistance and exertions in promoting this desirable object." (Jackson, *Timbuctu and Houssa*, p. 251.)

59. MacQueen, *Northern Central Africa*, p. 192.
60. MacQueen, *Northern Central Africa*, 212–57.
61. J. Hume, Commons, 15 June 1830, 2 H 25, c. 398.

plan lay dormant in a climate of opinion where even the humanitarian champions of Sierra Leone were nearing the nadir of discouragement. In 1830, Fowell Buxton, who had now replaced Wilberforce as parliamentary leader of the group, admitted in the House of Commons that Sierra Leone had failed. His only saving qualification was to claim that it had not failed quite so miserably as some of its critics had said.[62] Yet, in the longer run, it was to be Buxton and his followers who breathed life into MacQueen's project and with it a renewed activity in West Africa on a scale not seen since the 1790's.

62. Fowell Buxton, Commons, 15 June 1830, 2 H 25, c. 399.